SAINTS ALIVE!

SAINTS ALIVE!

The Lives of Thirteen Heroic Saints

ANNE FREMANTLE

DOUBLEDAY & COMPANY, INC.

GARDEN CITY, NEW YORK

Grateful Acknowledgments are made to the following sources:

Excerpts from *Catherine of Siena* by Sigrid Unset. Copyright 1954 by Sheed & Ward, New York. Reprinted by permission.

Excerpts from *The Dominicans* by Reverend J. B. Reeves, Macmillan, 1930.

Excerpts from *The Eagle and the Dove* by Victoria Sackville-West. Reprinted by permission of Curtis Brown, Ltd., London on behalf of Executors of the Estate of Victoria Sackville-West.

Excerpts from *Essay on Freedom and Power* by John Emerich Edward Dahlberg Acton, The Beacon Press, Boston, 1949.

Excerpts from *The Correspondence of Sir Thomas More* by Elizabeth Frances Roger, Princeton University Press, 1947.

Excerpts from the book *The Monk and the World* by Walter Dirks, translated by Daniel Coogan. Copyright © 1954 by the David McKay Company, Inc. and from *Saint Bridget of Sweden* by Dr. Johannes Jorgensen. Copyright 1947 by Johannes Jorgensen. Reprinted by permission of the David McKay Company, Inc.

Excerpts from *The Confessions of St. Augustine*, translated by E. B. Pusey. English translation copyright 1907 by E. P. Dutton and J. M. Dent & Sons Ltd. An Everyman's Library Edition. Reprinted by permission of E. P. Dutton and J. M. Dent & Sons, Ltd.

Excerpt from *Life of Sir Thomas More* by P. E. Hallet. Copyright © Burns & Oates Ltd., 1928. Reprinted by permission of Search Press Ltd.

Lines of poetry from "For the Time Being" in the book *Collected Poems* by W. H. Auden, edited by Edward Mendelson. Copyright 1942 and renewed 1972 by W. H. Auden. Reprinted by permission of Random House, Inc. and Faber & Faber Ltd.

Excerpts from *The Essential Erasmus* by John P. Dolan. Copyright © 1964 by John P. Dolan. Reprinted by arrangement with the New American Library, Inc., New York, N.Y.

Excerpt from *The Cocktail Party* by T. S. Eliot. Reprinted by permission of Harcourt Brace Jovanovich, Inc.

Extracts from Saint Luke: *The Acts of the Apostles*, translated by C. H. Rieu (Penguin Classics, 1957). Copyright C. H. Rieu, 1957. Reprinted by permission of Penguin Books Ltd.

Excerpt from "The Son of God goes forth to war" by Bishop Heber. In *Hymns Ancient and Modern* (London: Wm. Clowes & Sons, 1916).

Library of Congress Cataloging in Publication Data

Fremantle, Anne Jackson, 1909–
Saints alive.

1. Christian saints—Biography.   I. Title.
BX4655.2.F66   209′.2′2   [B]
ISBN: 0-385-12441-4
Library of Congress Catalog Card Number 78-4789

Contents

INTRODUCTION	vii
PAUL	1
HELENA	18
AUGUSTINE	23
BENEDICT	35
FRANCIS OF ASSISI	52
BRIDGET OF SWEDEN	67
CATHERINE OF SIENA	82
THOMAS MORE	90
FRANCIS XAVIER	114
FRANCIS DE SALES	141
MARTIN DE PORRES	158
THÉRÈSE OF LISIEUX	164
FRANCES CABRINI	171
CONCLUSION	183

Introduction

There are over twenty thousand saints mentioned in martyrologies and breviaries. Just what is a saint? How is it that ordinary people sometimes become saints? Why should they want to? And what good does it do them—or anyone else—to try? Or to succeed?

Basically, what is required of anyone who aspires to become a saint is to become what they were meant to be. The people in this book came from every walk of life, from every ethnic and educational background, from differing genetic strains, and different family environments. Some had radiant childhoods and devoted families—Thérèse of Lisieux, for example, and Francis de Sales. One was abandoned by his father (Martin de Porres), one by her husband (Helena). But the empress and the haberdasher's daughter, orthodox Jew and illegitimate Peruvian, French aristocrat and Italian peasant, wherever, whenever, or however they were born and raised, these thirteen (and the twenty thousand others!) realized, often when they were very young (but not always, for Augustine told God: "Late have I loved Thee!") what they wanted to be, and what they wanted was what God meant them to be. And they became just that. They never whined that they could not help themselves, that the dice were loaded against them, that they hadn't a chance because their fathers, mothers, siblings or schools had made them what they were. Where most people make excuses, rush to psychiatrists, or sink into mediocrity, explaining themselves by the fact that their husbands, wives, children or employers don't understand them, the saints realized that the first of all non-attachments is to the self, including its sins, mistakes and stupidities. Saints are quite sure they are here on earth for a purpose and that their job is to find out what that purpose is and do the best they can to fulfill it. In so doing, they succeed both in helping themselves and the rest of humanity, too. Sounds simple? Read on and see.

St. Paul (5?–67?)

It seems correct to begin a study of thirteen canonized Christian saints, relevant to us today, with one who considered himself the thirteenth apostle. And how he went on about that, continually asserting he was just as good as the Twelve! Using the word "boast" almost sixty times in his extant letters, he "boasted" he was their equal. Indeed, Dr. Grant, in his *St. Paul* (1975: p. 106) states Paul claimed "his apostleship was equal or *superior* to the status of the apostles who had known Jesus in his lifetime and had seen his risen body while it was still on earth." "Am I not an apostle? Am I not free? Have I not seen Jesus Christ our Lord?" Paul asks (1 Cor. 9:1). And he writes later: "By God's grace I am what I am. . . . I have worked harder than all of them [i.e., the other apostles]." (1 Cor. 15:10)

There were only five years between the death of Jesus and the conversion of Paul, and some of his letters—in spite of endless squabbles about their date—are the earliest Christian writings that have survived. Whether Galatians, placed by some scholars as written in A.D. 49, or 1 and 2 Thessalonians, which were, as is generally agreed, written to the Christian communities in Salonica (Macedonia) in A.D. 50, were written first, Paul's account, in 1 Corinthians 15:1–11, of the death and resurrection of Jesus Christ is the oldest testimony extant to these events. Here are Paul's words:

"The chief message I handed on to you, as it was handed on to me, was that Christ, as the Scriptures had foretold, died for our sins; that he was buried and then, as the Scriptures had foretold, rose again on the third day. That he was seen by Cephas [Peter], then by the eleven apostles, and afterwards by more than five hundred of the brethren at once, most of whom are alive at this day, though some have gone to their rest. Then he was seen by James, then by all the apostles, and, last of all, I too saw him, like the last child, that comes to birth unexpectedly."

What did this "last child" and thirteenth apostle look like? By second-century accounts—there are no contemporary portraits—he is said to have been small, bald, bowlegged, with eyebrows that met in the middle, a large nose, blue eyes, a thick, pointed, gray beard, and a florid complexion.

According to St. Jerome, Paul's family originally came from Gischala, in Galilee. But Paul's father somehow acquired Roman citizenship, which Paul inherited and later was to find very convenient, and moved to Tarsus, thus joining the *diaspora*—the six million Jews then living outside of Palestine. Another some two and a half million lived in Palestine, where Rome had set up a series of puppet princes; only Judea was directly governed by a Roman procurator.

The two most densely Jewish centers outside of Palestine were Alexandria, where the Jews made up between one fifth and two fifths of the population, and Rome, where they controlled a large share of the import trade.

Paul's parents were strict Pharisees, and Paul declares in Philippians 3:5: "I come from the stock of Israel, from the tribe of Benjamin, Hebrew-speaking as my parents were before me." He was circumcised on the eighth day after his birth and given the name of Saul, though he also from childhood used the Roman name of Paul. Paul read the Jewish Scriptures in the Septuagint, the Greek version. But after his conversion on the road to Damascus, he declared that Christ had spoken to him in Hebrew. He also declared, in Acts 22:3, that he was trained in Jerusalem, under the Rabbi Gamaliel, in exact knowledge "of our ancestral law," which suggests he went to Jerusalem when he was about fifteen. Dr. Grant doubts this, as Paul had stated, in Galatians 1:22, that he was unknown by sight to Christ's congregation. In any case, he is first mentioned by name, in Acts 7:58, as a very junior member of the synagogue of Roman freedmen, men from Cyrene, Alexandria, and Asia, who "started a controversy with Stephen, but in intelligence they were no match for him or for the Spirit behind him." Acts goes on to quote Stephen's speech at length, and to give the listeners' reaction: "They gave a great shout and stopped their ears, then hurled themselves on him in a body. They dragged him out of the city and got ready to stone him, and the witnesses laid the clothes they took off at the feet of a young man called Saul." After describing Stephen's last words and death, the chapter ends with the words: "Among those who approved the killing of Stephen was Saul." The next chapter—8—begins with an account of the first recorded persecution of Christians, which began on the day of Stephen's death.

As a result of this persecution, all "except the Apostles fled to different parts of Judaea and Samaria. Stephen was buried by some devout men with full ceremonial lamentations. Saul proceeded to ravage the Church, going into their homes and dragging people off, even women, and throwing them in prison." The story is continued in Acts, Chapter 9:

"Saul, meanwhile, still with threats on his lips and murder in his heart for the disciples of the Lord, approached the high priest with a request for letters to the synagogue in Damascus, empowering him to arrest and bring back to Jerusalem any men and women of the Way that he might find there. On the journey, when he was approaching Damascus, a light from heaven suddenly flashed around him. He fell to the ground, and heard a voice saying to him:

Saul, Saul, why are you persecuting Me?

Who are you, sir? he asked.

I am Jesus. It is I whom you are persecuting. But get up and go into the city, and you will be told what to do."

Saul's traveling companions stood speechless, for they heard Saul speaking but could see no one else. Saul rose from the ground, but though his eyes were now open he could not see, so they led him by the hand, and brought him to Damascus. For three days he was blind, and ate and drank nothing.

At Damascus there was a disciple called Ananias. The Lord called to him in a vision, "Ananias."

"Yes, Lord, I am here," he answered.

The Lord said to him, "Go to Straight Street and inquire at the house of Judas for a man called Saul, from Tarsus. He is saying his prayers, and has had a vision of a man called Ananias coming in and laying on his hands to restore his sight."

"But, Lord," Ananias answered, "many people have told me that this man has done a lot of harm to your followers in Jerusalem, and here in Damascus he has authority to arrest anyone who worships you."

"Go all the same," the Lord said, "because he is the man I have chosen to carry my name to the Gentiles, to kings, and to the children of Israel, and he must learn what he will have to suffer for my sake."

So Ananias went to the house and laid his hands on Saul, saying, "Saul, brother, I have been sent by the Lord—the Jesus who appeared to you on your journey here. He has sent me to help you regain your sight and receive the Holy Spirit."

Immediately, the scales fell from Saul's eyes and he could see. He rose and was baptized, and after he had had a meal he recovered his strength.

Saul later stayed some time with the disciples in Damascus. Without delay he began to proclaim the gospel in the synagogues, and his message was, "Jesus is the Son of God." Everyone who heard him was amazed. "Isn't he the man," they asked, "who caused such havoc among the worshipers of this name in Jerusalem, and wasn't the sole reason for his coming to Damascus to arrest them and take them back to the chief priests?"

Saul's power, however, went on increasing, and he nonplused the Jews of Damascus by proving from the Scriptures that Jesus was the Messiah.

After some time the Jews made a plot to kill Saul, but he heard about it. They were keeping a watch night and day at the city gates to catch and kill him, but his friends took him by night and let him down in a basket, along the face of the wall, lowering him to the ground.

On his arrival in Jerusalem he tried to join the disciples, but they were all afraid of him, not believing that his conversion was genuine. However, Barnabas took him to the apostles and told them how Saul had seen the Lord on his journey and what the Lord had said to him, and he described how courageously Saul had preached in the name of Jesus in Damascus, so Saul became one of their company in Jerusalem and preached fearlessly in the name of the Lord. He also began to engage in discussion and controversy with the Hellenist Jews, but they plotted to kill him. However, the Brotherhood found out about this and escorted him down to Caesarea, from where they sent him to Tarsus.

As to what happened to Paul after his baptism, there is a contradiction between this account in Acts 9, which describes his going to Jerusalem, and Paul's own, earlier account, in Galatians, which declares (Gal. 1:15–17), "My first thought was not to hold any consultations with any human creature: I did not go up to Jerusalem to see those who had been apostles longer than myself: no, I went off into Arabia, and when I came back, it was to Damascus." He writes that it was three years after his conversion that he went to Jerusalem, and then spent "fifteen days with Peter, but saw no one else except James, the Lord's brother."

As a result of the persecution suffered by the Jerusalem Christians after Stephen's death, those who fled went to Phoenicia and Cyprus and Antioch, preaching only to the Jews. "But there were some of them . . . who, when they found their way to Antioch, spoke to the Greeks as well, preaching the Lord Jesus to them. And the Lord's power went with them, so that a great number learned to believe, and turned to the Lord." (Acts 11:19–21)

These were the first Gentile Christians, and the "news of this activity reached the church in Jerusalem, and Barnabas, an honourable and deeply religious man, full of the Holy Spirit, was sent to Antioch." Antioch was the third-greatest city in the Roman Empire, and the principal one in the prefecture of the East. Now, for the first time, Christianity appeared in one of the metropolitan centers of the world. After Barnabas arrived, "he was overjoyed to discover that the grace of God was at work. . . . Many other people were converted to the faith. Barnabas then went to Tarsus to find Saul, and when he had found him brought him back to Antioch. Here they stayed for a whole year, joining in the worship of the church and teaching large numbers of people. It was at Antioch that the disciples were first called 'Christians.' "

Antioch became, from then until the conversion of Constantine, in 312, central to Christianity, indeed the chief Christian center, from which Christianity radiated all over Asia Minor. Christianity thereafter became Greek in thought and language, and the Jerusalem Christians, gathered under James, Jesus' brother, and Peter, diminished in importance until in the second century what remained of them were called Ebionites, from *ebionim*, (poor). They had become a despised and shabby Jewish sect. They held doctrines very similar to, and possibly derived from, the Essenes of Qumran, being vegetarians and ascetics. They declared Jesus to be the Messiah but to be the son of Joseph and Mary, and they accepted only the Gospel of Matthew, rejecting Paul as an apostate from the Jewish law.

The emperor Caligula reigned from A.D. 37 to A.D. 41, and with him began the enforced adoration of the emperor as the Supreme God, which was to produce many Christian martyrs. Caligula sent a statue of himself even to Jerusalem to be erected in the Temple to compel the Jews to worship him, and riots broke out in Alexandria against the Jews because of their refusal to render divine honors to the emperor.

In A.D. 44 there was a famine in Palestine, and Barnabas and Saul brought relief from the Antioch Christians to those in Jerusalem.

They then "returned from Jerusalem, their mission fulfilled, and took John, also called Mark, in their company." (Acts 11:29–30; 12:25)

About a year later, Paul and Barnabas set out on Paul's first missionary journey to Syria, Cyprus, and Asia Minor. This journey lasted about four years. The idea was that the two men were, in each place they came to, to speak in the synagogues. But the diaspora Jews were horrified at the story of the crucified Son of Man whom Paul and Barnabas declared was Son of God, so in A.D. 46 Paul frankly turned from the Jews to the Gentiles, who were eager to listen. But two problems immediately arose: must the Gentiles be circumcised? and must they keep the Jewish dietary laws? Paul, as he later wrote the Galatians, considered that "the gospel of uncircumcision was committed to me, as the gospel of circumcision to Peter (for he that wrought effectually in Peter to the apostleship of the circumcision, the same was mighty in me towards the Gentiles), and when James, Cephas, and John, who seemed to be pillars, perceived the grace that was given me, they gave to me and Barnabas the right hand of fellowship, that we should go unto the heathen, and they unto the circumcision." (Gal. 2:7–9) As a result of this decision, Titus, a Greek disciple of Paul's, was not compelled to be circumcised, whereas Timothy, another disciple, because his mother was Jewish (which made him a Jew) was circumcised, at Lystra. But when Peter came to Antioch, he and Paul had a flaming row, which Paul describes (Gal. 2:11–14):

"But when Peter came to Antioch, I opposed him to his face, because he was clearly in the wrong. For, until certain persons came from James, he was taking his meals with Gentile Christians, but when they came he drew back and began to hold aloof, because he was afraid of the advocates of circumcision. The other Jewish Christians showed the same lack of principle; even Barnabas was carried away and played false like the rest. But when I saw that their conduct did not square with the truth of the Gospel, I said to Cephas, before the whole congregation: 'If you, a Jew born and bred, live like a Gentile, and not like a Jew, how can you insist that the Gentiles must live like Jews?'" (Gal. 2:11–14) Even in Antioch the Jews "stirred up the opposition of the city authorities and the influential women attached to the synagogue, and had Paul and Barnabas persecuted and driven from the district. So they shook the dust of the place from their feet and went on to Iconium." (Acts 13:51–52) Iconium, which is now called Konya, is today the center of the

Muslim "turning," the "Dervish dancing" initiated by Rumi in the thirteenth century. The town, with its earlier, Christian history, is now holy also to the Muslims.

Acts 14 describes the adventures of Paul and Barnabas in Konya:

"In Iconium as in Antioch, Paul and Barnabas went into the Jewish synagogue, and converted large numbers of Jews and Greeks by their preaching. The unconvinced Jews, however, succeeded in poisoning the minds of the Gentiles and stirring up animosity against the Brotherhood. Nevertheless, they stayed there for a long time and, confident in the Lord, taught the gospel of his grace, and he proved the truth of their words by the miracles and wonders he enabled them to perform. But now a split occurred among the citizens, some supporting the Jews and others the apostles. Eventually, some members of both communities, Gentile and Jewish, including the leaders, made a plot to attack and stone them, but they came to hear of it and escaped to Lycaonia. Here, in the cities of Lystra and Derbe and in the neighborhood, they continued preaching the gospel."

Here (Acts 14:8–20) follows the account of a genuine, if embarrassing, miracle. "At Lystra there was a cripple who had never walked; he had been lame from birth. One day as he sat listening to Paul, Paul turned a searching eye on him, and seeing he believed he could be cured, called out loudly, 'Stand up on your feet.'

"The man jumped up and began to walk. When the crowd saw what Paul had done, they shouted out, in Lycaonian, 'The Gods have come down to us in human form,' and they called Barnabas 'Zeus,' and Paul, because he was the spokesman, 'Hermes.' The priest of Zeus from the temple outside the city now brought bulls and garlands to the gates and prepared to offer public sacrifice.

"When Barnabas and Paul heard of this they tore their clothes and rushed out into the crowd, shouting, 'You men, what are you doing? We are human beings like you; we have the same feelings as you. We are here to bring you good news, the news that there is a living God, who made heaven and earth and sea and everything in them. Leave these meaningless things and turn to him. In the past he allowed men of all races to go their own way, though even then he showed that he existed by the good things he gave you—rain from the sky, seasons of harvest, food for your bodies, and happiness for your hearts.' With this explanation they managed, though with difficulty, to prevent the crowds from offering sacrifice to them.

"It was after this that some Jews from Antioch and Iconium arrived in Lystra. They won the people over, stoned Paul, dragged him out of the city, and left him for dead. But while the disciples were standing round him he got to his feet and re-entered the city."

According to Eusebius (256–340), the earliest Christian ecclesiastical historian, Acts was written by the physician Luke, a disciple of Paul, and was intended by him as a continuation of his Gospel. Luke, "the beloved physician" (Col. 4:14), treated Paul possibly for ophthalmia or possibly for epilepsy. Luke certainly traveled on some of his journeys with Paul, and Eusebius writes that Luke's authorship of Acts was already an ancient tradition in Eusebius' time. Acts gives a long account of the Council of Jerusalem, which some modern authorities (Dr. Grant among them) doubt ever took place: Dr. Grant considers Acts a reconciling document written later—possibly after the deaths of both Paul and Peter, in order to present the Church as united. Acts says the Council was called because some Jerusalem Jews arrived in Antioch and declared, "Unless you are circumcised, in accordance with the law of Moses, you cannot be saved." Paul and Barnabas "vigorously opposed them and contested their doctrine." So a delegation, "which included Paul and Barnabas, was sent to Jerusalem to settle the question with the Apostles and Elders." Once they were in Jerusalem, "some members of the sect of Pharisees who had embraced the faith rose to say that converted Gentiles should be circumcised." Peter, "after a lengthy discussion," addressed them and asked, "Why are you trying to outdo God by placing a burden on these converts which was too heavy even for us and our forefathers to bear? Our hope of salvation, no less than theirs, lies in the grace of the Lord Jesus." Paul and Barnabas spoke next. After they had finished, James spoke. "Members of the Brotherhood," he called them, and proposed that "we do not trouble the Gentile converts in this way, but instead write and tell them just that they must abstain from meat that has been sacrificed to idols, from fornication, from the flesh of animals killed by strangling, and from flesh which still has the blood in it." (Acts 15:20) Verse 22 triumphantly concludes: "with the concurrence of the whole church the apostles and elders then passed a resolution to elect delegates to go to Antioch with Paul and Barnabas." And the delegates were given a letter quoted in full in Acts. After delivering this the delegates returned "to those who sent them" and by then "peace had been restored." Paul and Barnabas, however, remained in Antioch, but subsequently quarrelled over Mark, whom Barnabas wanted to take on another missionary journey as one of their company, but Paul "thought it wrong to have with them a man who had deserted them in Pamphylia instead of accompanying them on their work." As a result of their quarrel, they separated. Barnabas took Mark with him and sailed away to Cyprus. Paul chose Silas as his companion, with whom he "traveled through Syria and Cilicia, strengthening the churches." On this second missionary journey, they were "told by the Holy Spirt not to preach in Asia" (Acts 16:6) and, when they tried to go into the Province of Bithynia, "the spirit of Jesus forbade them," so they went on to Troas. Here Paul had a vision one night of a Macedonian "standing imploring him with the words: 'Come over to Macedonia.'" And so "we prepared to go to Macedonia." They then took ship to Samothrace, and next day to Neapolis, and on to the Roman colony of Philippi, where they met Lydia by the riverside. "She was a native of Thyatira, in the purple-dye trade," and she and her household were baptized and afterward invited Paul and Luke to stay at her house. "And we agreed to do so." Here, too, they met a slave girl with second sight, who kept "following Paul and us, and calling out: 'These men are servants of the Most High God and can tell you how to save your souls'. She went on doing this day after day, till Paul grew angry and turned around and said to the spirit, 'I command you in the name of Jesus Christ to come out of her.' After which she could no longer tell fortunes, and so her owners lost their means of income. They therefore caught hold of Paul and Silas, and dragged them off to the authorities" and told the chief magistrates that these Jews were "advocating customs which it would be illegal for us as Roman citizens to accept and practice." The chief magistrates ordered them to be stripped and flogged. After a severe beating they were thrown into prison, and the prison governor was given strict orders to guard them closely. On receiving these orders, he flung them into an inner cell and secured their feet in the stocks. But at midnight there was suddenly a violent earthquake. The prison foundations rocked, the doors flew open, and the fetters of all prisoners were pulled loose. The prison governor awoke and saw the cell doors open, and thinking the prisoners had escaped, drew his sword to kill himself. But Paul shouted out loudly, "Don't harm yourself, we're all here." The man called for lights, rushed in, and fell trembling at the feet of Paul and Silas. He then led them out and asked: "Gentlemen, what must I do to be saved?" "Believe in the Lord Jesus," they answered, "and you and your household will be saved." (Acts 16:25–33)

After the "gospel of the Lord" was explained, "then and there, at that late hour, after washing the wounds caused by their flogging, he and all his household were baptized. He conducted them into his house and gave them a meal."

When day came, orders for the release of the prisoners was conveyed to Paul by the prison governor, but Paul was indignant. "They have beaten us publicly, without trial, though we are Roman citizens, and have thrown us *into* prison. Are they now trying to throw us *out* secretly? No! they must come in person and conduct us out." This scared the magistrates, who had had no idea the two were Roman citizens. They were conducted out of the prison and asked to leave the city. So they went first to Lydia's house (Acts 16:14), and then went on their way. (Acts 16:40)

When they got to Thessalonica, they preached in the synagogue for three weeks, and made a lot of converts. But, again, the Jews enlisted "idlers from the market place" and declared that "these men have stirred up trouble all over the world, by saying there's another emperor, someone called Jesus." So "the Brotherhood" sent Paul and Silas away by night, to Beroea, where the Jews "eagerly accepted the Word" until the Jews from Thessalonica, who had again followed, arrived and stirred up trouble again. Paul was then sent off under escort to Athens, while Silas and Timothy stayed behind.

"While Paul was waiting in Athens, his indignation was aroused by the sight of idols everywhere in the city." So he started arguing with passers-by in the city center, including some Epicurean and Stoic philosophers—everyone in Athens spent all his time "communicating or listening to new ideas." Paul was brought before the Council of Areopagus, and there gave the splendid talk in which he declared he saw, among the objects of worship, an altar to THE UNKNOWN GOD. "The Deity you worship but do not know, I can make known to you." Then Paul quoted Aratus (*Phaenomena, 5,* as Dr. Grant points out op. cit., p. 200): "For in him we live and move and have our being"; and Epimenides, *Cretica:* "For we also are his offspring."

He went on to talk about a "Man whom he [God] has appointed," and whom he had resurrected from the dead, but the Athenians couldn't take that one, and began to laugh ironically, while others said they would hear what he had to say on *that* subject some other time.

Then Paul left Athens and came to Corinth, staying with a Jew called Aquila and his wife, Priscilla, who were "recently from Italy as a result of Claudius' edict banishing all Jews from Rome." They were leatherworkers, as Acts says Paul was, and he stayed with them and they worked together. Every Sabbath he held discussions in the synagogue, trying to convert the Jews and the Greeks. But the Jews "ranged themselves against him and blasphemed Christ," so Paul rejected them with a symbolical shake of his robes. "From now on I am going to the Gentiles," Paul said, and left the synagogue to stay with a Gentile called Justus. Paul stayed in Corinth eighteen months, "and many Corinthians were converted and baptized."

Later, Paul was brought before Gallio, the proconsul of Achaia, by the Jews, but Gallio told the Jews to "settle the matter yourselves . . . Gallio was indifferent to the whole affair."

Then, with Priscilla and Aquila, Paul, having cut his hair as part of a vow, sailed to Syria. Arrived in Ephesus, he left Priscilla and Aquila there and went on up to Jerusalem, and "he paid his respects to the Church and then went down to Antioch."

Then he went back to Ephesus, and found a group of disciples whom he asked: "At your conversion did you receive the Holy Spirit?" To which they replied, "No: we did not even hear that there was a Holy Spirit." "Then, what baptism were you baptized with?" Paul asked them, and they replied, "With the baptism of John." Paul explained that "when John baptized with the baptism of repentance he told the people of 'one coming after him' whom they were to believe in and that one is Jesus."

"When they heard this they were baptized in the name of the Lord Jesus, and with the laying-on of Paul's hands, the Holy Spirit descended on them and they cried out in ecstasy and uttered prophecies." (There were about twelve men in this group.) (Acts 19:1–7) This is, of course, the text best beloved by all "charismatics" of whatever denomination, all of whom are united by their belief that "glossolalia," i.e., speaking in strange tongues (whether real languages and comprehensible, or incomprehensible because "utterances" in no language) is a manifestation of the Holy Spirit.

Paul's third missionary journey, after some eighteen months in Corinth, began, Dr. Grant says, "presumably in spring 53 and lasted five years, of which about three were spent at Ephesus." Dr. Grant tots up the mileage for these enormous voyages: first journey, 625 miles; second, 875; third, 710. And as far as is known, all these on foot, except where Paul himself specifies he took a boat. And all the time, he was preaching: nothing stopped him. Paul describes himself as "in presence base among you, but being absent am bold towards you" ("I am so feeble when I am face to face with you. So brave when I am away.") (2 Cor. 10:1) And then again a boast: "I suppose I was not a whit behind the very chiefest apostles." He next describes the vicissitudes of his travels: "Are they ministers of Christ (I speak as a fool)? I am more: in labors more abundant, in stripes above measure; in prisons more frequent, in deaths oft. Of the Jews five times I received forty stripes save one. Thrice was I beaten with rods, once I was stoned, thrice I suffered shipwreck, a night and a day I have been in the deep; in journeyings often, in perils of waters, in perils of robbers, in perils by my own countrymen, in perils by the heathen; in perils in the city, in perils in the wilderness, in perils in the sea, in perils among false brethren; in weariness and painfulness, in watchings often, in hunger and thirst; in fastings often, in cold and nakedness." (2 Cor. 11:23–27) And on top of all this, he had the "care of all the churches."

After the end of the third journey, Paul returned to Jerusalem for a third or, if we prefer the account in Acts to Paul's own letters, a fifth visit. He was dragged out of the Temple by the Jews, and "while they set about killing him a report was taken up to the military tribune in command of the cohort that the whole of Jerusalem was in riot. He immediately rushed centurions and soldiers to the spot. At the sight of the tribune and the soldiers they stopped hitting Paul." Paul spoke Greek to the tribune, and was by him allowed to address the crowd. But the crowd, which had been quiet until Paul began to relate that Jesus was "sending him far afield among the Gentiles" at that word "raised a great shout: 'Wipe him off the face of the earth! Such a man isn't fit to live.'" The military tribune ordered Paul to be brought into the fort and questioned under the lash. But again Paul's Roman citizenship came in handy: "I was born to it," he told the tribune. Next day, the tribune "had him unchained and brought before the Sanhedrin," where Paul claimed to be a Pharisee and was defended by these against the Sadducees. The tribune, afraid Paul would be torn to pieces in the melée, "gave orders for the guard to come and rescue him and take him into the fort." (Acts 23:10)

Next day, "some Jews banded together and made a vow not to eat or drink until they had killed Paul." They plotted with the Sanhedrin to have Paul brought before the high priest and elders; "our plan is to kill him before he gets there." But Paul's nephew, his sister's son, heard of the plot and went to the fort and told Paul. Paul called a centurion and asked him to take the young man to the military tribune; Paul's nephew said: "The Jews have planned to ask you to take Paul before the Sanhedrin tomorrow, pretending they want a more thorough inquiry. But don't listen to them, as more than forty of them are going to ambush him—they have vowed not to eat or drink anything till they have killed him. They're all ready, waiting for you to agree." The tribune sent for two centurions and told them: "Make preparations for two hundred heavy infantry, seventy horsemen, and two hundred spearmen to go to Caesarea, setting out at nine tonight. Provide mounts for Paul, and take him safely to Governor Felix." (Acts 23) When Paul arrived in Caesarea, a lawyer called Tertullus opened the case against him, but Paul defended himself saying, "I admit this much: I DO follow the Way which they call a 'sect,' but I worship the God of our fathers." He went on, ending with the words, "I am on trial before you because I believe in the resurrection of the dead." And Acts goes on (24:22) to say that Felix, who had a fairly accurate knowledge of the Way, adjourned the hearing. He kept Paul in custody "but allowed some freedom, and that his friends should be permitted to see to his wants without interference." After a few days, Felix, with his wife, "who was a Jewess," listened to Paul's exposition of the faith in Christ. "But when Paul began to discourse of the good life, self-control, and the judgment to come, Felix became alarmed and said, 'For the time being you can go. I will call for you when I have time to spare.' And he did send for Paul and talked privately with him, quite often—especially as he was hoping for a bribe." (Acts 24:24–26) Acts goes on, succinctly: "Two years passed. Felix was succeeded by Porcius Festus, and in his anxiety to ingratiate himself with the Jews he left Paul in prison."

The Jews' hostility to Paul did not diminish. Only two days after arriving to take over the province, Festus left Caesarea and went up to Jerusalem, where the chief priests and Jewish leaders laid their case against Paul before him. "They asked him as a favor to have Paul brought to Jerusalem, planning to ambush him and kill him on the way." But Festus was not as green as he was cabbage-looking, and suggested instead that, as he was shortly returning to Caesarea, where Paul was, the Jews from Jerusalem should come and accuse Paul there. Which they did, making a variety of serious charges, none of which they could prove. Festus, however, "hoping to gain popularity with the Jews," asked Paul if he would go to Jerusalem and "stand trial before me there." To which Paul replied that he was standing in the court of Caesar, and that was where he ought to be tried. And then made his historic statement: "I appeal unto Caesar." Whereupon Festus declared, "You have appealed to Caesar. To Caesar you shall go."

A few days later, King Agrippa came to Caesarea to pay a state visit to Festus, and "Festus referred Paul's case to the king," explaining that the Jewish chief priests had "asked me to pronounce him guilty. 'It is not a Roman custom,' I told them, 'to hand over an accused man before he has been confronted by his accusers and had the opportunity of defending himself on the charge.'" (Acts 25:15, 16) Agrippa was the son of Herod Agrippa I, who had beheaded James, the brother of John, and put Peter in prison (from which he had been rescued by an angel); Agrippa was a third-generation pro-Roman Idumaean, whose sister, Berenice, accompanied him on this state visit to Festus. Berenice had been married to Herod of Chalcis, who died in A.D. 48. She had then moved in with her brother, and their incestuous relations had driven the Roman poet Juvenal to mirthful verse.

Festus explained to Agrippa that he didn't think Paul had done anything to deserve the death penalty: "And as he himself appealed to the Emperor I decided to send him to Rome. But I have nothing definite to write about him to the Emperor. So I have brought him before you, your Majesty, and you, ladies and gentlemen, in the hope that the inquiry may produce material for my letter." (Acts 25:25)

Agrippa gave Paul permission to state his case, and Paul then gave his (second) version of what happened on the road to Damascus. But when he said ". . . nothing of what I say differs from what the Prophets and Moses foretold, that the Messiah would have to die and that he would be the first to rise from the dead and bring light to the Jews—and the Gentiles," Festus "cried out loudly, 'Paul, you're mad. Your great learning is turning you mad.'" Paul countered by asking Agrippa if he believed in the Prophets, adding, "I know you *do*." Upon which, "Agrippa said to Paul: 'Almost thou persuadest me to be a Christian!'" And then the king, Festus, and Berenice retired, and Agrippa told Festus, "This man could have been set free, if he had not appealed to Caesar." (Acts 26:27–32)

Instead, Paul and some other prisoners were put into the charge of a centurion called Julius and took ship. In one day they reached Sidon, where "with great kindness Julius allowed Paul to go on shore and be cared for by his friends." They sailed slowly for many days, and "coasted along with difficulty till we reached a place called Fair Havens," in Crete. Paul gave a warning: "I foresee," he said, "that before the voyage is over the ship and cargo will be seriously damaged." (Acts 27:10)

Then came a great storm, which lasted fourteen days. Neither sun nor stars were seen for many days; spare tackle was thrown overboard. Paul said, "You men should have listened to what I said and not sailed from Crete. Then there would never have been this loss and damage. As it is, keep your spirits up, for though the ship will be lost, none of you will lose your lives. Last night an angel of the God to whom I belong and whom I serve stood at my side: 'Do not be afraid, Paul,' he said, 'you have to stand before Caesar. And for your sake God will save the lives of everyone on board.' So, courage, men." When daylight came, Paul advised everyone to eat, and all 276 men on board watched as he took a loaf and gave thanks and, "breaking off a piece," began to eat. Then "they, too, had some food. When they had had enough to eat they further lightened the ship by throwing the wheat overboard." (Acts 27:21–24, 32–38)

They had come to a bay, and a beach; the ship ran aground, the bow stuck fast, while the stern broke up. The soldiers wanted to kill the prisoners, but the centurion was anxious to save Paul and told those who could swim to jump overboard, and the rest to follow on planks; everyone reached land safely. The land was Malta, and "the natives showed us remarkable kindness. They lit a fire and invited all of us around it, for rain had set in and it was cold." Paul was collecting a bundle of sticks and putting them on the fire when a viper, roused by the warmth, came out and "fastened its fangs on his hand." The natives thought Paul must be a murderer. "He escaped death by drowning but justice caught up with him all the same." Paul shook the creature off into the fire, and came to no harm. When nothing happened, the natives "changed their opinion" and began saying Paul was a god. They remained three months on the island, and Paul laid hands on many, first on his host, Poplius, and then on all the sick who were brought him, and all were cured. When the winter was over, they sailed for Rome on an Alexandrian ship called *The Heavenly Twins*, which had wintered at Malta. They spent three days in Syracuse, and stayed a week with the Brotherhood at Puteoli. And from Puteoli they walked toward Rome. The Christian community there, hearing of their coming, came out as far as Appius Market and the Three Taverns, to meet them; "when he saw them Paul thanked God and his spirits revived." (Acts 28:15) In Rome, "Paul was allowed to live by himself with the soldier who guarded him." There he remained for two years; then, sometime between 64 and 67, he was put to death, tradition has it by beheading, under Nero, the Caesar to whom he had appealed.

"On the day when the apostle offered up his head to the Emperor's sword in the street of a Roman suburb, he could rejoice in having remained true to his oath that nothing would separate him from the love of Christ. For him, a citizen of the kingdom, death was truly a gain," writes Ernesto Buonaiuti (*Eranos Yearbook 6* [Princeton University Press, 1968], p. 160), and Buonaiuti goes on to declare that "the central problem of Christian history is the relation between the personality and teachings of Christ and the personality and teachings of St. Paul presented in the New Testament." (*Ibid.* p. 120)

For the Jews, God was "the universal order by which all things fulfill the law of their being," as Matthew Arnold described Him, and was apprehended chiefly as "the moral order in human nature." Christ himself invited all to an inner renewal which would bring them to the Father; for Paul, it was Christ's death and resurrection which "redeemed us." But to become participators in the Redemption one thing was necessary: "to die with Christ to the law of the flesh, to live with Christ to the law of the mind." As St. Paul wrote in 2 Cor. 4:10, "Always bearing about in the body the dying of the Lord Jesus, that the life also of Jesus might be made manifest in our body." Thus, dying with Christ, resurrection, and growing into Christ, here, now, are the supreme essentials. And consequently, as Matthew Arnold noted, "whoever identifies himself with Christ, identifies himself with Christ's idea of the solidarity of men." (*St. Paul and Protestantism* [London: Smith, Elder & Co., 1906], p. 54) The whole of humanity is conceived by St. Paul as one body, having to die and rise with Christ; indeed, in one passage St. Paul speaks of "the whole creation groaning and travailing in pain until now, waiting for the adoption." (Rom. 8:22–23) And for the "adopted," "neither death, nor life, nor angels, nor principalities nor powers, nor things present nor things to come, nor height, nor depth nor any other creature, shall be able to separate us from the love of God which is in Christ Jesus our Lord." (Rom. 8:38–39) Furthermore (Eph. 4:25) St. Paul says every man must "speak truth to his neighbour, for we are members one of another."

Christ had warned that "except a grain of wheat fall into the ground and die it abideth alone, but if it die, it bringeth forth much fruit (John 12:24) and Paul declared "we must all be buried with him [Christ] in baptism" in order to be "risen with him." (Col. 2:12) Also, referring to the Eucharist, Paul insists that we being many are one bread, and one body, for we are all partakers of that one bread. (1 Cor. 10:17) Augustine would later interpret this as meaning: "You eat what you yourselves are: the body of the Lord."

Christ's "I am the vine, and ye are the branches," is clearly echoed in Paul's "I no longer live but Christ lives in me" and by his statement in 1 Cor. 2:16, "we have the mind of Christ."

Everything about Christ's humanity is attractive: in almost twenty centuries no one has found His sinlessness priggish, or His personality maudlin. Paul, on the other hand, constantly scolding, continually boasting, often whining, admittedly was a squabbler from the start. Indeed, the thorn in his flesh, of which he complained and which some writers think was a sexual problem, might possibly have been his inability to stay friends with any individuals or any communities, his touchiness and grouchiness. Yet, in spite of this, Paul is the architect of the Church, and Christian theology, whether Catholic, Protestant, or Orthodox, all claims to derive from his hastily dictated letters, some sent from various prisons, others from stopping places on his arduous missionary journeys. And these letters are masterpieces, even in their sloppy Greek or archaic English. Indeed, 1 Corinthians 13 had been twinned with Cleanthes' earlier *Hymn* as two of the greatest poems in the Greek language.

But Paul certainly fostered—if he did not originate—Christian anti-Semitism. While frankly admitting his own Jewishness, even stressing it "to Jews becoming like a Jew, to win Jews" (1 Cor. 9:20), Paul declared, in 1 Thess. 2:15-16, "the Jews killed the Lord Jesus and their own prophets, and have persecuted us, and they please not God, and are contrary to all men, hindering us from speaking to the Gentiles to lead them to salvation. All this time they have been making up the full measure of their guilt, and the wrath is come upon them to the uttermost."

Indeed, Paul's relationship with the Jews after his breakaway from their ranks was disastrous. Moreover, it clearly pointed the way "towards a total breach between Jews and Christians . . . this final split occurred long after Paul's death. But it had been very largely his doing (Michael Grant, *St Paul*, pp. 158–59). It seems a pity that Paul's wonderful opening of Christian salvation to all peoples should have somehow been at the expense of his and his Master's own people. And it certainly provided an excuse to many Christian rulers— from the leaders of the Crusades to *Isabel la Católica*, of Spain, to persecute or exile Christ's countrymen.

Paul's ten letters were probably first collected in one volume, the *Apostolicon*, circa A.D. 150, by Marcion of Smyrna; they now occupy one fifth of the entire New Testament. Paul influenced Augustine, Martin Luther, John Wesley, and Karl Barth; in fact, it is possible to assert that within the Christian Church he has been the greatest single source of all its spiritual revivals.

What is Paul's relevance for us *today*? First of all, his complete internationalism. "For there is no difference between Jew and Greek, for it is the same Lord of all." (Rom. 10:12) "For as many as are led by the Spirit of God, they are the sons of God. (Rom. 8:14) Again and again, in letter after letter, Paul repeats this, often in almost the very same words, and always making the same point. Then, too, his insistence that "there is nothing unclean of itself, but to him that esteemeth anything to be unclean, to him it is unclean" (Rom. 14:14) is relevant for us.

Another, immensely important aspect of St. Paul is his insistence on the necessity, for the Christian, of work: "The man who refuses to work must be left to starve" (2 Thess. 3:10) or, as the King James translation has it, "if any would not work, neither should he eat."

But perhaps it is Paul the mystic who matters most to us today. His identification of Christ, himself, and the Church is so complete that he can say that in this mortal frame of his he helped to pay off the debt that the afflictions of Christ still left to be paid, for the sake of His body, the Church.

St. Helena (d. 329)

The most extraordinary fact about Helena is that she, rather than her distinguished son Constantine, the first Christian emperor of Rome, was canonized. Is it possible that there was some early *"vox populi, vox Dei"* form of canonization, such as prevailed over five hundred years later in the case of the emperor Charlemagne, the first emperor of the Holy Roman Empire (which was dismissed by Gibbon as "neither holy, nor Roman, nor an empire")? For even Gibbon, whose anti-Christian bias is as amusing as it is strong, doted on Constantine, and praised him extravagantly. Perhaps Constantine himself arranged for his mother's canonization? However it came about, canonized Helena was, and Constantine was not, and this retiring, gentle woman (whose feast is on August 18) shines not only with the aura of her established sanctity but also as a testimony to the wisdom of the Church, which chose to bestow its highest accolade on the meek mother rather than on the victorious son.

There are two versions of Helena's meeting with Constantine's father, Constantius Chlorus (chlorus means green-faced—he was so called because of his pallor). According to one tradition, Helena was about twenty-seven when Constantius, passing through Bithynia on his way to fight Zenobia, queen of Palmyra, stopped at an inn, fell in love with the innkeeper's daughter, and married her. The second, or variant, version is that Helena was the young (teen-age) daughter of a British king whom Constantius Chlorus met at a banquet given for him either in Colchester or York by this king, called Coel, whom British legend has it was the "Old King Cole," the "merry old soul," who "called for his fiddlers three." If the latter story is true, Helena was descended, via Brutus, Aeneas' great-grandson, from the "pious Aeneas" of Virgil's *Aeneid,* who fled the ruins of Troy carrying his father, Anchises, on his shoulders—and from Cymbeline. Whichever version is true, Constantius and Helena were married in 273, and their son Constantine was born in 274. Various places contend for the honor of being Constantine's birthplace: Gibbon prefers Drepanum, a town on the gulf of Nicomedia, which Constantine later renamed Helenapolis; while most British, rather naturally, prefer him to be British born. Evelyn Waugh, who wrote a book about Helena, declared Constantine to have been born at Nish, in Illyria. Constantine's father's family was distinguished: Constantius' mother was a niece of the emperor Claudius; his father, Eutropius, was one of the greatest Dardanian (Danubian) nobles. Constantius was given charge, by Diocletian, of Gaul, Spain, and Britain, but Helena remained at Nish with her baby son.

Diocletian, in fact, had already divided the Empire between himself and Maximian. Now he further divided it by conferring an equal share of authority on two generals "of approved merit": one was Galerius, the other Constantius. They were invested with the secondary honors of the imperial purple and were called caesars, not emperors. Diocletian obliged them both to divorce their wives. Galerius was required to marry the daughter of Diocletian, and Constantius was made to marry the daughter-in-law of Maximianus Heraclius.

Diocletian reigned for twenty-one years, and the frontiers of his empire were thousands of miles in extent. There were constant irruptions of barbarians, and revolts of subjugated people. Constantius was once surrounded by a host of Alemanni and wounded, but got to Langres, where he was drawn up a wall by a rope, as the citizens refused to open the gates. Roman troops, however, came to his aid from all sides, and he killed six thousand Alemanni the same evening. In 305, Diocletian abdicated, and for nine years lived on as a private citizen in Split, growing cabbages. On the same day as Diocletian, Maximian also resigned the purple, and Constantius and Galerius were raised to it in their stead.

Constantine was about eighteen when his mother was divorced (292). He was handsome, tall, agile, "intrepid in war, affable in peace," and his youth and energy made Galerius jealous. Constantine asked leave to join his father and traveling posthaste he covered the enormous distance through Bithynia, Thrace, Dacia, Italy, and Gaul, and got to the Channel just as his father was preparing to set out for Britain. Constantine accompanied his father, Constantius, who easily conquered the Caledonians but died in York, on July 25, 306. Immediately, Constantine was proclaimed Augustus in his stead. The troops acclaimed him emperor, and Galerius, bowing to the *fait accompli,* accepted him as sovereign of all the Cisalpine provinces. Constantius had three boys and three girls by his second wife, the eldest of whom was thirteen at their father's death. The dying Constantius bequeathed his second family to Constantine, and as Gibbon put it, "their liberal education, advantageous marriages, the secure dignity of their lives . . . attest the fraternal affection of Constantine."

But Constantine's warmest feelings were reserved for his own mother, Helena.

Though he had married Minervina, and had a son, Crispus, one of his first acts as Augustus was to divorce Minervina and proclaim Helena empress dowager. She had lived thirteen years alone. Now, for four years at Treves, she had her grandson Crispus with her; then he went off to join his father. Of course Constantine and Maxentius (co-emperor with Constantine, 280–312) quarreled. In fifty-eight days Constantine marched at the head of forty thousand soldiers to encounter his rival, who had four times as many troops. He crossed the Mont Cenis pass, in the Alps, and in the plains of Turin won a signal victory. Then, taking Milan, he went on to besiege Verona; it surrendered, and nine miles from Rome Constantine fought Maxentius at the battle of the Milvian Bridge, where he declared he saw a cross in the sky with the words "*In hoc signo vinces*"—"in this sign you will win." Which he did, in 312. Maxentius drowned in the Tiber in 313.

Constantine and Licinius (the new co-emperor) then decreed liberty of religious worship and the equality of all religions within the Empire. This was an extraordinary step, for after almost three hundred years, the Christians were still a persecuted minority, probably only 10 per cent of the population of the Roman Empire.

Constantine, who was a magnificent soldier and a great and wise ruler for the first part of his reign, was *literis minus instructus*—what today would be called a "functional illiterate"; and many historians have doubted—from Gibbon to Maisie Ward—how much he understood of the Christianity he first protected then embraced.

By the Edict of Milan, Constantine had restored the civil and religious rights of the Christians, of which Diocletian had deprived them. Christians, and all others, were now granted "a free and absolute power of following the religion which each individual thinks proper to prefer, to which he has addicted his mind," as Constantine decreed.

Constantine's mind, such as it was, appears to have been confused. The cross he saw may well have seemed to him the emblem of the sun god; after his victory, he "publicly invoked the Deity as one and the same in all forms of worship," as Cardinal Newman wrote; Newman goes on to note that, in 321, Constantine ordered both the observance of Sunday and the consultation of omens. He continued to accept his imperial position as the high priest of the hitherto official paganism. Gibbon declares, moreover, that the imperial convert was "permitted to enjoy *most* of the privileges before he had contracted *any* of the obligations of a Christian. Instead of retiring from the congregation when the voice of the deacon dismissed the profane multitude, he prayed with the faithful, disputed with the bishops, preached on the most sublime and intricate subjects of theology, celebrated with sacred rites the vigil of Easter, and publicly declared himself not only a partaker, but, in some measure, a priest and hierophant of the Christian mysteries. . . . As he gradually advanced in the knowledge of truth, he proportionally declined in the practice of virtue, and the same year of his reign in which he convened the council of Nicaea was polluted by the execution, or rather murder, of his eldest son."

This was 325, when, possibly at the suggestion of Hosius of Cordova, Constantine convened the first great ecumenical council of the Christian Church, in order to deal with the heresy of Arius. Arius, a native of Libya, was educated at Antioch. He declared that God was not always a father: "the self-existing God made the Word, who once was not, out of what once was not." Three hundred bishops were present at Nicaea, and Constantine, who when he had first heard of the Arian heresy had declared it were better for Christians not to entangle themselves in such minutiae of theological dispute, now, at the Council, arrayed in purple and gold, forced through an agreement on a creed that declared Jesus Christ to be "the sole-begotten of the father, God of God, light of light, very God of very

God, begotten, not made, of one substance with the Father [*homoousion tò Patri*]." Only two of the three hundred bishops refused to sign, and these two were sent into exile. Constantine stated triumphantly that "the decision of three hundred bishops must be considered no other than the judgment of God."

The murder of Crispus (Constantine's eldest son and his only son by Minervina) by Constantine's orders, much annoyed Helena. The young man had been sent to Pola, in Istria, where he had been executed. It was his stepmother, Fausta, who had suggested that Crispus made advances to her, thus poisoning Constantine's mind against his popular eldest son. But Fausta was discovered to be having an affair with a slave, and Constantine had her suffocated in the steam of a bath. Yet her three sons inherited the Empire.

One thing was certain about Constantine: his devotion to his mother. He converted her to Christianity and sent her on a mission to Jerusalem to find the site of Calvary, which she did, as Herbert Muller notes (see below) "with a speed and sureness that archeologists must envy." Constantine, who had already given the Roman Empire a new capital, called Constantinople after him; a new religion, Christianity; and a new policy, caesaropapism—that the emperor was above the Church!—now proceeded to build over the site of Calvary a monument worthy of it, the Church of the Holy Sepulcher, a shrine for pilgrims from that day to this and a major incentive for the crusaders to win back the Holy Land.

Helena brought back with her many fragments of the True Cross, also the Lance, the Sponge, and the Crown of Thorns. Constantine meanwhile adorned his new city, Constantinople, with libraries, stocked it with Greek manuscripts, and indeed inaugurated the first truly cosmopolitan city, "populated by assorted Asiatics who alike professed Christianity, spoke Greek, and called themselves Roman" (Muller, *The Loom of History* [New American Library, 1954], p. 273). After her return from Jerusalem, Helena, then over eighty years of age, gave many of the relics she had found to the city of Treves, where she died.

What has she to teach us, today? Like so many women caught up in the lives of famous men, she suffered greatly, but she survived. In an age in which life was nastier, more brutal, and shorter than usual, she seems to have managed to edify and to console, to exercise her womanly virtues through all the states of life she traversed. It is never easy to be a woman, a wife, a mother, and a grandmother; never easy to be an empress, yet she succeeded in all her roles. Not

only did her son love her, but her erstwhile slaves, her tutors, and
even the crotchety, squabbling bishops. Whatever she did, she did
well and without fuss. Rabindranath Tagore declared that "all reality is relationship," and Helena, so far from us in time, is a good example of Tagore's reality.

St. Augustine (354–430)

Born on November 13, 354, at Tagaste, today called Souk Ahras, a
small town in what is now Algeria, about 120 miles east of Constantine, Augustine was the son of a smallholder named Patricius and
his wife, Monica. The family was of pure Berber stock but completely Romanized; its ancestors probably received Roman nation-
ality, as did all other provincials, from the emperor Caracalla's constitution of 212. Augustine and his parents, though not Negroes,
were black, being Berbers. Patricius was baptized only on his
deathbed; Monica was a devout Christian. She was much envied by
the other wives of Tagaste, because she managed her husband very
well: she seemed never to get beaten, as the other wives did. As a
child, she had acquired a taste for drink by sipping wine in the big
cool containers in her parents' cellar, when sent down to draw some
by them. A maid once found her drinking and called her a sot; she
had bridled, but as a result of the scolding became abstemious for
life.

Augustine was her first child, and he has left us a wonderfully
complete account of his childhood: of how he remembered being
suckled (children then were suckled until two or three) and resented
the breast being removed; of how greedy he was, and demanding;
how jealous of a younger brother; and later, of how he loved to play.
He was brilliant as a schoolboy, but very lazy, and his parents, who
had made tremendous sacrifices to give him the best education of
the day, were stern with him; indeed, as an old bishop of seventy-
two, he wrote, "Who would not recoil in horror and prefer death,
were he offered the choice between dying and becoming once more a
child." He was beaten, and all his life remembered those beatings.
He mentions in a sermon what fun it was to sit with his small

friends playing knucklebones in the Tagaste square. When he grew bigger he stole pears with his companions and analyzed the reasons for the gang action: it wasn't for the sake of the pears—every one of the boys could get better pears at home without stealing them; it was partly the pleasure of the illicit chase, partly the delicious danger of getting caught.

One day, however, Augustine fell ill, and his mother wanted him baptized—he had already been listed among the Christian cate-chumens—but he grew better and baptism was deferred. At fifteen, seeing him naked in the public baths, his father was delighted at the thought of grandchildren; his mother wept at the thought of her son's future sexual sins. At sixteen, lack of funds interrupted Augustine's schooling for a whole year, during which the juvenile became delinquent. "I was tossed about and wasted and poured out and boiling over in my fornications," he wrote of himself. "I was like a forest: I grew a whole vegetation of loves."

Then, when he was nearly seventeen, a friend of the family, Romanianus, paid for the gifted boy to continue his studies. Augustine had already been to high school in Madaura (a local metropolis); now he went—in 370—to Carthage, the capital of Roman Africa and the most important town then in, and of, the West, after Rome itself. But while Augustine was studying at Carthage, his father died, before Augustine was twenty, and he had to leave and get a job, since he had now become the sole support of his mother, of a sister, and of a concubine, with whom he had taken up in Carthage, who bore him his only son, Adeodatus, in the summer of 372. He lived with her for fourteen years, and then sent her back to Africa—they were in Milan at the time—keeping with him her son, who died in 389, aged seventeen. She must have loved Augustine very much, for she vowed to remain faithful to him and did; whereas he, as soon as she had left, took another mistress while waiting for a young girl, chosen by his mother to be his wife, to become nubile.

Also in 372, Augustine became a Manichaean, but he remained an auditor, never even aspiring to become one of the elect. Mani (216–77) was born in Persia. He called himself "Apostle of Jesus Christ" and said he was the promised Paraclete. But in Persia he claimed to be the successor of Zarathustra, and in China of Buddha. Mani taught a strict dualism: There were two sources of beng, one of good and one of evil, and the whole cosmos was the result of a temporary, but unfortunate, mixture of good and bad elements. To help the good in its fight with evil—a fight that would endure as long as the world—it was necessary to free the particles of Light from their dark prison. So the elect abstained from marriage and from procreation, which were evil, and kept to a strict diet: meat, blood, and wine were "dark" foods; fruits and green vegetables were "luminous." Augustine has a very funny description of Manichaeans stuffing themselves, and above all, any young children whom they could coax to their feasts, with cabbage and lettuce, until some even swelled from too much gas and eventually died of indigestion. This was considered the equal of martyrdom, for the child—or adult— who so perished had done so while releasing the Light stored in the green vegetable into himself, a higher container of Light. Certainly, for all their errors, the Manichaeans seem to have gotten hold of two truths: photosynthesis and the nature of vitamins.

Mani also taught much that appealed to Augustine's inquiring mind. Mani did not deny Christianity but pointed out the many contradictions in the Gospels and the discordances among the Synoptics, and above all, he promised to give a rational explanation of the origin of evil.

"The Light shall go to the Light
The fragrance shall go to the fragrance. . . .
. . . .
The Light shall return to its place, the Darkness shall
    fall. . . ."

Such phrases from the Manichaean Psalmbook were far more attractive to Augustine than the horrific utterances of the Jewish God on Sinai commanding his followers to put innocent babes to death and constantly screaming against every other people. For Mani believed all people to be the same and all capable of salvation, once they had "awoken" and secured their own release. Monica, Augustine's mother, was appalled at her son's new interest; she shut him out of her house.

So Augustine returned from Tagaste to Carthage, where he won a poetry prize and wrote his first book: *On the Beautiful.* He converted his two greatest friends, Alypius and Nebridius, to Manichaeanism. In 382, Augustine set off on the long trip to Rome, Alypius having preceded him, Nebridius following. Monica tried to stop Augustine from leaving Africa, but he lied to her, saying he was seeing a friend off. Then, when he had persuaded her to spend the night in a place near the ship on which he intended to sail, "I stole away from her. She remained, praying and weeping. . . . The wind blew and filled our sails. . . . She went home and I to Rome."

Augustine's year in Rome was not a success, but at the end of it he became professor of rhetoric in Milan, thanks to the recommendation of some Manichaean friends. It was in the fall of 384 that Augustine arrived in Milan, already bored with Manichaeanism, but Ambrose, the Catholic bishop of Milan, snubbed him. Ambrose treated Augustine *"satis episcopaliter"*—in a sufficiently bishoplike way—Augustine wrote, but went out of his way to be nice to Monica, who had followed Augustine.

In Milan, Augustine spent his mornings giving lectures and his afternoons lobbying; he hoped, through influence, to be named governor of a province.

He had been a Manichaean for nearly ten years when he met the Manichaean leader, Faustus, and found him to be a fraud, for he would not (or could not!) answer Augustine's questions. Augustine now was worse off than before, believing in nothing and no one. Monica, who had never despaired of him, persuaded him to attend Ambrose's sermons. Ambrose was an easy man to approach: a prince by blood and a prince in the hierarchy of the Church though he was, anyone could come to him at any time, and Monica often did and wept to him about her delinquent child. Ambrose told her the child of so many tears could not be lost. But Augustine, when he diffidently went to consult Ambrose, found him reading alone and, afraid to bother him, crept shyly away.

It was Ambrose's confessor and later successor, the priest Simplicianus, who helped Augustine by introducing him to the neo-Platonists: to the *Enneads* of Plotinus and the Latin translations of Porphyry as well. From the neo-Platonists, Augustine learned that man was body and soul, and that the body was not to be despised but respected as the soul's fellow creature. As he wrote to his benefactor, Romanianus, the neo-Platonists lit in him a "flaming conflagration." But, as he wrote later, though from Plato he learned that in the beginning was the Word, and that the Word was with God and the Word was God, nowhere in Plato did he find it written that the Word was made flesh and dwelt among us.

Then, one day, when he was at home in Milan with his pupil and devoted friend Alypius, an African friend, Pontitian, came to call and described the recent conversion of two young soldiers to Christianity by reading the life of St. Anthony. Neither Alypius nor Augustine had heard of St. Anthony or knew about the Egyptian monks. Pontitian was "eager to introduce so great a man to men ignorant of him, and marveled very much at our ignorance." For Anthony had been still living when Augustine was born, and his monasteries were then flourishing; all Augustine could do was to repeat over and over:

"And we had not heard of it." After Pontitian had left, Augustine was in a turmoil: "The unlearned arise and take heaven by force, and here are we with all our learning, stuck fast in flesh and blood." (*Confessions VIII*, vii, 18)

He took up the Epistles of St. Paul, which he had been reading, and went out into the garden, wretched at the contrast between his life—for he was still living in sin—and his desires. In the garden, he thought he heard a child chanting in a singsong voice, loudly: "Take and read! Take and read!" Augustine then remembered that what had converted Anthony was listening to the gospel read aloud, so he opened St. Paul at random, at Romans 13:13, and read: "Let us walk honestly, as in the day; not in rioting and drunkenness, not in chambering and wantonness, not in strife and envying. But put ye on the Lord Jesus Christ, and make not provision for the flesh, to fulfil the lusts thereof." (*Confessions VIII*, xii, 28–30) At once, he felt as though these words were "spoken directly to himself"; a light of utter confidence shone in his heart, and he was able to "come clean." After a few more weeks of teaching, he resigned from his job and decided to enter the Church and give up the world.

So Augustine retired, with his mother, Monica, his son, Adeodatus, his beloved disciple, Alypius, and a few other students and friends, to Cassiciacum, some twenty miles north of Milan. There he spent the few months until Easter, when he was to be baptized; there he began to live the life of retreat, prayer, and study that he ever after regarded as ideal. Monica took care of the household, and Augustine describes how shocked she was when he insisted on singing hymns when in the bathroom. Of course he should, he told her: suppose death overtook him there, how regrettable were he not singing hymns! There, at Cassiciacum, Augustine wrote his first *Dialogues*. The months there were the happiest of his life.

After Augustine's baptism, as they were all on their way back to Africa: (*Confessions IX*, x, 23–25)

> The day was approaching when my mother was to leave this life, a day you knew, my God, but which we knew not, and it so happened, by a secret dispensation of your Providence, that we found ourselves alone together, she and I, leaning against a window, from which there was a view over the garden of the house in which we were living at Ostia, and in which, after the fatigues of a long trip, we were waiting for the moment to embark. In this solitude we were talking very quietly, and, forgetting the past, in order to throw ourselves into the future, we

were seeking together, in the light of the Truth that is You
Yourself, what might be the life eternal of the saints, which eye
has not seen nor ear heard nor the heart of man imagined.
Therefore, we were aspiring with the lips of our heart towards
the celestial streams of Your fountains, of those living fountains
which dwell in Thee (Psalm 35) in order that we might quench
our thirst as much as we could and thus lift ourselves in some
fashion up to such a high idea . . . and very sweet our talk was,
and *forgetting those things which are behind, and reaching
forth unto those things which are before*, we were discussing between ourselves and in the presence of Truth, which you are,
what the eternal life of the saints could be like, *which eye hath
not seen, nor ear heard, nor hath it entered into the heart of
man*. Yet with the mouth of our heart we panted for the heavenly streams of your fountain, the fountain of life, which is with
you, so that, if some drops from that fountain—all that we
could take—were to be scattered over us, we might in some way
or other be able to think of such high matters.

Our talk had reached this point: that the greatest possible
delights of our bodily senses, radiant as they might be with the
brightest of corporeal light, could not be compared with the joys
of that eternal life, could not, indeed, even deserve a mention.
Then, with our affections burning still more strongly toward the
Selfsame, we raised ourselves higher and step by step passed over
all material things, even the heaven itself from which sun and
moon and stars shine down upon the earth. And still we went
upward, meditating and speaking and looking with wonder at
your works, and we came to our own souls, and we went beyond
our souls to reach that region of never-failing plenty where
Thou feedest Israel forever with the food of truth and where life
is that Wisdom by whom all these things are made, both what
is past and what is to come; but Wisdom herself is not made;
she is as she has been and will be forever; or rather, there is no
place in her for "to have been" or "to be going to be"; one can
only say "to be," since she is eternal and "have been" and
"going to be" are not eternal. And as we talked, yearning toward
this Wisdom, we did, with the whole strength of our hearts' im-
pulse, just lightly come into touch with her, and we sighed and
we left bound there *the first fruits of the Spirit*, and we returned
to the sounds made by our mouths, where a word has a beginning and an ending. And how unlike is this to your Word, our

Lord, you who abide in yourself forever, without becoming old, making all things new!

So we said: if to any man the tumult of the flesh were to grow silent, silent the images of earth and water and air, and the poles of heaven silent also; if the soul herself were to be silent and, by not thinking of self, were to transcend self; if all dreams and imagined revelations were silent, and every tongue, every sign; if there was utter silence from everything which exists only to pass away (for, if one can hear them, these all say: we did not make ourselves. He made us that abideth forever) but suppose that, having said this and directed our attention to Him that made them, they too were to become hushed and He Himself alone were to speak, not by their voice but in His own, and we were to hear His word, not through any tongue of flesh or voice of an angel or sound of thunder or difficult allegory, but that we might hear Him whom in all these things we love, might hear Him in Himself without them, just as a moment ago we two had, as it were, gone beyond ourselves and in a flash of thought had made contact with that eternal wisdom which abides above all things—supposing that this state were to continue, that all other visions, visions of so different a kind, were to be withdrawn, leaving only this one to ravish and absorb and wrap the beholder in inward joys, so that his life might be forever like that moment of understanding which we had had and for which we now sighed—would not this be: *Enter into Thy Master's joy?* And when shall that be? Shall it be when *we shall all rise again,* though we *shall not all be changed?*

Something like this I said, though not precisely in this way and in these words. Yet, Lord, you know that on that day when we were talking together as I have described and when, as we talked, this world with all its delights seemed to us so worthless, my mother said: "My son, as to me, I no longer find any pleasure in this life. What more I have to do here and why I am still here I do not know, since I have no longer anything to hope for in this world. There was only one reason why I wanted to stay a little longer in this life, and that was that I should see you a Catholic Christian before I died. Now God has granted me this beyond my hopes; for I see that you have despised the pleasures of this world and are become His servant. So what am I doing here?"

What reply I made to these words of hers I cannot clearly remember. Within five days, or not much more, she fell into a fever. And one day while she was ill she had a fainting fit and temporarily lost consciousness of her surroundings. We hurried to her side, but she soon regained consciousness, and, seeing my brother and me standing by her, she said to us, as though she were trying to find the answer to some question, "Where am I?" Then, as we stood dumb with grief, she looked in our faces and said: "Here you will bury your mother." I remained quiet and kept back my tears; but my brother said something to her to the effect that he hoped that she would have the good fortune to die in her own country and not abroad. On hearing this an anxious expression came over her face, and she gave him a reproachful look for still savoring of such earthly things. Then she looked into my face and said: "See what he is saying!" Soon afterward she said to both of us, "You may lay this body of mine anywhere. Do not worry at all about that. All I ask you is this, that wherever you may be you will remember me at the altar of the Lord." This was what she said, speaking with difficulty, and then she became silent as the force of her illness grew heavier upon her. (*Confessions IX*, xi, 27–28)

Monica died a few days later, in the fifty-sixth year of her age. Augustine returned to Tagaste, sold his father's lands, and began to lead a monastic life.

He lived for less than three years thus, from the fall of 388 until the spring of 391. Then, one day, by chance, he happened to be in Hippo, in church, and Bishop Valerius was asking his people to find him a priest to help him—Valerius was old and Greek-speaking, and found it difficult to express himself in Latin. The congregation, which had seen Augustine arrive, shouted, "Augustine, priest," then seized him, dragged him to the choir, and in spite of his cries, insisted on his being ordained. So, at thirty-six, Augustine became priest, and at forty-one, auxiliary bishop. Shortly after this, Valerius died, and thereafter for thirty-four years, Augustine was in his stead bishop of Hippo.

Bishop though he now was, he wished to remain a monk, and he organized a kind of monastery in the shadow of his cathedral, where Valerius had given Augustine a house and a garden. Augustine lived a community life with his priests, deacons, and other clerics, following a strict rule. It was moderately ascetic as to food, rigorously chaste—the "cloister" was absolute—and absolutely poor, for every member gave up everything he possessed upon joining. This community of priests, under the bishop's aegis, was a nursery of bishops, about a dozen whom were inspired by Augustine, including his biographer Possidius, who had been a member of Augustine's community before becoming bishop of Guelma.

Augustine's rule was founded on the apostolic life, and the ideal Augustine and his priests set themselves was, above all, that of doing their jobs properly. "The key to Augustine the Christian lies in his inner relation to monasticism," writes Dr. Walter Nigg, a Protestant pastor. (*Warriors of God* [New York: Alfred A. Knopf, 1939], p. 107) "Augustine considered that monks came closest to putting the Christian ideal into practice, and he resolved to do likewise. He joined their ranks and became, in the end, one of the great fathers of monasticism." Augustine attempted three monastic foundations: at Cassiciacum, at Tagaste, and finally at Hippo. Cassiciacum was "hardly more than a debating society, a sort of nursing-home for convalescent souls." Whereas "Tagaste is a landmark in the development of Western monasticism. Here . . . was to come into being—for the first time, perhaps, in history—a monastery that was truly Western in spirit." (A. Zumkeller, *Das Monchtum des heiligen Augustinus* [1931], p. 10) For the first time, too, by his insistence that he was, and would remain, a monk, even after ordination, even after his elevation to the episcopal throne, Augustine showed the way to all the priest-monks, bishop-monks, even pope-monks, who were to follow him.

Altogether, Augustine founded three monasteries in Hippo, and near them one convent for women, of which his sister, Perpetua, was head. His 211th letter is to these women and has been called St. Augustine's rule for nuns.

St. Augustine was the first to prove that the monastery need not be in the desert but can be in the market place. Yet he insisted that every man must have time to himself for mental prayer. "No man has a right . . . to be so immersed in active life as to neglect the contemplation of God." (St. Augustine, *City of God*, Book xix, Chap. xix [New York: Library of Nicene and Post-Nicene Fathers, 1907], Vol. 110) God did not say, he pointed out, "Go to the East to find peace, travel to the West to seek rest. There where you seek, there shall you find; to Him Who is everywhere present, one comes by love and not by sail."

In his monastery, Augustine cared more for the conversation at meals than for what was served: only the spoons were of silver; the dishes were of clay, wood, or stone. But if the talk became slanderous, Augustine rose and left the table even when visiting bishops were present. And carved into his monastery dining table were the words: "If anyone in his conversation attempts to injure the character of some absent one, let him consider himself unwelcome to this table."

St. Augustine's rule has been followed by many. In the eleventh century, as the result of Pope Nicolas II's recommendation to priests, deacons, and subdeacons "that they live together near the churches for which they had been ordained, and that there they have in common their table, sleeping quarters, and church revenues," the Augustinian, or Austin, canons, also called canons regular of St. Augustine, appeared. They were priests bound by the vows of religion, who lived in community under St. Augustine's rule. Canons secular, who were attached to cathedrals and colleges, took no vows of poverty or obedience. Augustinian canons sing the Divine Office in choir and normally lead the life of monks, but they are at all times prepared to undertake the works of the active apostolate, and they must be in holy orders. They wear a white linen rochet as a distinguishing mark. In 1256 the Austin friars, or the hermits of St. Augustine, and the Augustinian order proper were unified; in the thirteenth century a third order of Augustinians began, and in the sixteenth, the discalced Augustinians.

Once he had been consecrated bishop, Augustine had to celebrate the liturgy publicly each day; he had to administer the sacraments; he had to preach, on Sundays and holydays, several times a day (over five hundred of his sermons, as taken down by stenographers, have come down to us). He also was the sole resort of the guilty or the oppressed; he had an enormous correspondence, and had to distribute the considerable episcopal charity; to manage the episcopal finances; to direct many souls; to listen, sometimes from morning to night, to plaintiffs seeking justice or mercy at his tribunal. And in spite of all this press of work, Augustine remained a contemplative. He also managed to leave 113 books and 218 letters as well as the sermons. "In the beginning was the Word: behold Him to Whom Mary hearkened; and the Word was made flesh; behold Him Whom Martha served." Augustine waited upon his Lord in both capacities, equally attentive in Mary's role as in Martha's. Augustine's cry, from the moment of his conversion, was *Noverim me, noverim Te*: May I know myself, may I know Thee! He took his episcopal duties, even the least, most seriously. The following is from his *Enarratio in Psalmum 106, 107*:

Supposing that, cured of error, having overcome the difficulty of doing good, freed from torpidity and from all distaste for God's word, perhaps you have deserved the care of the faithful: you have been given to care for and to conduct one vessel, a church. Now appears a fourth temptation. The sea's tempests shake the church and trouble the pilot. Any believer can suffer the first three temptations, but the fourth one is especially ours, and the danger increases with the honors conferred upon us. Anyone can fear lest the danger of error turn him away from the truth; anyone can fear he may be overcome by concupiscence, preferring to yield rather than to cry to the Lord from among the difficulties to which it gives rise; anyone may fear lest the taste for God's word leave him, so that he risks death by his lukewarmness. But the temptations which come from directing souls, the temptations arising from the dangers attached to governing a church, these are especially ours. And you—can you be indifferent to this danger, if the whole bark is in danger of going down? . . . You, my brothers, although you do not hold the tiller, you are nevertheless passengers in the same vessel. . . . You must therefore continue to pray for us, being exposed to shipwreck with us. . . .

Augustine's was one of the most seminal minds that has ever been. Perhaps because he knew little or no Greek, and so could only make use of such Greek writers as had been translated into Latin, he had, so to speak, to think through everything the Greeks had discovered for himself; that is, he actually had to invent anew many ideas that he might otherwise have got at second hand. The whole problem of time and of duration; the whole problem of the relation of sign to meaning in language; the whole problem of predestination and grace; the whole problem of causality and accident—these are but some of the areas in which Augustine's original thought has reached out and reacted upon all subsequent thinkers. In the Lateran is a sixth-century inscription which says: "The various Fathers explained various things, but only he [Augustine] has said it all, in Latin, explaining the mysteries in the thunder of his great voice." He was quoted and commented on, from one end of the *Romanitas*, of the Romanized world, to the other: from the edge of the Black Sea, where Scythian monks—Romanians—around 518, in a theological quarrel in Constantinople decided the issue by quoting Augustine: their training and theology were wholly Augustinian; Gaul, where St. Caesarius of Arles, and Rome, where Gregory the Great, regarded St. Augustine as their master, whom they adapted and commented on. Gregory the Great, Supreme Pontiff though he was, warned a correspondent in Africa: "Beware lest you prefer our bran to his pure wheat." And Isidore of Seville, himself the last of the Fathers, put Augustine above *all* the Fathers, Greek or Latin.

After fifteen hundred years Augustine is still one of the most original of Western minds, constantly commented on, taught, edited. His major contributions to the development of Western understanding are threefold: His idea of justice—that kingdoms are bands of robbers—has been the wellspring of all subsequent political ideas, whether orthodoxly Christian, like St. Basil's, for example, or even such ideas as Godwin's, that property is theft, or Kropotkin's, that history is the history of crime. Augustine's social gospel was based on his recognition of the fear of death as the basis of selfishness. Though he has had fathered on him the idea that the visible Church is the kingdom of God, he himself called such an idea *insania*: insanity.

The second time one of his ideas was to sweep Europe was at the Reformation, when Calvin and Luther claimed Augustine's ideas of predestination and grace were theirs. A third time, in the nineteenth and twentieth centuries, Augustine's ideas of time, eternity, and creation influenced Kierkegaard, Hegel, Bergson, and Freud. Mankind's destiny, for Freud as for Augustine, is "departure from, and effort to regain, Paradise, and between these two terms man is at war with himself."

For Augustine, the pagan used God to enjoy the world; the Christian must use the world to enjoy God.

Augustine accepts the individual as totally responsible: "I that will and I that will not am the self-same I." "Neither make of your righteousness a safe-conduct to heaven, nor of God's mercy a safe-conduct to sin." "Our whole business in this life is to heal the heart's eye by which God is seen." Yet he can be stern: "The price of charity is yourself. If you give not yourself, you lose yourself. He requires the whole of you who made the whole." And, writing of the Eucharist, he declares, "It is the sacrament of yourselves at our Lord's table. Be what you receive and receive what you are: we are one Christ loving Himself." Again, he makes Christ say, "I am the food of the adult; grow, and you shall eat Me; but not I into you, but you shall be changed into Me." Elsewhere he writes, "I entered into my inner self and saw, above my seeing soul, above my recording spirit, the changeless Light." For Cardinal Newman, Augustine "founded the mind of Christian Europe," and this African keeps reappearing in every generation of thinkers. Descartes's great cry "I think, therefore I am" is only an echo of Augustine's "I doubt, therefore I am." And Kafka would agree with Augustine that "the only victor is the victim." How contemporary too is Augustine's cry "Give me a lover, he will *feel* whereof I speak." And "My love is my weight" (*Pondus meum amor meus*).

His continuing concern with time is contemporary also: he is always relating it to music: he sings a verse of a psalm: where are the notes he has sung? what of the interval between the verses? Such problems interested Einstein profoundly at the end of his life.

Of all the saints, Augustine is possibly the one who, as the Quakers phrase it, "speaks most clearly to our condition." Today as fifteen hundred years ago.

St. Benedict (d. 543)

On the rough wall of an abandoned cave chapel of San Lorenzo, in Fasano, in the province of Brindisi, in Italy, there is a faded painting of ample design showing Basil and Benedict standing side by side, the twin founders of the oldest continuously used monastic rules in East and West. For six hundred years after Benedict, to be a monk in the West was to be a Benedictine. Today, after more than fourteen hundred years of uninterrupted use, Benedict's rule is perhaps more admired, more commented upon, and more widely known than ever before.

During the fourth and fifth centuries, the Roman emperors had found that by admitting large masses of barbarians into the Empire and allowing them to settle and become Roman citizens, they could avoid the continual wars that had otherwise to be fought to keep the barbarians outside and on the frontiers. But more and more barbarians poured in, and those already settled within the Empire did not want to remain on the *sors barbarica,* as it came to be called, on the lands allotted to them, but penetrated farther and farther into the heart lands of Rome until they conquered the city itself. Alaric and his Visigoths, who sacked Rome in 410, were succeeded by Attila and his Huns, who in 452 invaded Italy and were advancing on

Rome. Leo the Great, the then Pope, was asked by the emperor to try to stem Attila's advance. Leo went to Attila's camp, near Mantua, and persuaded him to leave Italy. Three years later, in 455, the Vandals came over from Africa under their leader, Genseric, and marched on Rome and sacked it.

Leo could only persuade Genseric to spare the lives of the citizens and promise not to fire the city: Genseric's Vandals kept their word but plundered and pillaged Rome for fourteen days. In 476, Odoacer persuaded the emperor of the East, Zeno, to accept him as vice-regent after deposing the Western boy emperor, Romulus. Odoacer ruled well for thirteen years, and it was during his reign that Benedict was born, in Nursia, an old Sabine town about seventy miles from Rome.

The Nursians were known to be a grave, rather stern people, and Benedictine authorities incline to think that Benedict's father may have been a councilor, or even a magistrate, of his town. St. Gregory, the only authority for St. Benedict's life, says he was of a "goodish birth." Benedict had a twin sister, Scholastica, and they were probably raised in a genuinely Christian home. Most likely early in his teens Benedict set off to Rome for his "liberal studies," accompanied by his nurse, whom tradition has called Cyrilla.

When Benedict arrived in Rome, the city was between devastations. It was around the year 500. The aqueducts still carried water to and from the Campagna; the baths were still a feature of Roman life. The gladiator fights in the Coliseum had been ended by the heroism of a Christian monk, but there were still many savage and pagan sights as well as many Christian ones, such as the tombs of the apostles and martyrs and the dark catacombs, to visit and explore.

St. Gregory describes the young Benedict, and tells how soon he "abandoned the schools and left his father's house and possessions, and desiring to serve God alone sought the habit of a monk." He was about nineteen when he made this decision, and he and his nurse left Rome and at first stayed awhile in the little hill town of Affile (then Enfide), "detained by the charity of many good people." The two lived on the property of the church of the apostle St. Peter. As Jesus Christ wrought His first miracle for His mother, so Benedict performed his first for his nurse. She had borrowed an earthenware sieve from some women of the place in order to sift some grain but had imprudently left it on a table; an accident befell it, and the sieve was broken into two pieces. When the nurse returned and saw what had happened,

she began to weep most violently because the vessel she had borrowed was broken. But Benedict, pious and loving youth that he
was, had pity on her sorrow, and taking with him the two pieces
of the sieve set himself to earnest prayer. When he rose from his
knees the sieve beside him was whole and entire, nor was there
any mark to show that it had been broken. Going then he com-
forted his nurse with kindly words, and restored the sieve whole
which he had taken away broken. The fact became known to all
who dwelt in that place, and caused so much admiration, that
they hung the sieve in the porch of the church, so that all, both
then and afterwards, might know in what perfection Benedict
began his holy life. The sieve was there for many years, obvious
to all, and hung over the door of the church down to these
times of the Lombards. (*The Dialogues of Saint Gregory the
Great* [London: Phillip Lee Warner, 1911], Book II, Introduction, p. 52)

Benedict, like any other twenty-year-old, was embarrassed by the
fuss made over his (to him) simple act of kindness, and fled once
more, still attended by the faithful nurse. He explored about three
miles to the north of Enfide, at a place called Sublaqueum. Here
there were two artificial lakes, made by the emperor Claudius by
damming up the river Anio; the second lake escaped in a waterfall of
some twenty feet back to the river bed, and beside it Nero had built
a villa and baths. While he was prospecting among the ruins for his
hermitage, Benedict met a monk, Romanus, who led him to a cave,
gave him a sheepskin garment such as then was worn by Eastern
monks, and promised to bring him bread at regular intervals without
revealing Benedict's whereabouts to anyone.

There, in the place now called Subiaco, this twenty-year-old lived
absolutely alone for three years. Once, when some shepherds caught
sight of him, they at first thought he was an animal. While alone,
Benedict was tempted; the form taken by the enemy was that of a
blackbird that "persistently beset his face," and when he drove it
away with the sign of the Cross "there followed such a temptation of
the flesh as the holy man had never before experienced." The evil
spirit brought before his mind the image of a woman he had once
seen and by this picture inflamed the servant of God with such a
heat of passion that his breast could hardly contain it. Almost overcome with desire, he was on the point of abandoning his solitude.
Then suddenly, being moved by heavenly grace, he returned to himself, and seeing hard by a dense thicket of nettles and briars, threw

off his garment and cast himself naked amid the sharp thorns and stinging nettles, and "rolling in them for a space came out with his body torn and wounded. . . . From this time forth—as he used afterwards to tell his disciples—the temptation of lust was so conquered in him that never again did he feel any such thing." (Ibid., Chap. 2, p. 55)

After three years Romanus "rested from his toil," and a certain priest who lived at a distance and had prepared himself an Easter meal had a vision in which the Lord said to him, "Thou preparest a feast for thyself but My servant in yonder place is tormented with hunger." So writes St. Gregory, and goes on:

> The priest forthwith arose and set out on Easter Day itself, taking with him the food he had prepared. Over the rugged hills and through the valleys and in the holes of the ground he sought the man of God, and at last found him hidden in his cave. They prayed, and blessing Almighty God sat down together. After sweet talk of heavenly things the priest said, "Arise, let us eat, for today is Easter Day." The man of God replied, "I know it is Easter Day, because I have been granted the sight of thee." For he was so removed from men that he knew not that the feast of Easter fell on that day. Then the reverend priest insisted again, "Verily, today is the feast of the Lord's Resurrection, and it by no means befits thee to abstain. Yea, and for this was I sent, that we might partake together of the gifts of God." So with blessing they took the food. And when the meal and talk were finished the priest returned to his church. (Ibid., Chap. 2, p. 54)

Gradually the name of Benedict became known to the shepherds and farmers of the district, who "brought him food for his body while they carried away in their hearts the food of life that fell from his lips." Benedict found himself bringing to a knowledge of the spiritual life some of his scattered neighbors, and presently the monks of the neighboring monastery of Vicovaro—which still exists, being hewn out of rock—came to Benedict and asked him to be their abbot, as theirs had just died. Benedict did not wish the job, and told them "their way of life and his would by no means agree." But the monks were very insistent and finally Benedict agreed to go and stay with them. But the monks found Benedict a stern father, and after complaints and sulks, they decided to poison their new and too strict abbot. They put poison into the wine and brought it, as was the custom, to be blessed and tasted by the abbot. Benedict stretched out his hand and made the sign of the Cross over the jug of wine, and

> at that sign the vessel, though at some distance from him, was broken, and broken exactly as though he had cast a stone at it and not a blessing. The man of God at once understood that it had held a deadly potion which could not endure the sign of life, and rising immediately from the table, called the brethren together and thus addressed them: "My brethren, may Almighty God have mercy on you. Why would ye treat me thus? Did I not tell you before that my ways and yours would never agree? Go then and seek an abbot according to your way of life, for me ye can have no longer." With these words he returned to his beloved solitude, and alone under the eye of God dwelt with himself. (Ibid., Chap. 3, p. 57)

But still many came flocking to Benedict, and now he could no longer put them off by advising them to join other, neighboring monasteries, as he knew too well what they were, or might be, like. So he built a monastery near the lake and gathered around him several young men who wanted to be monks. As soon as there were twelve monks and an abbot, he built another monastery, and soon there were twelve monasteries, each housing twelve monks and an abbot, at Subiaco. Benedict's fame now began to spread far outside the Anio Valley, and as St. Gregory puts it:

> At that time the nobles and pious folk of the City of Rome began to flock to him and to give him their sons to be brought up for the service of Almighty God. It was then that Equitius brought his son Maurus, and the patrician Tertullus his son Placid, two youths of great promise. (Ibid., p. 61)

Maurus and Benedict one day were both in the monastery, near the lake, when Placid, who had gone to fetch water, leaned over too far, and his full bucket pulled him in. The current quickly dragged him an arrow's flight from the bank. Benedict, in his cell, sent Maurus to help the youth (Placid was still "a boy of tender years"). Maurus ran straight to where Placid was, and pulled him out—not realizing, until both were back on land, that he had walked on the water. When they got back to Benedict, he ascribed the miracle to the obedience of Maurus, while Maurus ascribed it to Benedict's prayers. Placid settled the matter: "When I was being drawn out of the water," he said, "I saw the abbot's cowl over my head and I judged that it was he who was taking me out of the water." (Ibid., Chap. 7, p. 64)

On another occasion, the head of a billhook flew off its handle and fell into the lake. The monk who was working with it when the accident happened was cast down, but St. Benedict caused the head to rise from the water and returned it to the monk with the words, "Behold, here is thy billhook back again, work on and be sad no more."

St. Gregory also tells the story of the priest of a near-by church, one Florentius, who was a man of bad life (one of Gregory's own subdeacons was a grandson of this Florentius). This priest hated Benedict, and sent him a poisoned loaf of bread. Benedict had a tame raven, which came daily to take bread from his hand. The saint threw the raven "the loaf which Florentius had sent, bidding it take it in the name of the Lord Jesus Christ and cast it in such a place that no one might find it. Then the raven opened its mouth and spreading its wings . . . after a long delay took the bread in its mouth, picked it up, and departed. After three hours' space, having cast the bread away, it returned and received from the hand of the man of God its usual portion." (Ibid., p. 65)

According to St. Gregory, it was the hatred of Florentius that decided Benedict, now around fifty, to move away from Subiaco. Although on his way there Benedict heard of the sudden death of Florentius, he refused to defer his departure and pursued his way south accompanied by some of his young monks. In the year 529, he arrived at Monte Cassino, a massif of rock midway between Rome and Naples. There, on the ruins of a temple to Apollo, Benedict started building. Perhaps the site had been given him by the rich Roman Tertullus, the father of Placid. In any event, from the first, Benedict behaved as though he owned the place: broke the pagan statues, preached to the peasants (then wholly devoted to their idolatry), and taught them the worship of the true God, to whom Benedict built a church. As St. Gregory puts it, "When the man of God arrived, he broke to pieces the idol of Apollo, overturned the altar and cut down the sacred groves. In the temple of Apollo he put an oratory dedicated to St. Martin; on the site of the altar of Apollo he erected an oratory in honor of St. John, and preaching continually to the people round about he summoned them to the faith." (Ibid., p. 68)

And now again Benedict was building. And now again, as the monks worked, the "ancient Enemy" did all he could to thwart Benedict's purpose: by adding to the weight of stones, so the monks could not raise them; by burying a young monk, who was crushed to death under a wall, so Benedict had to raise the boy from the dead; by showing himself to Benedict and letting the brethren hear his cries. But still the monastery grew, and soon another was built near the town of Terracius.

At what exact moment Benedict wrote his rule is not known, but Abbot John Chapman's well-argued theory is that it was written at the suggestion of Pope Hormisdas, sometime between 514 and 523. Abbot Chapman points out that it was then the great era of codes: Justinian's was contemporary, and the abbot suggests that Benedict copied the style of Justinian's canons and that his rule is a well-ordered code of monastic law, designed for use in all monasteries.

Abbot Justin McCann, in discussing what were Benedict's sources for his rule, says that he displays a deep knowledge of the texts of other, previous rules, including those of St. Basil, St. Pachomius, St. Macarius of Alexandria, St. Orisius, and other, anonymous rules. Benedict also knew St. Augustine's rule, and may also have known the rule of Caesarius of Arles—but if this is the case, then Benedict's rule could not have been written before 534, the probable date of that of Caesarius. But Benedict's chief teacher was John Cassian, who had brought to his monastery at Marseilles, and written down in his *Institutes* and *Conferences*, all he had learned from the Desert Fathers. However, in spite of his debt to Cassian, and whatever Benedict's other sources, and however much he owes to them, his rule is his very own, an inimitable and unique document, composed with Roman sobriety and common sense and with, too, a single-minded attention to the end in view: the achievement, by each human being following it, of a right relation with his Creator, through obedient love.

Benedict declares that to wish to be a monk is first and foremost to wish to renounce one's will. Through the rule, the whole person—body, soul, and spirit—is subjected to a careful and methodical system of training until the will has become tamed and humble. And this system Benedict calls the "practical life" or "practical discipline," which, for him, is synonymous with moral discipline. Whether the rule be active or contemplative or both, is an enduring topic of discussion among Benedictine theologians, but St. Benedict's fundamental conception of the monastic life is "a practical, moral discipline of which the goal is the perfect love of God . . . to this end he provides an ordered life of prayer, study and manual work, and a regime of moderate austerity." (*St. Benedict* by Abbot Justin McCann [New York: Image Books, 1958], p. 135) Compared with all former rules, that of St. Benedict is wonderfully mild and benign: during the greater part of each year, the Benedictine monk is given eight hours of unbroken sleep in a bed provided with a mattress, blankets, and a pillow. As Montalembert put it, "Compared with the previous Oriental rules, the rule of St. Benedict bears the seal of Roman wisdom, and that adaption to Western customs which has made it . . . a masterpiece of clearness and discretion, in which judges who are above all suspicion have not hesitated to recognise a character of good sense and gentleness, humanity and moderation, superior to everything that could be found up to that time in either Roman or Barbarian laws, or in the habits of civil society." (*The Monks of the West*, [Boston: Thomas B. Noonan, Vol. I, p. 341)

The Benedictine monk's weekday is divided into six hours of Divine Office (liturgical worship in common), four hours of reading (and by that Benedict meant spiritual reading, not profane study), six hours of work, and eight hours of sleep. Above all, the Benedictine life is a community life: in prayer, in work, in discipline, there is to be no individualism. The monks who would practice private prayer apart from the Divine Office are bidden "just to go in" to the oratory to pray, but St. Benedict warns them continually to beware of spiritual pride. Even in Lent, special mortifications must have the specific approval of the abbot. And the rule is, above all, simple and practical. First things first: first one's vices should be rooted out, and the Ten Commandments observed. Everything else—the contemplative life, the practice of the Presence of God, the solemn engagement by vows—comes after the observance of the Ten Commandments. As Pius XII noted in his sermon for the fourteenth centennial of the rule of St. Benedict, he is the father of Europe:

> When the Roman Empire, wasted by age and vice, collapsed, when the barbarians overran the provinces, St. Benedict . . . united *Romanitas* (if we may use a word coined by Tertullian) and the gospel. Out of this fusion he revived the resources and the power that proved so conducive to the uniting of the peoples of Europe under the banner and sovereignty of Christ. . . . For behold, from the Atlantic Ocean to the green plains of Poland, the Benedictine legions spread out, and with the Cross, with books and with the plow, tamed the intractable and barbaric nations.

Yet neither the reclamation of vast areas to cultivation, nor the evangelization of Holland, Germany, Belgium, France, and England, nor the salvation of pagan letters, nor the enormous economic, social, intellectual, cultural, or even apostolic work done during fourteen hundred years by the Benedictines, is an excuse for their existence; they know that they are in the world for one thing only: truly to seek God. "The novice is asked one thing only, and a senior assigned to him . . . who shall watch over his conduct most minutely and consider carefully whether he truly seeks God. . . . Let him be told all the difficulties and trials whereby one goes to God." (Rule, Chap. 58) The entire rule—the prologue and the seventy-three chapters, of very unequal length—is to be read to the novice three times: after the lapse of two months, of six months, and again four months later. And then "let him who is to be received make in the oratory, in the presence of all, a promise of stability, conversion of manners, and obedience." The monk's whole person—body, mind, and spirit—must thereafter be subjected to a careful and methodical system of training and pruning, until the will has become tamed, notes Dom David Knowles, writing of Benedict's monastery, which is "a school of the Lord's service."

Of the three vows, the most important for Benedict's age was the first, that of stability. What Benedict had most disapproved were the two then prevalent types of bad monks, the Sarabaites, "as soft and yielding as lead, who live in twos and threes and whose law is their own good pleasure," and the Gyrovagues, who spent their life "wandering from province to province, staying three days in one monastery and four in another, ever roaming and never stable, given up to their own wills." To avoid becoming Gyrovagues, the vow of stability was made by all Benedictines, who became and become monks of one monastery; to avoid becoming Sarabaites, the monks were to renounce their own will by the promise of obedience—nor was Benedict afraid to give the abbot absolute authority over his monks.

The stability Benedict made his monks promise, he gave to Europe, for, more than any other single man or agency, he ended the wanderings of the peoples. By binding the monastery to one place, and the individual monk to the one definite community he had chosen, Benedict, as Walter Dirks points out, said, "Stop," which he meant

> very literally. He by no means questioned the previous results of the migrations and mixture of peoples; he criticized nothing, made nothing retroactive. He did not say, "Back," but he did say, "Stop." For example, he received men of all different back-

grounds into his monasteries—nothing was less his intention than to further "Roman" or "homogenous" fraternities. . . . The Goths in his monasteries received the same treatment as Italians and Romans, just as the slaves, the free, and the nobles received equal treatment. He recognized the mixture of races, but he said, "Stop." Whoever wanted to come to him had to decide to put down his staff . . . the Benedictine existence was the end of the Great Migrations. To this extent it was also the end of the Roman-German dualism. (*The Monk and the World*, by Walter Dirks [New York: David McKay, 1954], p. 116)

The action of St. Benedict's monasteries on Christianity was collective. And it was lay action: Benedictines were not in the beginning—or were only very rarely—priests, and indeed, Chapter 60 of the rule begins: "If anyone of priestly rank ask to be received into the monastery, let not permission be too quickly granted him." And if he perseveres, "he is to know that he shall be obliged to the full rigor of the Rule and that nothing will be relaxed in his favor." Above all, the vice of private ownership was relentlessly attacked in the rule: the tools with which the monks worked, the clothes used in traveling, were taken from, and returned to, a common stock. "In order that this vice of private ownership may be completely rooted out let all things that are necessary be supplied by the Abbot," declares Chapter 53 of the rule.

Toward the middle of Benedict's life the lull between devastations ended, and Italy was once more ravaged. Justinian (483–565) refused to rule the West from Constantinople through Goths or Ostrogoths, such as Odoacer or Theodoric. Unfortunately, in reconquering first a great part of Roman Africa and then Italy, he began the Gothic War, which "caused more ruin and devastation than any of the barbarian occupations." (Abbot McCann, op. cit., p. 25) Rome fell now to Belisarius, an imperial general, now to Totila, the Gothic king.

Benedict had a memorable encounter with Totila in 542. St. Gregory tells how Totila dressed up one of his guards, by name Riggo, and gave him three counts of his bodyguard, Vultheric, Ruderic, and Blidi, to walk by his side and make it appear to Benedict that he was King Totila himself. But Benedict waited until Riggo was within hearing, and then cried out, "Put off those robes, my son, put off those robes, they are none of thine." Riggo fell down in terror, and he and his escort would not dare come near Benedict, but returned to their king and with fear told him how quickly they had been detected.

Then King Totila came in person. He saw Benedict sitting some distance away, and threw himself to the ground. Benedict rebuked him for his deeds, and in a few words foretold all that was to happen to him: he would enter Rome and cross the sea, and reign for nine years, and in the tenth die, all of which came true exactly as Benedict had predicted. Totila occupied Rome twice—in 546 and in 549. In 547—the probable year of Benedict's death—Rome was recaptured by Belisarius, and for forty days in that year the city was emptied of all its inhabitants.

In 568 the Lombards took Rome, and about 581 they destroyed Monte Cassino, and the Benedictines fled to Rome, taking with them, as Paul the Deacon wrote in his history of the Lombards, "the book of the Holy Rule . . . some other books, the weights for bread and the measure for wine, and what furniture they could get away with." This book of the rule is generally conceded by scholars to have been the autograph of the rule, which was returned to Monte Cassino when it was restored under Abbot Petronax.

In 883 Monte Cassino was attacked again, this time by the Saracens, and the monks fled to Teano, near Capua. The Teano monastery was destroyed by fire in 896, and the autograph of the rule with it, but by this time many accurate copies had been made, of which the best was one made for the emperor Charlemagne by Abbot Theodemar, in 787.

Benedict, looking around him at the general devastation, foresaw that the first thing his monks must do was to stay alive. And to stay alive meant to farm; to remain quietly in one place, clear the ground, plow, sow grain and reap it, plant vines and olives, make bread and wine and oil; make clothes and shoes and books; build cells and churches, also barns and byres, pig sties and chicken coops. And as it was in the beginning of Benedictine life, so it is today. When a new Benedictine foundation begins, whether at Cuernavaca, in Mexico, or at Elmira, in New York State, whether in Korea, Ceylon, West Africa, or Mauritius, its first human concern is to become self-supporting. All manual labor is good, Benedict decreed, and no monk may regard any work as beneath him. But each monastery must be careful not to become a factory. If monastery products—whether milk or manuscripts—are sold "as regards price let not the sin of avarice creep in, but let the goods always be sold a little cheaper than they are sold by people in the world, that in all things God may be glorified." (Rule, Chap. 57)

Gradually, largely owing to the Benedictines, the Dark Ages became light. Europe became studded with great abbeys: Lérins and Lindisfarne, Bec and Cluny, Montserrat and St. Gall, Einsiedeln and Westminster, Wearmouth and Jarrow, Fountains and Fontevrault, until at the beginning of the fourteenth century there were thirty-seven thousand Benedictine monks in Europe, and at the beginning of the sixteenth there were still thirteen hundred Benedictine abbeys there. Gradually it became the custom, and then the rule, that all choir monks become priests. This led to differentiating between those capable of serious studies, who were chosen to prepare for ordination, and the uneducated men, engaged in manual labor, who were directed by the choir monks: these devoted fewer hours to the *Opus Dei,* the four hours of public prayer in common, and generally remained intellectually the peasants they were before they became monks. From the choir monks, when they became priests, popes and bishops chose their emissaries, as Gregory chose Augustine, and from the choir monks, bishops and popes were also chosen—there have been twenty-five Benedictine popes.

Idleness, Benedict had declared, is the enemy of the soul (Chap. 48 of the rule), and the Benedictine day is divided by the seven offices and the two meals. The monks sleep in a dormitory; at their two meals only the sick may have meat, but there must always be two cooked dishes, so that if any cannot eat of the one they can eat of the other. Half a bottle of wine is allowed daily, and a pound of bread; the Abbot can allow more to heavy workers. The monks' dress is to be made in color and quality "such as can be obtained in the region where they live or can be bought more cheaply." (Chap. 55)

In Benedict's own lifetime, his beloved disciple, St. Placid, was sent to found a monastery in Sicily. This was the first foundation made by a Benedictine. The Venerable Bede, himself a Benedictine monk, has told for all time how Gregory the Great, also a Benedictine, saw the Anglo-Saxon slave boys in the Roman market and was impressed by their white skins, beautiful faces, and fine, bright hair. "Who are these?" he asked, and was told, "Angles." "Not Angles, but angels they shall be," he said, making one of the world's best-known puns, and proposed to go and evangelize them himself. But having failed to escape being elected to the Papacy (he smuggled himself out of Rome in a carrier's wicker basket to no avail), soon after he became Pope he sent thirty-nine monks under their leader, Augustine, to the English people. Gregory provided the evangelists with letters to the rulers of the countries through which they would pass, but when they arrived at Aix-en-Provence, they were so terrified by the reports of the savagery of the Anglo-Saxons that Augustine, leaving his thirty-nine companions comfortably at Lérins, scampered back to Rome. There he was told by Gregory not to chicken out, and sent back to Lérins. He and his companions set out again via Aix, Arles, Vienna, Chalons, Autun, Sens, Tours, and Anjou, and reached England in the spring of 597. They landed at Ebbsfleet, in the kingdom of Kent. There King Ethelbert, whose Frankish wife, Bertha, was a Christian, received them courteously, and gave them Canterbury as a residence. They were given, too, permission to preach and to make as many converts as they could. In a small chapel in Canterbury, Augustine baptized Ethelbert on Pentecost, and ten thousand followed his example. Augustine became the first archbishop of Canterbury.

Benedict Biscop (628–90) founded the abbeys of Wearmouth in 674 and Jarrow in 682, while Wilfred, another Benedictine monk, founded Ripon, and Cuthbert brought Lindisfarne under Benedictine rule, and was prior there under the abbot of Melrose. In Scotland, Margaret (d. 1093), wife of Malcolm II, founded Dunfermline Abbey around 1075, and twelve other Benedictine abbeys were subsequently founded. To Germany, Boniface brought the gospel, and Pirmin, fleeing from the Moors, who had overrun his native Spain, became the founder of Reichenau (724), and in 580 Marmoutier was founded by the Abbot Leobard (d. 618). Other founders of Benedictine abbeys were Boniface's beloved disciple Storm, who with eight disciples began the building of the abbey of Fulda, on March 12, 744, on land given Boniface by Frankish nobles. Soon there were four hundred monks at Fulda, for whom Boniface obtained from Pope Zacharias many privileges, confirmed by King Pepin. Fulda became a nursery of missionaries; yet these missionary-monks, who existed from the seventh to the ninth centuries, were as much exceptions to the Benedictine norm as were hermits or recluses. Other famous Benedictine founders were Willibald (d. 787) and Wynnebald (d. 761), Anglo-Saxons from Waltham, in Essex. The two brothers had gone with their father on a pilgrimage to Rome; the father died in Lucca, and Wynnebald remained in Rome, while Willibald traveled to Constantinople and the Holy Land and in 730 became a monk in Monte Cassino. Both brothers were sent to help Boniface, and founded Eichstatt and the double monastery, for men and women, of Heidenheim. Their sister, St. Walburga, (d. February 25, 779) was the first abbess. By the middle of the eighth century, at the first German National Council, the seventh canon insisted that all "monks and nuns shall follow and obey the rule of St. Benedict," and at the first Frankish general synod, in Hennegau in 734, the first canon decreed that "Abbots and monks shall take the Rule of St. Benedict as the model of the cloistered life." At the Synod of Aachen, in 802, one of the questions asked of all was "whether the Rule of St. Benedict should be preferred in all monasteries." In France, St. Benedict's own beloved Maurus founded St. Maur-sur-Loire, where the body of St. Benedict now lies, and by 640 the synod of Autun assumed the rule of St. Benedict to be in general use in France. In Spain the rule of St. Isidore coexisted with the rule of St. Benedict for more than four hundred years, from the time of Bishop Tajo of Saragossa, who translated St. Gregory's *Dialogues* and made a compilation of his works, until the synod of Coyaca, in 1050, which ordered, in its Canon 2, that in "all monasteries either the Rule of St. Isidore or that of St. Benedict must be followed."

Two hundred years after Benedict's death, his rule was not only known in all the monasteries of the West but had in almost all of them supplanted all other rules. Only in England the Benedictine missionaries had found the Welsh and Scottish Christians hostile to the Rule because they resented the idea of converting their Anglo-Saxon conquerors. "We will not preach the Faith," the abbot of Bangor is reported to have said, "to this cruel race of strangers, who have treacherously driven our ancestors from their country and robbed their posterity of their heritage." An anti-Christian reaction, too, followed the death of Augustine of Canterbury, in 605, and that of his convert King Ethelbert of Kent. Only in the North, where Edwin, king of Northumbria, had become a Christian upon his marriage to Ethelburga, Ethelbert of Kent's daughter, did Christianity flourish. But in 633 Edwin was defeated and killed at Hatfield by the Angle leader Cadwalla and the heathen Mercian king Penda. Christianity almost disappeared from among the Anglo-Saxons, and when it was re-established, it was from the North.

Oswald, a Northumbrian prince educated in Scotland, reconquered his kingdom and brought Aidan from Iona to evangelize England. Aidan established himself at Lindisfarne, and as Montalembert says, ". . . from the cloisters of Lindisfarne, Northumbrian Christianity spread over the southern kingdoms. What is distinctly visible is the influence of Celtic priests and missionaries everywhere replacing or seconding the Roman missionaries, and reaching districts which their predecessors had never been able to enter. The stream of the Divine word thus extended itself from north to south." The greatest light of the Anglo-Saxon Church was the Benedictine monk the Venerable Bede (672–733), whose *Ecclesiastical History of the English People* is astonishingly accurate and one of the great sources of English history. Bede was most exact in observing all the precepts of St. Benedict's rule. "If the angels do not find me among my brethren in the choir, will they not ask, 'Where is Bede?'" he said, but as he lay dying, he dictated the last words of his translation of the Gospels into Anglo-Saxon.

Gaul suffered terribly from Roman tyranny and taxation on the one hand and from the terrible Frankish invasions on the other. The peasants refused to till the land for fear of the taxgatherer or the barbarian, and dense forests or wastelands covered the neglected countryside. The monks chose these wastelands, or deserts, or the depths of the forests, but families fleeing from brigands or invaders would often seek out the monks and place themselves under their protection. Clearings were made, houses built, and the land farmed, by families dependent on the monks; about half of all the towns and villages of France came into being in this fashion. Columbanus, an Irish monk from Bangor, in Wales, came to Gaul in 590 as a missionary, and protected by King Gontran, a grandson of Clovis, the Frankish king who had embraced Christianity on Christmas day 496, built the monastery of Luxeuil. The rule of St. Columbanus was very harsh: "Absolute obedience was required and food was reduced to an absolute minimum, and the punishments, such as flogging, were most severe." Driven from Luxeuil by a grandson of King Gontran, Columbanus founded the abbey, now called St.-Gall, in what is now Switzerland, with Gall, one of the twelve companions who had originally come with him from Ireland. Columbanus went on to Italy, where he founded Bobbio, in the territory of the Lombard king Agilulf. Columbanus died in 615 and within fifty years of his death, the rule of St. Benedict had been adopted in all the monasteries founded by Columbanus.

In spite of the savagery of the times—St. Boniface was murdered at the end of his life by the Germans he evangelized—the Benedictine monk Ansgar brought the Benedictine way of life to Scandinavia, Rupert to Austria, and Swithbert to the Netherlands. Benedict's own relics were translated from Monte Cassino to Gaul, to the abbey of Fleury, which became a great center of pilgrimage, and later to St. Maur.

Among the great Benedictine writers, after Gregory the Great and the Venerable Bede, are Harbanus Maurus, abbot of Fulda and from 847 to 856 Archbishop of Mainz, and Walafrid Strabo, abbot of Reichenau, who died in 849. Others are the historians Paul the Deacon (d. 789) and Willam of Malmesbury (d. 1143). Lanfranc of Bec, and Anselm, who succeeded him as archbishop of Canterbury, were outstanding theologians; Notker Balbulus, who died in 912, and Ekkehard I, who died in 973, were great musicians; Peter Damian and Bernard of Morlaix were but two of many great Latin poets; Adelard of Bath in 1161 translated Euclid from the Arabic into Latin; and mathematics, physics, and astronomy found their only medieval hopes in Benedictine monasteries.

The great Benedictine schools at Jarrow, Wearmouth, Fulda, Corvey, St.-Gall, Jumièges, Cluny, Einsiedeln, etc., kept Greek and Latin alive throughout the Dark Ages, and many of them, including Eton (which still preserves the Benedictine grace said before meals), are still extant, though some, like Eton, became Protestant at the Reformation. Libraries, bookbinding, painting, glass painting, stained glass, and bellmaking were all outstanding Benedictine activities: yet all these were by-products: more than five thousand canonized and beatified Benedictine monks are better proof that the "one thing needful" was, and is, given first place. "The names of the great abbeys," wrote Abbot McCann (op. cit., p. 187), "are inseparably associated with the political and social history of the countries to which they belonged: they are even more deeply associated with their civilized culture. It is not too much to say that for the early Middle Ages, the period of their greatest influence, the Benedictine monasteries were the chief cultural centers of Europe."

And how quietly, unobtrusively, all this work was done. As Cardinal Newman put it, "Silent men were observed about the country, or discovered in the forest, digging, clearing, and building, and other silent men, not seen, were sitting in the cold cloister, tiring their eyes, and keeping their attention on the stretch, while they painfully copied and recopied the manuscripts they had saved. There was no one that . . . drew attention to what was going on, but by degrees the woody swamp became a hermitage, a religious house, a farm, an abbey, a village, a seminary, a school of learning and a city." (*An Essay on the Development of Christian Doctrine* [London: Longmans, Green, 1949], p. 372)

And under what difficult circumstances Benedictines did their work! The seventh century saw Monte Cassino sacked twice; in 793 on a winter's day the Viking fleet sacked Lindisfarne and killed all the monks they could find; in 845 Nantes was sacked by Vikings and all the clergy massacred; in 843 Paris was sacked on Easter Day. In 842 the Saracens captured Arles, and in 848 they sailed up the Tiber and pillaged St. Peter's; indeed, the history of the ninth century is composed of the shock of the invasions, the rapacity of the nobles, the selfishness of the kings. The tenth century saw the Normans taking up where the Vikings had left off; then came the investiture struggle between popes and emperors, with the Benedictine abbeys used as arsenals; later, at the Reformation, in the countries that went over to Protestantism, the Benedictine abbeys were confiscated, their monks dispersed, many abbots martyred. In England alone three hundred Benedictine monasteries were closed, and everything they had owned, from chasubles and chalices to lands, was taken by the king. At the French Revolution, the continental monasteries fared hardly less badly; at the time of the peace of Tilsit, only thirty Benedictine monasteries were left in all Europe. But with the nineteenth century a revival began; in France and Germany, in America, Africa, and Australia, new foundations were made, and in England six abbeys for monks and four for nuns have been restored. Abbot McCann gives 372 as the current number of Benedictine monasteries and convents, with thirty-two thousand religious.

St. Benedict had laid great stress upon the fact that each monastery should be an independent unit, governed only by an abbot, counseled by the chapter. By the end of the eighth century, at the time of the coronation of Charlemagne (Christmas Day, 800, in Rome), there were all over Europe many Benedictine monasteries, each one a separate entity, all observing the same rule but, as Abbot McCann puts it, "admitting considerable variety in minor points of observance." (Op. cit., p. 180) He adds, "We are too often inclined to think of relaxation and reform as great and catastrophic things; whereas, the whole history of monasticism would be more truly conceived as a constant tension between observance and relaxation, as a conflict in which the ideal struggled incessantly with opposing forces and was on the whole decisively victorious." Again and again Monte Cassino has been physically destroyed, most recently in World War II; again and again, too, it would seem as though the Benedictine ideal had withered, had become externalized, had decayed; each time, just as, physically, Monte Cassino has been rebuilt, so also the many and various saintly Benedictine reformers have restored the spirit of the rule.

St. Francis of Assisi (1182–1226)

Continually, throughout all the Christian centuries, young men have
asked the question the rich young man asked Jesus, "What must I
do to attain eternal life?" and have pondered Christ's answer: "If
thou wilt be perfect, go sell what thou hast and give to the poor, and
thou shalt have treasures in heaven; and come, follow Me." The rush
to the desert of the early Fathers, the disciplined communities of
Basil and Benedict, these all had taken the counsels of perfection
to heart, controlling hunger, thirst, sleep, and sexual desire. Gradually,
after the barbarian invasions, the monastic communities, surrounded
by lay communities that grew up around them, at first physically
near them, sheltering them from barbarian attack and hostile armies,
later sheltered spiritually under their care and benefiting intellectually
and socially from them, fused together into one society, which became what now we call Western Christendom. This was

> the union of a vast congregation of Christians under a common
> language, a common social structure (feudalism), common eco-
> nomic conditions, common political and military aims and insti-
> tutions. . . . The common social structures and economic con-
> ditions were very thoroughly worked out, even to the detriment
> of religion, which was the first principle making for unity and
> order . . . the later history of the monasteries is a more con-
> stant witness to the working of social and economic laws than to
> that of the religious laws which first produced them . . . the
> monks as landowners became social personages. The monastic
> lands became the chief sources of wealth. Abbots became tem-
> poral rulers, controlling the services of burgesses and villeins,
> equipping them for war, administering justice to them in their
> courts, minting coinage for their use. The same process of
> feudalization extended itself for the rest of the clergy. The
> Church was as zealous for their admission into European society
> as that society was to absorb them. Hence the equal enthusiasm
> of the Church to receive, and of the State to grant, ecclesiastical
> benefices in the form of territorial and feudal rights. By com-
> mon consent bishops ranked with abbots and barons as feudal

lords and because of their closer organization they became the most powerful body of all. (*The Dominicans,* by Rev. J. B. Reeves, O.P. [New York: Macmillan, 1930], pp. 10–11)

This state of affairs produced a society which, eventually and after much suffering, absorbed and civilized the barbarians, though taking several centuries to complete this process. Thanks to the Church, the language, law, and discipline of the Roman Empire were preserved, at first only within the monasteries. Then gradually the law, language, and discipline expanded their influence over the administration of secular fiefs, and, still later, they became paramount in the government of cities, and later still, of nations.

From the first, the towns had tried to reject the feudal authority of the barons, and had sided, now with the king, now with the nobles against him, playing, from within the comparative safety of their walls, the one against the other in order to wring great privileges for themselves, the burghers, the townspeople. The clergy, within and without the city walls, secular and regular, also took sides. At the signing of Magna Carta, for example, in 1215, the Church sided with the nobles against King John; in the eleventh-century investiture struggle, the towns, especially in Tuscany, sided with the Church in its struggle with the German emperor over his claim to have the right to invest bishops with the *pallium,* the external expression of their power. The new class that grew up within the medieval city walls was rich and worldly, and depended on trade. It aped the nobility, marrying them, and quite often buying them, when, impoverished by war, they sought loans. It was from these new-rich townsfolk that the Church was to receive one of her major institutions, that of the friars. The hallowing of the middle classes, and their education, was to be accomplished first by the Franciscans, then by the Dominicans, just as the Christianizing of the kings and the barbarian nobility, and eventually the reform of the secular clergy, had been accomplished by the Benedictines, though begun by their predecessors, the monks of Ireland and of Gaul.

In the Eastern churches, to be a religious is still to be a monk. In the Western church, this was true only until the twelfth century and the coming of the friars. A friar is any member of one of Chaucer's "ordres foure": the Franciscans, or Friars Minor; the Dominicans, or Friars Preachers; the Carmelites; and the Augustinians, or Austin Friars. These are the four mendicant orders of the Common law.

The Servites, the Trinitarians, the Mercedarians, the Hieronymites, the Minims, the Brothers of St. John of God, and the members of the various penitential orders constitute the lesser friars.

It has been said that the dominant fact of the monastic experience is a belief in the necessity and efficacy of prayer, and the religous have been called anonymous well-wishers who reduce the moral overdraft of mankind, who act, as it were, as the lightning conductors for society. One of the most enduringly efficacious human beings in all history, who is thought by many to have been that Christian who in his life most conformed to Christ, was St. Francis of Assisi, the founder of the Franciscans.

Francis was born in Assisi in 1182. His father, Pietro Bernardone, was a rich cloth merchant; his mother, Pica, was a Provençal girl Pietro had found on one of his frequent trips to Provence. Their first son was christened John Baptist, but he was early nicknamed Francesco, the little Frenchman. Francesco went to the local Benedictine school, then entered his father's shop as his assistant. From the East, as a result of the Crusades, had come new fabrics, and also new methods of accounting: the Arabic numerals, and asset and debit columns (double-entry bookkeeping); and Francis, quick-witted and young, enjoyed his work. Thomas of Celano, who wrote an early life of him, says Francis was "skilled in the art of making money, but rash and ready to spend it." Also, Francis loved giving parties, and though he was small and thin "with a low forehead, black eyes and narrow lips," yet he quickly became the leader of the youth of Assisi. His father's store was the richest and most fashionable in Assisi, and on market days, when he opened his stall, wealthy noblemen and dealers from neighboring towns would stand in line to buy. Francis was immensely popular with all his father's clients, and sold more fine velvets, rare brocades, and exquisite laces than even his father could. But where Pietro saved, Francis spent; and though Pietro was proud that his son "outdid all the young noblemen, and was the uncontested leader of the younger set," yet Francis was wildly extravagant, night after night wielding a floral staff as scepter, wearing particolored trousers (a French troubadour fashion), singing songs, playing the viol, and seeing that no glass was ever empty. Francis was also generous to beggars. And one market day, when Francis was alone in charge of his father's stall, he was so busy selling whole bales of expensive stuff to a rich customer that he took no notice of a beggar who had approached. The deal concluded, Francis looked around for the beggar, who had disappeared. He went off, leaving the stall with unguarded bales and cashbox, and went hunting for the beggar. The locals he asked thought he was pursuing a thief. He caught up with the beggar at the city gate and gave him all the money he had on him and also his coat. Then he dashed back to his father's stall, where his father had arrived to find cashbox and bales unguarded. He scolded Francis volubly.

Francis loved the new troubadour songs, which celebrated human love, women's beauty, knightly prowess, and devoted loyalty, and until his father's outburst, he had not really thought about the contrast between his rich, easygoing life of pleasure and the discomforts of the poor. But soon after this incident, when Francis was twenty, war broke out between Assisi and Perugia, and Francis headed a group of lancers that marched to San Giovanni, halfway between the two towns. There, at the bridge, Francis and his men were taken prisoner, and he was kept in jail for a year. In the jail he managed still to be the life of the party, jesting and singing.

But soon after his release he fell ill. He remained for some weeks delirious, in a high fever, and in pain. When he began to recover, the first thing he noticed was the sun shining through his window. As soon as night fell, he fell back into fever and delirium: day after day he recovered while the sun was shining, and at night relapsed. His parents and his friends had been, and were, constantly in his sickroom, but he was not aware of them and did not recognize them. When they spoke to him, he was impervious to their voices.

But now, when the sun was shining in his room, he heard them. But when the sun disappeared, they did too. Gradually the sun helped him move his stiff limbs, and gradually he began to sit up in bed, the better to see the sun. He would walk to the window and watch the sun move in the sky and, little by little, he began to see the sky through which the sun moved and the earth it illumined, and he grew more and more in love with the sun, longing for it, aching for it. One morning, he asked his mother for his clothes: he wanted to go out into the sunlight. He had promised his mother he would only go to the end of the street, and kept his word, but next day he walked as far as the town gates, and soon he would walk from morning until sundown, completely recovered. But although he once more spent whole nights drinking with his friends, or leading torchlight processions through the streets, singing and dancing, he did not find the same pleasure; he was happier, he found, walking alone on the sunny hills.

Soon war broke out again, and Francis mounted a fine horse and rode off down the Spoleto road. At the city gate he called out to his friends, "I shall come back a great knight."

But, arrived at Spoleto, his fever and delirium returned. He thought he heard a voice telling him to return to Assisi. But, in the morning, the fever had gone, and he was ashamed to go back. So he rode on, as he thought, to Apulia. But found himself, after a long ride, back at Assisi. So, ashamed and embarrassed, he rode home, laughed at by those he had told he would come back a great knight. He drifted for some months, then was persuaded to give a banquet. But when everyone was drinking his health, Francis rose and left the table. His friends took their musical instruments, and he went with them into the streets but could not participate.

He hung back, and when his friends noticed his absence, they looked for him and found him alone, staring into space. The friend who found him first joked, "I suppose you are thinking of marriage." Francis did not reply for a moment, then said, "You are right. I intend to be married. But to a lady purer and more lovely than any you ever saw. Her name is Lady Poverty." He had replied without knowing what he said. But, once the words were uttered, Francis made a complete break with his former life. He had found a deserted cave on one of his solitary walks, and now he hid there.

On his way there one day, on horseback, he saw a leper coming toward him. His first instinct was to spur his horse in the other direction: lepers were forbidden all contact with their healthy fellow humans, and had to live outside the city walls in special huts, or lazar houses, and had to wear special clothes that made them recognizable at a distance. But Francis, impelled by some power outside himself, found his horse moving toward the leper. He could see the man's lips were gone, and that a hole was all that was left of his nose. He reached the man, got down from his horse, and put into a hand that was a festering sore all the money he had. Francis felt nauseated, but then took the leper's hand and kissed it, remounted, and rode on toward his cave. He returned to wave farewell, but the leper had disappeared.

Next day, he went to the lazar house and asked the prior of the Lazarists for permission to help them care for the lepers (the order of St. Lazarus of Jerusalem was a hospital order that cared for the lepers). Francis came daily with gifts and found a new joy in his service. At this time, Francis started going to the little church of St. Damian, in the fields below Assisi. There he asked God to tell him what he should do; and one day it seemed to him he heard a voice say: "Francis, do you not see my house is in ruins? Go and restore it." Francis thought the voice referred to the little church of St. Damian, which was in a very bad state of repair. So he went back home and, as his father was away on a business trip, Francis simply helped himself from the shelves to several bales of expensive stuff and went off to the Foligno fair, where he sold the bales very well and brought the money back to the priest of St. Damian. The priest was doubtful if Francis' father would approve the gift, and hesitated to take the money.

Indeed, when Pietro Bernardone came home, he was furious and accused Francis of stealing. Francis refused to give the money back. His father dragged Francis into the cellar of their house and locked him in. He kept Francis on bread and water, but Francis still refused to repent or return the cash. Called out of Assisi on urgent business, Pietro told his wife Francis was to be kept on bread and water and locked up. His mother brought him delicious food but urged him to obey his father. Still he would not. "God told me to restore his church. I must obey him," Francis said. So she left the cellar door open and Francis left. When his father came home, he went to the Assisi courthouse and denounced his son, asking for his arrest. The officials knew where to find Francis, either in the church of St. Damian or in one of the nearby caves. But when arrested, he refused to answer to a secular court. He must be called to account before a church court, he said.

The local authorities did not wish to argue their competence in front of the canonical court, so they told Pietro Bernardone to take his case there. Which he did, happily; his son had stolen, and was as much a thief in a church court as in the secular court. When the trial came up, the courtroom was crowded with everyone who was anyone in Assisi: merchants, knights, clerics, and anyone who could squeeze in. The bishop, Guido, asked Pietro to present his case against Francis. Pietro described the stolen goods, estimated their value, and asked the court to oblige his son to restore the money, and also to impose a penalty on the thief. Then the bishop asked Francis to present his side. Francis raved about "voices" he had heard, and said he had taken the money at the orders of God himself, only to rebuild the ruined house of the Lord. The bishop said to Francis: "You intend to serve the Lord, but however worthy your motives, the means you employ are not just. The money you have taken cannot benefit the church. Restore it to its rightful owner."

Whereupon Francis replied, firmly and clearly, that he would restore to his father not only the money but "everything I have of him." Then he took off his splendid garments and fine linen, and clad only in a hair shirt, threw his clothes at his father's feet, and put the money on top. Then he called out "into the tense silence of the courtoom: 'Hear and understand! Until now I have called Pietro Bernardone my father, but now I wish to say: "Our Father, who art in heaven!'" Bishop Guido, greatly moved, walked across the courtroom and put his own cloak around Francis' shoulders. Pietro picked up the money and the clothes, and walked back to his shop without a word.

Francis went off to his cave, but on the way, as he was singing with joy, a group of waylaying bandits came out from the undergrowth and blocked his path. They were furious to find he was only a pauper in a strange hair shirt, and asked him, "But who are you?" To which Francis replied, "I am the herald of the great king." They were outraged, and rolled him into a ditch filled with snow. When Francis scrambled out, he went on singing as though nothing had happened. He found an old peasant's coat, with a hood, thrown out as useless by its owner, tied it around him with a bit of rope, and started to rebuild St. Damian.

In his youth he had helped rebuild the ramparts of Assisi after they had been torn down by the Perugians, and found he had some skill at building. And so he went from house to house begging for materials. He sang so agreeably that people gave him what he asked, and soon he had enough heavy stones and bags of lime. But he had no horse or mule, so he told himself, "Now, Brother Donkey, carry these to St. Damian." And he did just that, carrying all the stones, bags of lime, a shovel, a ladder, and spent many days, working hard, and singing to himself. Whatever hours of rest he allowed himself, he spent at the lazar house. And when St. Damian's was finished, he had set up an entirely new form of pointed arch which presaged the new style of the early Renaissance.

The priest at St. Damian offered to share his bread, his bacon, and his grapes with him, but Francis said God could care for his donkey. And went begging. He was roundly abused by the citizens of Assisi as he came around with an old pail begging scraps. Some said his father's son should be ashamed, others laughed at him as noble knight and troubadour, and offered him the bones they had saved for the dogs. Francis accepted all, but when he came to eat the swill in his pail he turned away in disgust. But he forced himself, sitting by the roadside, to eat it all, and then he walked through the night, singing for joy, and slept on the grass in an open field. He restored not only St. Damian but two other little churches, St. Peter and St. Mary of the Angels. The work was finished by St. Matthew's Day, when the priest wanted to reconsecrate St. Mary of the Angels (later called the Portiuncula). At the mass, at which the only congregation was Francis and a shepherd who was passing by, Francis realized that he was not just to rebuild little Umbrian churches, but the whole, universal, Catholic Church. So September 21 is regarded by all Franciscans as the birthday of their order.

Then Francis began to preach in the Assisi market place, standing on the step of a staircase. "This impossible dunce," a disgrace to his father, to his native town, dressed in rags, had the gall to declare that poverty was the true way to Christ, and that peace and love of one's neighbor, even of one's enemy, was the only way to God. He was called a vagabond, and mocked, yet this pauper, who begged for cast-off crusts from the rich, dared tell the rich what was real wealth. And this in a small, affluent town, where his own father was one of the richest men. Francis was laughed at and scorned. Yet he began to attract not only interested attention but also followers. The first was one of the wealthiest Assisi merchants, Bernardo de Quintavalleo, splendidly dressed as Francis once had been. Bernardo stopped the first time to listen to Francis out of curiosity. Next day, he came again, and when Francis had finished, Bernardo asked the beggar to accompany him home. Francis spent the night at Bernardo's home and instructed him.

After Francis' next sermon, a canon, Pietro dei Cattani, vicar of the church of St. Nicolas and a most respected figure, asked Francis why the word of God as preached in the churches was not enough. Francis replied that the priests taught the doctrine of Christ but did not put it into practice in their lives. "Let me prove it to you." So the three of them, the rich merchant in grand clothes, the canon in his soutane, and Francis the beggar in his rags, went into the church and opened the Gospels at random. The first time, the book opened at the saying of our Lord to the rich young man: "If thou wilt be perfect, go and sell all thou hast and give to the poor"; the second time, at the advice to the disciples "Take nothing for your journey, neither purse nor bread, nor yet two coats." And the third time, the book opened at: "He that taketh not his cross and followeth after me is not worthy of me." "Let us act according to the words of the

Lord," Francis said, and the rich merchant in his velvet and the canon in his soutane obeyed the beggar.

On April 16, 1209, Assisi witnessed Bernardo, Canon Pietro, and Francis giving all Bernardo's wealth, stacked in several bags full of money, at noon, on the Piazza San Giorgio, to all who came, a crowd of paupers. It took only a few minutes. Then the three went to the city gate and offered Bernardo's velvet clothes and the canon's soutane, with both their pairs of shoes, in exchange for two "badly mended and threadbare coats." Daily the three begged together for scraps and daily went to the lazar house to serve the lepers. They lived together in a hut they had made of branches, leaves, and clay, near the Portiuncula. And they were always singing. And helping people. If the people they helped—an elderly farmer plowing, a woodcutter, a drayman—offered them money, they refused, but if offered a meal they would accept bread and water. It was a woodcutter who joined them next, a poor man whose only possessions were his ax and his hut. The four decided to go on a missionary journey, though Francis had given his last and most precious possession, his Bible, to a poor woman who asked him for money. "Sell it and buy bread for your children," he told her.

Francis and the woodcutter went south toward Ancona; Bernardo and Pietro went north. At first, people were afraid of the beggars, called them thieves and sorcerers, but soon they won everyone with their songs and cheerfulness. But though they sang and spoke, they would not accept a decent meal, only a little bread and water. When they got back they found three new recruits: a cured leper from the lazar house; a learned man, Sabatino, who found salvation was in living like Francis, not in books; and a young man, John, whose father, a merchant like Pietro Bernardone and Bernardo, was even more miserly. John's father attacked Francis in the street in Assisi: "You thief. You have stolen my son." Bishop Guido summoned Francis to ask him about cult of poverty. Francis explained, "If we keep property, we shall need arms to defend it."

Now Philip, a tall fellow, joined them. Winter came on, and the people of Assisi shut their doors in the faces of the eight beggars. Francis and his friends—he called them his "Knights of the Round Table"—shivered under the attentions of Brother Rain; and when their stomachs grew too noisy, rumbling with hunger, Francis would tell Brother Hunger to keep quiet so they could pray undisturbed. Then the snow came and Francis said, "Brother Winter has come. Tomorrow we must go out, two by two, and preach the gospel."

Francis withdrew to a cave to ask forgiveness for his past life. And he had a vision of hundreds of brethren coming toward him, and a voice from within the now-illumined cave told him his sins were forgiven and "I have chosen you to proclaim my kingdom." Francis came out of the cave into a howling snowstorm. Francis found, when he got back (having persuaded a young knight in splendid armor to get off his horse and accompany him) that his companions had also returned. He told them of the vision he had had in the cave, and soon three more joined them. "Now we are twelve, like the apostles," Francis rejoiced. They were rather crowded.

When the weather improved, Francis sent two of his companions to Assisi to beg for parchment, ink, and a quill, and he wrote his rule of life for himself and his followers: absolute destitution, love of all created things, and great humility. They were to be called Friars Minor. Then, in April 1210, the twelve set off for Rome to present their rule to Pope Innocent III.

Because there was so much heresy about—the Albigensian, for example—Cardinal John of St. Paul, who had met Francis and his followers, was suspicious of them. So he had quartered the twelve men in his own house, the better to observe them. He watched them most carefully, and came to report to Innocent: "I have found them to be men of the highest perfection who strive to live in the spirit of the holy gospel. I believe that the Lord intends to use their work to reform the faith of our holy church everywhere in the world." And he asked Innocent to receive the leader of the group and listen to him. The following day, Innocent received Francis in the audience room of the Lateran Palace.

Innocent recognized him as a beggar he had chased off the terrace of his palace a few days before. But he now asked Francis to read his rules. Innocent thought the rules too austere, but Francis disarmed him by saying: "Dear Pope Innocent, I rely on my Lord Jesus Christ. He has promised us eternal life, and will certainly not deny us so trifling a thing as what we need to support our lives here on earth." The Pope gave the new rule to six cardinals to study. Five of the cardinals thought the mendicants, if sincere, should enter one of the existing orders of monks. Much safer than being vagabonds spending their nights hiding behind a hedge. Francis replied: "Dear Pope Innocent, we are not afraid of the world and of men. Wherever we are, we always have our cell with us. Brother Body is our cell, and our soul is the hermit that remains within, praying to God. If the soul does not remain quiet in the body, little profits a cell made by hands."

Cardinal John of St. Paul warned his five colleagues against rejecting Francis, and the Pope withdrew, undecided. Then he dreamed the church of St. John Lateran was tottering and a man in ragged clothes hurried across the Lateran Square and held it up; when the man turned his face to the sleeping Pope, Innocent saw it was Francis. Next day, the cardinals still objected to Francis and his rule, but the Pope told them, "This is the man through whom the Church of God shall be erected anew." Then he bent down and embraced Francis, who was kneeling before him, and blessed him. On April 16, 1210. Now Francis went back to Assisi, and Bishop Guido gave him the church of San Giorgio, but it was too small, and so the bishop asked Francis to preach in the new cathedral of San Rufino. All of Assisi came, including Francis' parents, but Francis went back to his shed as soon as his sermon was over. Then the twelve friends were turned out by a donkey driver, who wanted their shed. So they went to an old Benedictine abbey near the Portiuncula and asked the abbot to allow Francis and his followers to settle there. The abbot, grateful for the work of restoration Francis and his friends had done, offered to give them the church and all the land around it in perpetuity. But Francis refused: "God forbid! But we would like to rent it and pay for it with our work." The rent was to be a monthly basketful of fish. And so it was.

Yet, as Walter Dirks says, Francis "did not want to be a monk and found an order, but only to be one who does what Jesus did and urged others to do. St. Francis did not even specifically want what St. Benedict specifically wanted: permanence, the order, the constitution. He resisted the desired effect, the decided answer. . . . St. Francis had no intention other than the following of Christ, from one day to the next. . . . The truth of the Incarnation was at work in St. Francis. Since God became man, one can love Him humanly in Jesus; but one cannot love the Godman if one does not love men, and if it is done rightly, one will love them in the same manner." (*The Monk and The World*, by Walter Dirks, [New York: David McKay, 1954], p. 154)

Francis and his friends also were very lucky in their Pope. Lotario di Segni, elected Pope in 1198, when not yet a priest although a theologian and a canon lawyer and author of three religious books, had found time to give the young Francis, still in his twenties, an audience, and to give him and his friends permission to preach the gospel and to live it literally by wearing the garb of peasants, and to live by begging food from other men's tables. Francis' mission was to the rich: he was himself a rich man. Walter Dirks points out (op. cit., p. 163) that although Francis encountered the "arrogant wealth of the church" contrasted with the fact of the poverty of the poor "he preached not contentment to the poor, but poverty to the rich. . . . He was not a poor man who did not want to be rich, but a rich man who became poor. . . . He did not preach justice or equality. . . . He was much less concerned with the poor man who received the alms than with the rich man who gave it. The threat to the rich man from his wealth caused him much greater anxiety than the hunger of the poor."

In 1212 a highborn Assisi girl of nineteen, named Clare, came to Francis and asked to be allowed to live in poverty following his way; her hair was shorn, she put on a rough dress and started the order of Poor Clares, the second order of St. Francis.

In 1215 the Pope formally approved the first order of St. Francis, the Friars Minor, and at the general chapter of 1217 Francis sent many brothers to the East. The whole idea of a friar is different from that of a monk, although they all make the three primary vows and base their lives on the evangelical counsels. Both are called to the religious life, both live cloistered lives. But the friars' activities are not only prayer, penance, study, and manual work; indeed, the early Franciscans strongly disapproved of study and did no manual work: like the flowers of the field, they toiled not, neither did they spin. Their main objective was missionary, and their later developments arose from their missionary activities, not from any extension of study or manual labor.

At the Pentecost chapter of 1219 Francis for the first time divided Italy and the lands beyond into provinces, and sent Brother John of Penna with sixty friars to Germany, Brother Pacificus to France, and other brothers to Tunis and Morocco. Honorius III, the Pope who had succeeded Innocent III, dearly loved Francis and directed the priests in all dioceses to welcome the Friars Minor. Francis himself set off on a crusade, and in Egypt preached the gospel to Sultan Malek-el Kamil. He returned to Italy only in the spring of 1220. In 1221 Francis was too ill from malaria to attend to the revisions necessary to his first rule owing to the enormous increase in the order: at Whitsun, 1221, there were so many friars—over three thousand— that they could not be accommodated in the Portiuncula and had to sleep in the fields in huts made of mats. At Christmas, 1223, St. Francis made the first crèche, and sang the Gospel of the Mass as deacon.

At the Assumption next year, Francis began a forty-day fast in honor of the archangel Michael. On September 14, the feast of the Elevation of the Cross, as he was on his knees, he saw in a vision a six-winged seraph, and from him received the stigmata: the heads of the nails were hard and black in his hands and feet; from the wound in his side often blood flowed, which soaked his clothes. The Church later established a feast of the stigmata of St. Francis.

When Francis returned from preaching in Egypt and Syria, he was horrified to find his brotherhood organized, with a splendid house at Bologna, and in the place where his little hut had been at the Portiuncula, a fine building for the friars. He was so angry he climbed onto the roof and began to throw down the tiles. "My free larks are imprisoned in the cages of their monasteries," he declared. And he resigned from administering his order, his place being taken by the faithful canon Pietro dei Cattani. Pietro died shortly after, and Brother Elias Bombarone succeeded him—with disastrous results. For Brother Elias abandoned completely the ideal of poverty at once—and changed the concept of "Friar" and of "Minor."

In 1220 Francis had met Dominic, and though the two great founders met that once only, they became great personal friends. In *The Mirror of Perfection*, compiled about 1318 and based on the *rotuli*, or parchments, upon which Brother Leo, the closest of all Francis' companions, wrote his reminiscences, there is an account of the two saints together in the presence of the cardinal of Ostia, later Honorius IV. The cardinal asked both men, "Why should we not choose bishops and prelates from among your friars, so that they may influence all the others by their witness and example?" Then there arose a humble and devout dispute between the founders as to which of them was to reply, for neither wished to take precedence, but each deferred to the other, urging him to answer. But at length the humility of Francis prevailed in that he did not answer first, while Dominic also prevailed, in that by answering first he also humbly obeyed.

So blessed Dominic said, "My Lord, my friars have already been raised to a noble state if they will only realize it; and in so far as I am able, I will never permit them to obtain any shadow of dignity." Then blessed Francis, bowing low before the Lord Cardinal, said, "My Lord, my friars are called Minors so that they may not presume to become greater. Their vocation teaches them to remain in a humble place, and to follow in the footsteps of Christ's humility, so that by this means they may at last be exalted above others in the eyes of the Saints. So if you wish them to bear fruit in the Church of God, hold them to the observance of their vocation. And should they aspire to high place, thrust them down to their proper level, and never allow them to rise to any prelacy."

Such were the replies of the Saints, and when they had ended, the Lord of Ostia was much edified by the answers of both, and gave profound thanks to God.

As they were both taking leave together, blessed Dominic asked blessed Francis if he would consent to give him the cord which he wore; but although he asked this favor out of love, blessed Francis refused it out of humility. At length Dominic's loving persistence prevailed, and having obtained the cord, he girded it beneath his habit and wore it devoutly from that time on.

Then each placed his hands between the hands of the other and commended himself to him with the most affectionate regard. And blessed Dominic said to blessed Francis, "Brother Francis, I wish that your Order and mine could become one, and that we could live within the Church under the same Rule." When at length they had taken leave of one another, blessed Dominic said to those standing by, "I tell you in all truth that every religious should imitate this holy man Francis, so great is the perfection of his sanctity." (*The Little Flowers of St. Francis and The Mirror of Perfection* [New York: E. P. Dutton, 1910], pp. 218, 219)

As is well known, that sanctity was appreciated not only by human beings but by birds, beasts, bees, and butterflies. The wolf of Gubbio, which Francis tamed, the birds to which he preached, the swallows that stopped twittering so his words could be heard, the fish that followed Francis' boat because Francis would not eat it but put it back in the water, the cicada that came when he called and sang with him, the caterpillar he picked up so no one should step on it, the bees for which he placed honey in a hollow tree after a hard winter—all testified to his universal appeal.

In Egypt Francis had contracted trachoma, and he, to whom the sun was the most godlike and glorious of created things, now often could not see it, and when it shone, it hurt his eyes dreadfully, so he had to pull his cowl over his swollen eyes. He fell very ill, and was taken to St. Damian, where Clare built him a wattle hut where he spent weeks in torment, bitten by gnats and rats, which he would adjure, "Sister Gnat, Sister Rat, I am tired. Please let me rest." One morning, to everyone's surprise, he was found by Clare and the sisters standing up, his cowl down over his eyes, and he sang to them what has been called the first poem in the Italian language, the *Canticle of Brother Sun*. He was carried to Rieti and Siena, to try to stem his sickness, but he only grew worse. He lingered on another six months. He wanted to go back to Assisi, and in August 1226 was taken to the very room where Bishop Guido had presided over the court that gave Francis' father back his money. Guido knelt and kissed the hem of Francis' garment, and this time it was Francis' turn to adjudicate between the bishop and the podesta (mayor). He made peace between them (they were quarreling about jurisdiction) and judged the same bishop who had once judged him. He added another verse to his canticle, in praise of Sister Death, "from whom no living man can escape." Then he asked to be taken to an isolated hut at the Portiuncula and to be laid naked on the bare ground, "for thus, in the arms of my dear Lady Poverty, I wish to die."

Which he did, at sunset on October 3, 1226. His last words were those of the 142nd Psalm: "I cried unto the Lord with my voice."

His feast is October 4. In 1228 a portrait of him was painted on the wall of a side chapel at the Sacro Speco at Subiaco.

Francis had been called a saint for all times. How is he a saint for ours? Firstly, perhaps, by his insistence that "money doesn't matter": it has no relevance at all to the interior life. Rich men have been saved, though we know it to be hard for them; but class, intelligence, temperament, money, all can be used in the pursuit of the Kingdom of God, as long as they are abandoned. Francis is also, in our sad century, an outstanding example of joy: he enjoyed the lovely

Umbrian countryside, the birds, the beasts, the elements. Lastly, he was quite, quite sure that evil was evil and must be dealt with instantly: he foresaw such tragedies as Brother Elias' treason in, and to, his order, and warned of it, but did not let it depress him. And he knew the good must never despair. His order provided for the hallowing of the new rich, whether haberdashers, like his father, or the new intellectual rich of the universities, and two of the greatest medieval poets, Thomas of Celano (d. 1255) and Jacopone da Todi (d. 1306), were Franciscans.

There were five Franciscan popes and eighty cardinals. Before 1414 the order had sixteen saints and thirty-five beatified members. It still flourishes.

St. Bridget of Sweden (1300–73)

How did it happen that a Swedish widow became, in the fourteenth century, one of the most influential personalities of her time? Sweden, in those days, was "the country which lies most northerly in the world, and beyond there is no country where men can live." Yet Sweden belonged to, and was part of, Europe, the "empire of Rome, all that which is north and west of Rome, and there is true Christendom." Europe was then one civilization, very much as Latin America is today: various nationalities and governments, but basically the same traditions and, over and above the various languages, a common language (Latin). The countries of Northern Europe were characterized then—as they are still—by an enormous feeling for law and by a natural sense of democracy. The Anglo-Saxon "dooms" were the basis of the English common law, and in Sweden the lawman "in the social order taken over from heathendom was *primus inter pares.*" (*Saint Bridget of Sweden,* by Johannes Jørgensen [New York: Longmans, Green, 1954], Vol. I, p. 2) Only later did the "lawman" become "King," and the peasants had still an active share in the making of the laws, "for no man must lack land, all shall have earth who have come from earth," wrote Birger Persson, who wrote the Uppland Law, which was confirmed in 1295. Around 1300, at his home, Finsta Gaard, was born his daughter Bridget.

Bridget's home consisted of a collection of wooden houses surrounded by a wall of earth: at the center was a tower of stone. Bridget was her mother's seventh child; her mother was preserved from drowning while pregnant with Bridget, who was given an excellent education by the dean of the cathedral of Uppsala, Andreas And. Bridget's parents were "pious persons of high rank." Her father, grandfather, and great-grandfather had all made the pilgrimage to Jerusalem, and also that to St. James of Compostela, in Spain.

When Bridget was eleven she had a vision, on Quinquagesima Sunday, of Christ crucified. When she was fourteen her mother died, and her father sent her to live with her aunt, her mother's sister Karin, married to the lawman of East Gothland.

Bridget moved from one "great house to another," for her aunt's husband, Knut Johsson, was constable and one of the Council of the Realm. Later he was a member of the Regency Council, guarding young Magnus Eriksson, who later became king. Their place, Aspanas, was on a lake in the midst of great forests. On Sundays Bridget with her aunt and cousins were ferried over to the small church at Malexander: the village consisted of a few wooden huts, an inn, and the priests' house. Aunt Karin watched over her pretty niece, and one evening, going her "last round to see that the fire was covered with ashes and all candles and lamps were put out," found the girl kneeling on her bare knees beside her bed. The aunt was afraid the girl might be invoking some of the troll creatures the servants talked about endlessly, and asked Bridget what she was doing. The girl looked up at her aunt and replied, "I only got out of bed to praise Him who is always near me, and always ready to help me!" "Who is that?" asked her aunt. "It is Jesus Christ who was crucified for our sakes and *whom I have seen*," declared Bridget. (Ibid., p. 42) Another time, as they were sitting sewing, embroidering with threads of gold, her aunt saw an unknown lady helping her niece. "Who was that?" she asked Bridget, who replied, "No one has been here, Aunt." But her aunt kept the piece of the needlework "as if it had been a relic." (Ibid., p. 43)

When Bridget was sixteen, her father promised his two motherless daughters in marriage to Ulf Gudmarsson and his brother Magnus, sons of the lawman of West Gothland. Bridget's husband-to-be was only eighteen; Bridget did not want to get married, since marriage "begins in joy and ends in sorrow." So she flung herself down on her bed and wept. Yet the weddings were celebrated in great splendor, and Bridget was given by her Ulf a golden girdle, gilded shoes, a bridal crown, and a gold wedding ring. She was married from her father's house, and then rode, accompanied by her father, to her new home, Ulfasa. On their wedding night Bridget asked Ulf to "live like the angels" with her, and these two virgins "for a whole year lived in a state of virginity" and constantly they prayed to God that, if they came together carnally, He would grant them children who might serve Him and never displease Him. And, when later they resolved to come together, they prayed each time that they might not sin thereby, and that He might grant them issue, ready always to serve Him. And that, although they were both young. They actually "knew each other," as the Bible puts it, only after *two* years of marriage, and then "they had between them firmly grounded a communion of hearts strong enough to bear the union of passion." (Ibid., p. 51) In the course of the following twenty years Bridget bore her husband four sons and four daughters, of whom two sons died. Bridget lived her married life fully: supervising the baking of bread, the brewing of ale, the making of cheese, and the washerwomen and gardeners as well. She took her children with her visiting the sick, and ran a hospital at Ulfasa itself, where she nursed scabies, skin diseases, boils, sores, etc., without fear of infection. She even taught her beloved Ulf to read, and when, in 1330, he became lawman in Narike, he had already been knighted. He and Bridget said the little office of Our Lady daily, as they both were Francisan tertiaries.

Bridget chose as tutor for her sons a young priest, Niels Hermansson, who later became archbishop of Uppsala (1324), and he lived to see his pupils' mother canonized a saint. For her own spiritual director she chose a canon of Linköping Cathedral, Master Matthias, through whom she became aware of the current plight of the church: the Babylonian captivity of the Pope in Avignon, of the growth of heresies, and of the falling away of the clergy, so many of whom like knights had horses and fine houses but did not fight; like well-born women, had fair and warm clothes, but did not suffer childbirth; ate, and above all drank, like peasants, but did not plow. Bridget, on the contrary, drank no wine, and ate only two dishes at any meal, and would get up at night and pray, while her husband held fast her hand and fell back asleep.

Her father, Sir Birger, went to Avignon, and when he came to die he was the richest man in Sweden, leaving twenty-two estates to his three heirs, of whom Bridget was one. So she became one of the richest women in the country.

Now Bridget built a wooden church on some of the land that came to her from her father, and her mounting block of stone is still outside it. She used to ride across the lake, her horse wading while he still found foothold and swimming after.

Bridget and Ulf really loved each other, but Bridget was indignant when Ulf gave their eldest daughter, Mereta, to one Sir Sigvid Ribbing, who was "notorious for his lewdness, and arrogant to boot." In Sweden, the father alone gave his daughter in marriage, and Sir Sigvid was a good match. Bridget would have nothing to do with the wedding; she was pregnant with her eighth child, and told Ulf to make that her excuse for not appearing at the wedding feast. But she thought the child she was about to bear reproached her, so she went to Ulf, took his hand, and joined in the reveling. A few days later she was brought to bed, and nearly died, but gave birth to a last girl, Cecilia, who lived to marry twice and died in 1399.

In 1332 the young king, Magnus Eriksson, attained his majority. (He had already forbidden the buying and selling of thralls, and ordained that no child born of a Christian father or mother could be called a thrall.)

In 1335 he married Blanche de Namur. She was very young, and Bridget was chosen to look after her education. Bridget left Ulf at Ulfasa, and their youngest children with him; she moved to Stockholm, where she watched over the royal couple. After two years, they had a son, and Bridget held him in her arms for his baptism. Another son was born two years later, after which Magnus wished to live in continence with his wife. Bridget's own second daughter had chosen this way, but she did not approve of the royal resolve. "Blanche has come to this far country in order to bear fruit," said Bridget. (Ibid., p. 86) The young queen gave her a box full of relics, which Bridget placed on the altar, yet Bridget thought Blanche frivolous, while Magnus took to unnatural vice and chose a favorite whom he loved "with all his heart more than himself." Bridget was horrified. "Three devils rule this land," she said, "the first is drunkenness, the second voluptuousness, and the third demon is worse than all the others, it excites men to unnatural intercourse with men." (Ibid., p. 89)

Sometime between 1339 and 1341 Bridget and Ulf went together on a pilgrimage to the martyr brother of Saint Erik in the cathedral, on the river Nid. They took thirty-five days to reach Nidaros. The interior of the cathedral had been burnt, but the casket with the saint's relics had been spared. Bridget rose from her knees determined to found a convent "for the salvation of the land." (Ibid., p. 96)

Bridget's family was very pilgrimage-minded, and she became so

too. She and Ulf first set off for St. James of Compostela: this was in
celebration of their twenty-five years of marriage. They took none of
their children: they left the two oldest boys at Ulfasa, and Cecilia
was taken care of by Dominican nuns, Karin and Ingeborg by Cister-
cian. (Ingeborg later became a nun, and died young.) Then Bridget
and Ulf set out, in June 1341, across East Gothland. Bengt, their
youngest son was left with the monks of St. Bernard at Alvastra.
They took the main road south, through Germany, France, and
Spain, making the first part of the journey by sea to Germany, which
they crossed following the Rhine, then down the Rhône to Taras-
con, where St. Martha is supposed to be buried.

They took with them on their pilgrimage Brother Svenung from
Alvastra. When they got to Compostela, Brother Svenung fell ill,
and he was much put out by Bridget's stern remarks about priests
and kings. "Once, there had been good priests, with five pieces of
gold: understanding, holy wisdom, chasity, moderation, and perseverance. Now it is no longer so. Today's bad shepherds buy a
woman's body with their gold pieces, and Christ is only a sheep from
whom they get their living, whose wool gives them clothes, whose
milk feeds them. All they preach is 'Come, give your money,' and
their sack is never full." Bridget would not even visit Avignon, and
she excoriated the kings of France and England, who were at war.
"They are like two wild beasts. One is greedy to swallow all it can
get, and the more it eats the hungrier it gets; the other wants to
exalt itself above all men." (Ibid., p. 111)

Brother Svenung was thinking Bridget very bold saying such
things about her betters, when, suddenly, he did not see the statue
over St. James's tomb any more, only a great light, and in the light a
woman crowned with seven crowns, and to his surprise, the woman
was Bridget. And above the woman was a darkened sun. A voice told
him that the darkened sun was the king of Sweden, and that the
seven crowns were a sevenfold grace of the Holy Spirit, to be given
Bridget. And he was further told that he would recover and go home
and be advanced. Coming out of his vision, Brother Svenung found
himself completely well; after he got back to Sweden he became
an abbot.

Ulf and Bridget came home by easy stages, stopping at Arras,
where a canon put them up in a fine house. There Ulf immediately
fell ill and was given extreme unction. While praying beside him,
Bridget asked him to grant when he recovered that they live in chastity together to the end of their days. Ulf agreed, and Bridget,
watching beside him, had a vision of St. Dionysius, who told her,

"Thou shalt come to Rome and Jerusalem, and by thee God will be made known to the world. And this shall be a sign to thee, that thy husband shall not die of this sickness." (Ibid., p. 119)

So Ulf recovered and they came back to Alvastra, where Ulf remained with his son Bengt, and Bridget rode on to Ulfasa, where the two big boys, Karl and Birger, ran to meet her, asking "But where is Father?"

Soon father Ulf was lying once more very sick in the monastery guesthouse at Alvastra, with his son Bengt, now eight, and Bridget beside him. He had still been functioning as lawman in March 1343, and appeared at a meeting in November. But early in 1344 he received extreme unction again. His last action was to take his wedding ring off and put it on Bridget's finger, saying, "Little Brita, I loved you so much." (Ibid., p. 129) Then he died. Bridget traveled home to Ulfasa, leaving Bengt with the monks. Ulf had been buried in the "right nave of the monastery church." Bridget divided everything she possessed among her children and the poor, keeping only enough to enable her "to live simply and dress modestly."

Bridget's eldest son, Karl, was already a lawman, and took over Ulfasa. One daughter, Karin, had been married, to Eggert von Kyren, a year before her father's death; one had been sadly and badly married earlier; one, Ingeborg, was a nun; Bengt would probably become a monk; Cecilia, who had no vocation, was later taken from the Dominicans, who had raised her, by her brother Karl and married off. So Bridget was now free. Sitting by her fire, looking into the flames, Bridget saw her husband, and asked him, "How are you faring?" Ulf replied he had sinned most in five things: that he had been too fond of his son Karl; that he had forgotten to pay a widow from whom he had bought some things: she would appear next day, sent by him, and Bridget was to pay her what she asked, for she did not ask too much; "the third was I carelessly promised to stand by a certain man in all his undertakings, and this made him bolder, so he defied the law; the fourth is that I exercised myself in throwing the lance and other knightly exercises, more that I might show how well I could do it than because it was of any use; the fifth is that I was far too severe with him of whom you know, and who was doomed to exile—he was guilty but I should have shown him greater mercy." And that was all. "O happy soul," said Bridget. (Ibid., p. 132)

That March, Bridget was in the chapel and on three mornings she was "rapt in spirit" and heard a voice saying, "Woman, hear me." Bridget was terrified, thought it was a delusion, went to confession, to communion. But, once again, the voice came, and in a shining cloud she saw the Christ she had seen as a child, and he said to her, "Fear not, I am the Creator of all things, who speaks to thee. And I will speak to thee, not only for thy own sake, but for the salvation of others. And I say to thee that thou shalt be my bride, and it is through thee I shall speak to the world. Thou shalt see and hear spiritual things and my spirit shall come upon thee and remain with thee to death." Bridget still doubted, so the voice added, "Go to Master Matthias, he is learned in spiritual things, and is able to discern between the spirit that is from above and that which comes from him who in the dawn of time fell from heaven like lightning because of his pride."

So Bridget left Ulfasa forever, and went first to Linköping to pour out her doubts about her revelations to Master Matthias. She sat at his feet, and read him the pages of warnings she had written down at the voice's command.

When she had finished, Matthias commanded her to look up (she never looked directly at anyone without her confessor's permission). She lifted her face obediently, her blue eyes full of tears, and sighed, "The judgment I must proclaim is hard, but Christ says that if the kingdom of Sweden will repent he will alter his judgment." Matthias bade her go to the monastery at Alvastra, where Bengt was, where Ulf was buried. "Stay there until you receive a message to go elsewhere." (Ibid., p. 140)

At Alvastra she was allowed to stay in a small house belonging to the monastery. She found a secretary in the subprior, Petrus Olai, who took down her visions. "God in his plenty inspired her with visions and divine revelations, not while she slept but while she was awake and at prayer. Her body was as it was otherwise, but she was rapt and caught away from the senses of the body in ecstasy and spiritual contemplation," he testified at her process of canonization. (Ibid., p. 94) He remained with her for thirty years, until her death.

Bridget lived at Alvastra from 1345 to 1349. During this time she seems to have conversed almost daily with the Blessed Virgin, who once asked her, "What do the proud ladies say in thy kingdom?" to which Bridget replied, "I am myself one of them, and I am ashamed to speak!" (Ibid., p. 150) But Our Lady insisted, so Bridget told her it was useless to speak to these ladies about humility and renunciation, or voluntary poverty. "Our mothers had many servants and brought us up with honor, why should we not teach our daughters the same lesson, to live in joy and be buried with honor?" they said. Then God "commanded Bridget to go to the king. She said she did not know what to say. God gave her this answer: 'Open thy mouth and it shall be given thee what thou shalt speak.' And immediately when she came to the king, it was given to her from God not only what she was to say to the king but many things that were to come to pass." (Ibid., p. 166) (Vita, p. 12) Bridget's brother Israel and her two eldest sons were often at court, and she was well aware that pride, gluttony, and lechery flourished there. Bridget told the king "he must apply himself to justice, he must not impose taxes without the consent of the people and not deprive any of their lawful possessions." Furthermore, he must build a convent in honor of the Mother of God in the place which would be shewn him." (Jørgensen, *supra*, p. 167)

The place shown Bridget (not the king!) was the king's castle of Vadstena, already almost a hundred years old, built of stone. Money was needed to make the alterations, and Christ said to Bridget, "It is my will that the lords of the land shall build a convent to the honor of my mother. I ask the poor people, too, to share in the work and to show their good will as far as they are able"; each unmarried man or woman to pay one penny, married couples two pennies. The convent Bridget founded was a double convent: an abbess was to be at its head, but next to the convent, and associated with it, must be a house for priests, and they must have lay brothers to help them.

"There shall be sixty sisters and not more. They shall have priests who shall say Mass and recite the Divine office daily. And they shall be completely separated from the sisters and have a house for themselves in which they shall live. There shall be thirteen priests, after the thirteen apostles, of which the thirteenth, St. Paul, did not work least." Bridget wrote the rule in twenty-eight chapters, in great detail. The bed is to be of straw, and each bed is to have two woolen blankets and two pillows but no sheet. Bridget ordered fasting for Advent and of course for Lent, and on all vigils. The nuns must keep careful accounts, and the sisters must not even call a thimble their own. "As fire comes of a spark, condemnation comes from private ownership." The sisters are to spend a third of their time in prayer, a third in work, a third eating and sleeping.

"In a very short space of time all the articles of this rule were said to me by Jesus Christ, and to me it was all, not like words written on paper, but I understood them one by one and with the help of the grace of Christ I hid them all in my memory. And when the vision was ended my heart was filled with so much warmth and rejoicing that nothing more could find an entrance into it, if I was to go on living, for it would have burst with joy. For many days my heart was so filled to overflowing, like an inflated sack. . . . But when it was all written down my heart and my body grew low as they were before." (*Regula*, Chap. 29—Jørgensen, p. 174)

Now Bridget went with her rule in her hand to King Magnus. Magnus was very polite. "You must be assured, dear Aunt, that personally I agree with the plan and will do everything to support this beautiful idea. But as to the king's house at Vadstena, you must understand, dear Aunt, that I must talk with Blanche about it first." (Ibid., p. 188) Yet in the spring of 1346, on May 1, King Magnus and Queen Blanche signed their will, leaving Bridget the king's castle of Vadstena, and chose it as their last resting place, adding land and money for the additional buildings.

Bridget now turned her attention to the war between England and France, and sent Bishop Hemming and Petrus Olai to Avignon with a letter to the Pope, Clement VI, telling him that he must "arise and make peace between the kings of France and England." But from Avignon Bishop Hemming wrote the Pope had taken no interest in making peace, had rejected the pleas to leave Avignon and go back to Rome, and had refused to consider Bridget's rule for a new order. The Pope pointed out that at the Lateran Council of 1215 it had been decided that there should be no new orders founded. Could Bridget not accept one of the orders already founded, the Pope asked?

Bridget was sad to see Bishop Hemming and Petrus Olai come back so unsuccessful. She was still at court, where the bishop had been scandalized by how much she ate at her two meals. Bridget had understood his feelings without his having any need to express them, and she wrote a note to him in which she said his feelings had been revealed to her; this so impressed him that he apologized. Others were not so impressed. A cousin of the king's pushed her so she almost fell, at which the king was so angry he scolded his cousin, who died three days after. Another courtier poured water over Bridget in the narrow street where he lived; "not clean water," the chronicle says. Bridget called up to him, "God bless you and may you not atone for it in the other world—I have only got what I deserve." (Ibid., p. 201) He, too, was soon found dead, in bed, choked in his own blood from a nosebleed. Bridget now entertained the king on her estate at Arboga, and there, walking in the woods, she met the king's tax collector, who was a priest. She got the king to dismiss him and give the job to a layman. The priest was furious, and rounded on Bridget. "I had a nice office, and you robbed me of it. You should stay in your own house, instead of going around making trouble." Bridget warned him, "Your mouth speaks out of the evil of your heart. If you do not take back your words and do penance, I tell you, as true as my name is Bridget, you shall not escape God's punishment." Soon after, while he was watching a bell being founded, the mold burst and the molten metal flowed out and killed him. Another priest, who was living in sin, told Bridget, "Our Lord is not so particular." (Ibid., p. 203) He went out into his field in a thunderstorm to bring in his horse, when he was struck dead by lightning as he loosed the tethering peg: his penis was burnt up. As they traveled from place to place, Bridget attracted more attention than the king or the young queen. Sometimes she cast out devils; sometimes she cured, as she did one of the priests traveling in the royal retinue who was so ill he could not sit on his horse. He was about to be left in a peasant's house, but groaned, "Will you leave me here among these wild animals?" Bridget was standing beside his bedside. "May I?" she asked Prior Petrus Olai, her confessor, who nodded. She laid her hand on the priest's head: "O sweet Jesus heal him." (Ibid., p. 218) At which he got up and rode better than before. A message came from Alvastra to tell Bridget her son Bengt was dying. She arrived in time, but the boy died on the fifth day after she came. He was buried in the abbey beside his father and brother Gudmar. Bridget decided she would not go back to the court; she would stay near her dead at Alvastra, and carry on with the building at Vadstena, only about fourteen miles away.

Bridget received her revelations in Swedish, and her confessor, Petrus Olai, translated them into Latin. By this time there were already five volumes—the fifth book alone contains sixteen thousand words in Swedish, fourteen thousand in Latin. In 1349, King Magnus was still doing what his "dear Aunt" bade him: he summoned a council and promulgated a new law, by which he promised not to deprive anyone of his property without a trial, to govern with the help of Swedes only, not foreigners, and to live off his estates; also not to impose new burdens on his people. This law came into force in 1351, and the king swore at Uppsala, his hand on the relics of St. Eric, to keep this law "towards young and old, towards born and unborn, towards friends and foes, towards absent and present."

Bridget had urged the king to make a crusade against the pagan Finns, but instead of putting to death the prisoners he took, he promised freedom to the captured if they accepted the Catholic faith and paid a big ransom. They obliged, but came back next year with a big army, and won back all that had been lost. Bridget told the king he should go to the Pope and apologize, but instead he made plans for a new war, against Russia. And now the king seemed to be regretting his gift to his aunt, as people around him were suggesting that Bridget wanted to put her son Karl on the throne instead of the king. The new part of Vadstena, built for and by Bridget, was pulled down in her absence: was the king involved? Anyway, Bridget decided to cut her losses. The year 1350 was a jubilee year, and Bridget determined that, as the king would not, *she* would go to Rome. She gathered a group of fellow pilgrims: none of her children, nor Master Matthias, but Petrus Olai, Prior Vetrus (also a chaplain), and a female friend, Lady Ingeborg, whose husband gave her leave to go. Bridget left Alvastra, and Sweden, never to return.

As she left, Black Death came. Two thirds of the inhabitants of Norway died, half as many in Sweden. As Bridget and her little group went through Swabia, one evening the pilgrims halted outside the town of Mainingen, letting their horses graze in a meadow outside the town gate. The peasant who owned the field asked for payment, so Bridget bought the whole meadow and gave it to the town. In 1472—a hundred and twenty-two years later—a Bridgettine convent was founded there.

Bridget and her group got safely to Milan, where, kneeling at the tomb of St. Ambrose in the cathedral, she was told by the saint that "at the prayer of thy friends God has called thee so that thou mayest in spirit see and hear and understand, and what thou hast heard in spirit thou shalt reveal to others." (Jørgensen, Vol. II, p. 9) In Milan poor Lady Ingeborg died. The rest went on, to Pavia, to the tomb of St. Augustine, thence to Genoa, and on by sea to Ostia. They arrived in Rome, where Cardinal Beaufort, a brother of Pope Clement VI, offered the Swedish princess his palace, as, living in Avignon, he did not use it. Bridget accepted. Petrus Olai ran the household, attended to the marketing, and saw to repairs. Bridget spoke the rule of the house she said she had from Christ Himself: eight hours' sleep, then the office of the day in the chapel, then a meal—soup or cabbage, two kinds of meat or fish—then two hours' recreation, more prayer, an evening meal, and bed.

"God who drew thee out of the nest, will care for thee till death." So Bridget was promised, and as they took "pious morning walks" every day in Lent, wonders never ceased. For example, among a crowd of beggars Bridget said to one holding a small boy by the hand, "That is not your son—you stole him to arouse people's pity. He's a Jew." She took the child away and saw to it he was baptized. Another time, she moved through the air in St. John Lateran. Indeed, soon "everyone" in Rome was talking about the Swedish miracle worker. She went to Faifa, a monastery, and while she was there

her confessor, in Rome, was accosted by a lovely girl with gold hair
and blue eyes: it was Karin, Ulf and Bridget's daughter, who asked,
"Where is Mother?" and said, "I longed so much for Mother I could
not eat or sleep. Eggert saw how I was and said I had better go. Eggert could not come with me, he is not well." (Ibid., p. 57) Bridget
told Karin it was God's will she stay with her in Rome, and when
Karin cried for her dear Eggert, she whispered, "No one knows but
me, but Eggert is dead, Karin; God told me." And so he was.

While Bridget stayed on in Rome—she was now fifty—her relations and friends died in Sweden: her daughter Ingeborg, her
brother Israel, and Archbishop Hemming of Uppsala. Bridget wrote
to the emperor, Charles IV, in Prague, heading her letter: "The Emperor Christ writes to the Emperor of Germany," recommending her
rule. But the emperor, who was sick in Prague, did not reply. She
also wrote again to the Pope, but he, too, was sick, and also did not
reply, and soon died.

The Roman people began to dislike this *principessa* who seemed
to have the evil eye: she was always having revelations that threatened people, and they always died; should she not be excommunicated? Maybe burned, like the Spiritual Franciscans, whom the new
Pope, Innocent VI, was consigning to the flames? The populace
tried to break into her palace, but Bridget, quietly praying in the
chapel, merely told Petrus Olai, "It's time for vespers, is it not?" And
the people dispersed.

Meanwhile, though, the Swedish group was running out of cash,
and Cardinal Beaufort wrote they had stayed long enough and must
move. However, a Roman lady offered them her house; they had
been ten years already in Rome and had made many friends. When
they got to the Papazuri house, Bridget recognized it: sitting by her
dying husband's bed, she had seen it in a vision and been told that
was where *she* would die.

Bridget's son Birger and his sister Karin were together in Rome,
visiting Bridget. On their way back through France they ran short of
money, and it was the Pope himself, Innocent VI, who lent, or gave,
them four hundred gold florins.

When her children had left to go home to Sweden, Bridget
started on a round of pilgrimages. Twice she went to Ortona, where
St. Thomas is buried, then on to the kingdom of Queen Joan of
Sicily.

Meanwhile, King Magnus, in Sweden, had borrowed from Pope
Innocent VI all the Peter's pence collected there in one year, a sum
of twenty-five thousand marks in silver. He did not attempt to repay

it, though the Pope gave him till May 1358. When he did not even offer an installment, Sweden was laid under interdict, and the king was excommunicated. He took no notice, but then King Valdemar of Denmark conquered Holstein and Scandia, and Gothland, too. Haakon, King Magnus' son, married the daughter of King Valdemar and rebelled against his father, taking him prisoner, though he soon let him go, in 1362, and was "reconciled with him in all matters." But another rebellion, which Bridget encouraged from afar, drove King Magnus into exile, and the duke of Mecklenburg was chosen to be king of Sweden in his stead. Bridget had hoped her grandson would be chosen; when he wasn't, she hoped the said grandson would become a priest, but instead he married and named his daughter for his grandmother. The child died aged nine and was buried in her great-grandmother's grave, in Vadstena.

Meanwhile Bridget spent two years in Naples, from July 1365 to October 1367. She stayed at the guesthouse of the Knights of Malta, and one of her spiritual sons was young Elzéar Orsini, who became a cardinal later. She cured the tubercular son of the lady Lapa, making, Bridget's daughter Karin said, "the sign of the cross over his abdomen and at once he recovered."

And in 1367 came the wonderful news Bridget had so long been waiting for: on April 30, the Pope left Avignon for Rome. It was no longer Pope Innocent, who had died in 1362; it was now Urban, a pious Benedictine who received a tumultuous welcome throughout Italy.

Bridget packed up and left Naples for the Farnese Palace, and no sooner was she back in Rome than she cured a seven-year-old, Gentile, son of Monna Golizia, who was dangerously ill of typhus and dysentery. Bridget just put her cloak over him, and the fever left him: later the boy would talk about the miracle with his mother and say, "Was it not strange, as soon as the Lady Bridget spread her cloak over me I was no longer ill."

And then, on October 16, 1367, the Pope entered Rome. Exactly a year later, in 1368, the emperor came. Bridget had prophesied so long that the Pope and the emperor would meet in Rome, and that she would be there, and now it really had happened. Did Bridget have an audience with the emperor? It is not sure. But she certainly had one with the Pope, accompanied by her two sons, one, Birger, simply clad as a knight, the other decked out in ermine so that the Pope said to Birger, "You are your mother's son," and to Karl, "You are a child of the world." In 1370 she had another audience with the Pope, who told her she should adopt the Augustinian rule for her order, but that she could certainly build a convent of nuns and next to it a monastery. However, he refused her the Portiuncula indulgence—the one granted St. Francis of Assisi. Bridget was mortified. To her great distress also, the Pope decided to go back to Avignon—which he did on September 16, and died there on December 19.

Bridget had more personal problems. Her son Karl became the lover of the wicked Queen Joan of Naples, who wanted to marry him—this Bridget was able to prevent, as he had a wife in Sweden. But he died in Naples, just as his mother was about to set off on a pilgrimage to Jerusalem.

On November 25, 1371, Bridget set off, and on April 14, 1372, she and her little company reached Cyprus, where she met Eleanor of Aragon, with whom she stayed at Nicosia. Eleanor was regent for her son. When Bridget spoke to the local people, a Dominican called out aloud, "The woman is crazy." Bridget's ship ran aground outside Jaffa, and everyone had to lose all his belongings; only Bridget did not complain, but sat quietly until she was rescued. It was May before they got to Jerusalem, and on Friday, May 14, she and her daughter Karin went to the chapel on Golgotha.

Bridget was now seventy-two. And in Bethlehem the Blessed Virgin revealed to her the truth of the Immaculate Conception, which was not to be promulgated by the Church for many centuries. "The truth is this, that I was conceived without sin . . . that hour in which I was conceived may well be called a golden hour, for then began the salvation of mankind, and darkness gave way to light." Mary also told Bridget, "I performed what I had to do, and went about as a human being among other human beings. But when some years had passed after my son's death, I began to long greatly to see Him again." An angel came to tell her "that the time has now come when you are to come to Him" and she asked: "Do you know the day or the hour when I have to depart hence?" And the angel answered, "When your friends come to lay you to rest." Then the angel vanished and . . . my soul was so filled with joy that it could no longer contain itself and in this joy my soul was loosened from the body. . . . Thereafter my son's friends came and buried my body in the valley of Jehosaphat. Fifteen days did my body lie in the grave, then it was taken up into heaven." (*Processus of Canonization of Bridget*, p. 330) From Bethlehem Bridget went with Karin and Birger and her confessors to Jordan, and Birger was made a knight of the Holy Sepulcher. When Bridget got back to Naples, she was interviewed by the archbishop and the inquisitor for the Kingdom of the Two Sicilies, but they found nothing amiss with her revelations. Bridget went to stay with Queen Joan in her villa at Aversa, and then went on back to Rome, where she fell ill. For five days, in which her understanding and memory were not affected, "as if she were not ill at all, and as if she were not so near death," she ate nothing except the Communion wafer. Then she received extreme unction and died as Prior Petrus was elevating the Host, on July 23, 1373, at daybreak. In December Karin and Birger took their mother's bones back to Sweden, having given one arm to the convent of the Poor Clares. And on July 4, her son Birger put his mother's coffin down in front of the high altar in the convent of Vadstena. Bridget of Sweden had come home.

What is there in the life of this remote woman for us today? She was rich, well-born, happily married, the mother of eight—as unlike most of us even in her life style as she could be. And she was continually scolding—she is a sort of essence of aunt, of auntiness, or aunthood! Yet two things about her are valid for us, and for always: One, at the purely human level: she exemplifies the fact that being a woman doesn't make a bit of difference to getting things done, or even to getting things said. Here was an obscure Swedish princess, who admonished popes, emperors, kings, queens, near and far—her own sovereign king was as impressed by her as were such remote royalty as the queens of Naples and of Cyprus. Bridget did whatever she set out to do: she founded her order, which continues to this day; she warned whomever she felt she was called to warn; she went wherever she wanted to go—including Jerusalem. And it would even appear that God did whatever she asked—whenever she wanted to cure a sick person or a cripple, she had only to pray. Miracles are tiresome things, because one doesn't like to believe that the higher powers (still less the highest Power) intervene on this plane: one prefers to think they are there and we are here. But, in some cases, there is just too much evidence to the contrary and Bridget certainly seems to have scattered prophecies that came true, and miracles that were attested, in prodigious quantities. She lived a far fuller life than (so far) any of the protagonists of Women's Lib, and left devoted children, grandchildren, and great-grandchildren as well as many followers and countless beneficiaries. In a little over seventy years, six hundred years ago, she won immortal fame simply by being what she was meant to be at every stage of her life: girl, wife, mother, seer, healer, and universal aunt.

St. Catherine of Siena (1347–80)

One of the relatively unexplored relationships is that between sanctity and sociology. Why, at "one point in time" (to paraphrase President Nixon) were Christian saints almost all fishermen, carpenters, and the like, and at another kings and their cousins, at yet another noblemen, at another highly educated academic types, at another merchants and rich upper-middle-class folk, at yet another small tradespeople? Saints seem to occur in class batches; the spate of "antimacassar" saints, such as Thérèse of Lisieux (1873–97) seems to have abated, while the last genuine peasant to be canonized, except for the virgin martyr Maria Goretti (1890–1902), was the Curé d'Ars (1786–1859). Now it seems again the turn of the professional classes to be canonized—St. Elizabeth Seton's father was a doctor. But in October of 1975 Pope Paul VI beatified an Austrian countess and a French aristocrat, so we may be right back to another mutation.

Catherine of Siena's parents, Jacopo and Lapa Benincasa, belonged to the well-to-do Italian middle classes, whose great exemplar was St. Francis of Assisi (1182–1226). The family of Jacopo were wool dyers, and they lived in Siena in the Via dei Tintori (the dyers' street) and worked as a family. Jacopo was a most saintly man "of unparalleled goodness, piety, and uprightness" (*Catherine of Siena*, by Sigrid Undset [New York: Sheed & Ward, 1954], p. 15) who never lost his temper, never allowed any quarrels in his home, and when almost ruined by a slanderer, would not allow any word to be said against his vilifier. Jacopo's wife, born Lapa di Puccio di Piagente, had already borne him twenty-two children of whom twelve had lived, when on March 15, 1347, she produced twin girls. She could feed only one, and chose Catherine. Giovanna, the other, was put out to nurse and died.

Catherine remained the youngest, as another daughter, born subsequently, also died in infancy. Catherine was much loved and petted by her large family: she was pert, pretty, and pious. Aged only five she taught herself the Angelus (the prayer said at 6 A.M., 12 noon, and 6 P.M., to recall the message of the Angel Gabriel to Mary) and would also kneel on each step going up or down stairs and say a Hail, Mary. One evening when Catherine was six, she was walking home with her older brother Stefano and another small boy, after visiting her married sister Bonaventura. Catherine looked across the Valle Piatta, and over the roof of the abbey church of San Domenico, on the other side of the valley, she saw Jesus Christ sitting on a throne, in bishop's robes, with the papal tiara on his head, and the apostles Peter and Paul and John the Evangelist beside him. Jesus smiled lovingly at Catherine, and blessed her with the sign of the cross. The child said she saw him "with the eyes both of her body and soul." (Ibid., p. 18) She stood glued to the spot, and her brother came back after a while to find the girl immobile, as though turned into stone. When he shook her crossly she seemed to wake, and burst into tears at being interrupted in so sweet a vision.

This vision matured the six-year-old, so she became quieter and ate less and less. She began beating herself on the shoulders with a small whip, imitated soon by her small friends. She went off one day with a loaf to look for a cave—she had determined to become a hermit. She found one, and knelt down, but felt she was floating up to its roof. Thinking it was the devil trying to scare her, she prayed harder and harder, and received a feeling that she was not meant to be a hermit—she was to go home and stay home. Aged eleven, she refused to eat meat, living only on bread and vegetables, and continuing her scourgings of herself. When she was twelve her mother tried to insist she dress her lovely face and figure becomingly, and prepare herself for marriage. She had a fair skin, dark eyes, and shining golden-brown hair. Her family tried to force her to take pains with her appearance, but she was so refractory they sent for a Dominican monk, Fra Tommaso della Fonte, to whom Catherine confided that she had promised God after her six-year-old visionary experience that she would remain a virgin for His sake. So Fra Tommaso suggested she cut off her hair, which Catherine did, to the horror of her family, who had found her a suitor. Lapa now dismissed her maid and made Catherine do all the chores. But the child did them so graciously, uncomplainingly, and efficiently that Lapa could not find fault with her. One day, Jacopo came into the girl's tiny room—a sort of closet on the stairs—and found her in prayer. On her head rested a snow-white dove. Shortly after, Catherine had a dream in which she chose St. Dominic, who showed her a robe like that worn by the Sisters of Penitence, of his third order.

Catherine now told her parents of her decision and that their opposition could not change her; if they would keep her in their house she would gladly remain there as their servant; if they chased her from their house she would accept their decision, but it would not change hers. Her family wept and raged, but her father declared that from now on, no one was to "tease or annoy my beloved daughter, or lay obstacles in her way. Let her serve her Bridegroom in complete freedom, and pray for us. We could never have obtained so honorable a marriage for her; instead of a mortal man we have been given the immortal God-made-man."

Now she refused to eat even bread, and lived on a few vegetables, while cooking rich meats for her family. She wore an iron chain around her waist and scourged herself with it three times daily; she only slept for half an hour a night, she drank only water. In 1366, when she was in her nineteenth year, she received in the Dominican church the white robe and veil and black cape of the Sisters of Penitence. This was most unusual, for mostly the sisters accepted only postulants of forty years and older, but she had persuaded them of her complete sincerity.

Now for three years Catherine lived in solitude in her little room at home, leaving it daily only to go to early mass in the Dominican church. She took her meals in her room—raw vegetables and water—and spoke only to her confessor, Tommaso. She enjoyed already an almost continual sense of the presence of Christ, Who told her: "Daughter, do you know who you are and who I am? You must know that you are that which is not, but that I am that which is. If you are truly possessed of this knowledge, the devil will never be able to cheat you. You will never consent to anything which is against my commands." (Ibid., p. 43) Sometimes her visions were without sight or sound; at other times she saw Christ on the Cross, or He seemed to be in her tiny cell and to talk with her. Sometimes He brought His mother, sometimes Mary Magdalen.

But now she also suffered from the most terrible temptations. She, who was so utterly pure, was assailed by sensual images and unchaste impulses; she seemed to see sexual orgies, and worst of all, except in church, she derived no comfort from prayer. Finally the demons jeered at her that she would never be free from these horrors until she gave in. She then declared, as her biographer, Raymond of Capua, relates, "I have chosen these temptations as my refuge, and I bear them, as I will bear all other sufferings, from love of my gentle Bridegroom." At this, the whole pandemonium left her, and she saw Christ. She asked him, "My beloved Lord, where were you when my heart was so filled with such terrible bitterness?" "I was in your heart," was the reply. (Ibid., p. 47)

She now tried to learn to read the breviary. She could not read, and accepted the fact that she found it too hard. Then, one day, she found suddenly that she could read. (It is not at all certain that she ever learned to write.) But she loved reading the Psalms, and the canonical hours. And then, one day, during carnival, when everyone was feasting except Catherine, she had the experience of the mystic betrothal. After which, the Lord told her to go and take her place at table with her family. She was overcome with shyness—she had not eaten a meal with them, had hardly seen them, for three years. Now she began to serve them, collecting the dirty clothes at night and washing them, scrubbing the stairs, baking the bread, setting the table, and doing the dishes. She now also acquired the confessor who was to be her biographer, Raymond of Capua, much older than she, yet who listened to her with great humility, for he already realized how far ahead of him spiritually she was, though he was her senior in years and in the ecclesiastical hierarchy. Now, too, she began giving away her father's possessions to the poor, and Jacopo let her take whatever she liked. But her siblings were not so happy, as she would go into their rooms and take shirt or socks for a beggar. Now, too, she began to levitate: she would be kneeling on the floor and suddenly be seen to rise in the air, still kneeling. She went to work as a nurse in the hospital of Santa Maria della Scala, and there nursed those no one else would go near: lepers, and old women dying of cancer of the breast. She managed to overcome her own physical revulsion against sickness and dirt—she was always, like Teresa of Avila, exquisitely clean—and also managed to make the grumpiest, most suffering patients fond of her. In 1368 Jacopo Benincasa died, and after his death Siena was wracked with civil war. Then Lapa fell ill and appeared to have died. But Catherine was horrified because her mother had died without the sacraments, and prayed her back to life. Lapa lived to be eighty-nine, and survived all her children and many of her grandchildren. Lapa finally told Raymond of Capua sadly after Catherine's death: "I think God has wedged my soul crossways in my body so it can't get out." (Ibid., p. 90)

Around 1370 Catherine gave up eating altogether; she only took Communion. Her confessor ordered her to eat, but food made her so ill he had to let her go her own way. It was at this time that she experienced the exchange of hearts: it seemed that God took out her heart and gave her His. And that same summer, just as she was saying the *Domine, non sum dignus* (Lord, I am not worthy that thou shouldst enter under my roof; speak but the word, and my soul shall be healed), Catherine heard a voice say, "But I, I am worthy to enter you." And as she communicated, it seemed to her that she entered into God and God entered into her "as the fish is in water."

(Ibid., p. 99) When she got back home, she was overcome with ecstasy, and lay down on her bed, and the neighbors who came saw her body floating above it. That same summer she, like St. Francis before her, received the stigmata—the wounds of Christ's Crucifixion in her own flesh—but asked that they be not visible until after death: they showed on her corpse. She began a remarkable series of conversions; hardened old sinners, robbers tortured on their way to execution, Catherine prayed for them and they died like innocent lambs. She now had a following, the Caterinati they were called, young people of both sexes who followed her, rarely left her alone, and told each other and everyone else of her ecstasies and miracles.

The current Pope, Gregory XI, was a French nobleman who lived at Avignon, which was safer than Rome. In spite of the efforts of such reforming popes as Gregory VII, the Papacy had not improved much in the more than three hundred years since Benedict IX had been elected Pope at the age of twelve. Pope Clement V left a fortune of one million florins, and had lent money to the kings of France and England to make war on each other. Now, because of the cruelties of Bernabò Visconti, the tyrant of Milan, and his rows with the Papacy, Catherine began to get into politics. In 1372 she wrote to the cardinal legate, Pierre d'Estaing, who was very attentive to the young saint. But he was recalled soon after he had made peace with Bernabò Visconti. A new legate came, anxious to meet Catherine. She wrote to him about Pope Gregory XI: "With regard to our loved Christ on earth, I believe . . . he would do good in the eyes of God if he hastened to right two things which corrupt the Bride of Christ. The first is his too great love and care for his relations. There must be an end of this abuse at once and everywhere. The other is his exaggerated gentleness, which is the result of his lenience. This is the cause of corruption among those members of the Church who are never admonished with severity." (Ibid., p. 141)

Under orders from her confessor, Catherine made a journey, her first, to Florence to attend the Dominican Chapter General in 1374. She came back to find Siena gripped by the plague—a third of its citizens died. Raymond of Capua took it too, but Catherine's prayer saved him. Yet he still doubted her powers and her ecstasies, while sure she was pure, good, and holy. But one day, when she was in bed with a raging fever, he saw her face change into the face of a man about thirty, with fair hair and beard. Raymond was very frightened, as the young man looked very sternly at him. "Who is it?" he asked. Catherine's voice replied, "It is that which is." (Ibid., p. 155) Then, as he looked, the face on the pillow became Catherine's again.

In 1375 Catherine went to Pisa to try to rally the city to the Pope, to whom she was now dictating letters frequently. Gregory XI told her to go to Lucca, where she made many friends but did not succeed in winning over that town to the Pope. And Catherine's own Siena joined Florence in a league against the papal legates which included also Naples, Milan, and Arezzo.

So Catherine wrote even more forcefully to the Pope, telling him: "My soul, which is united with God, burns with thirst for your salvation, for the reformation of the Church, and the happiness of the whole world. But it seems to me that God reveals no other remedy than peace." (Ibid., p. 177) She told him he must come back to Rome. And she demanded reform: the Pope must return to Rome, a crusade must be preached and peace made between Christians. Then she wrote to the Florentines and offered her services as peacemaker between them and the Pope. They accepted, and Catherine made her second visit to Florence. The Pope had placed the city under an interdict: no mass could be said in the whole city, no services held. Catherine was welcomed as the only person who could persuade the Pope to lift the ban. To do this, at the end of May 1375 Catherine set off for Avignon to see the Pope. She took with her several of her "followers" and three priests, one of whom was Raymond of Capua. They arrived in Avignon on June 18.

Two days after her arrival, Catherine met the Pope. Raymond of Capua interpreted for her, since she spoke only Tuscan, the Pope only Latin. How did this young tanner's daughter not only get to see the Pope but influence him and his successor? For it was even more astonishing than Joan of Arc's obtaining access to, and influence over, the dauphin. Gregory XI fell completely for Catherine, and was once and for all convinced that this lovely, articulate young woman was a saint. They spoke to each other with the greatest frankness. When the Florentine envoys did not show, Gregory told Catherine, "The Florentines are making fools both of you and me. Either they will not send any ambassadors at all, or when they come you will see they have not the necessary authority." (Ibid., p. 184) Which is what happened. Catherine told the Pope his court stank of the sins flourishing there. Fearing for French interests, three theologians came to Avignon specially to try to catch out this Italian girl. They asked why she, not a man, was sent by God on such a mission? They asked her about her fasting, her ecstasies; they plied her with difficult theological questions. They talked from early afternoon through nightfall, and then, being basically honest men, went to the Pope and told him Catherine had a clearer insight into spiritual matters than anyone they had ever met. She also made great friends with Bartolommeo Prignano, archbishop of Acerenza, a zealous reformer, who later became, after Gregory XI's death, Pope, as Urban VI.

Catherine urged Gregory to return to Rome. He said he just wanted to know God's will. Then she said, "Have you not bound yourself by a vow?" (Ibid., p. 186) Gregory, like the dauphin in Joan of Arc's case, was shaken, for he *had* made a vow, that were he ever elected Pope he would return to Rome. And he had never told a soul.

When the Florentine ambassadors finally came, they were rude to Catherine, and the negotiations broke down. In September the envoys were asked to go home, and the war between the Pope and the anti-papal league of cities went on. So Catherine concentrated on getting Gregory XI to return to Rome. The French cardinals warned him that if he went he would die, poisoned. Catherine, shown their letter, remarked, "There is no less poison in Avignon than in Rome." (Ibid., p. 187) On September 11, Catherine began her return journey to Italy; on September 13, Gregory XI left Avignon for Rome, suddenly, never to return, taking with him all the cardinals except six.

Catherine and her companions journeyed on foot, welcomed everywhere by crowds anxious to see this young woman who had gotten the Pope to end his Babylonian captivity. Raymond of Capua described the journey marvelously, including Catherine's joy at being home again in Italy. They took a long time, as several of their group fell ill—evidently of an infectious malady, as they succumbed to it serially. Poor Lapa was very worried, and got someone to write to Catherine. Catherine's answer was to tell her mother: "I think if you loved my soul more than my body all exaggerated tenderness in you would die, and you would not suffer so múch when you lack my presence in the flesh." (Ibid., p. 190) They stopped in Genoa, in the Palazzo Scotti, where crowds came to see Catherine. One night, a man dressed as a simple priest asked for her. When he entered her room, she fell at the feet of the vicar of Christ: Gregory XI had weathered a stormy passage to find his armies beaten in several battles against the Florentines. He had called a council and was about to yield to his timorous cardinals, who wanted him to go back to Avignon. But Catherine persuaded him to go on to Rome, and so decided his fate and the fate of the Church for many years to come.

In 1377 Catherine came home to Siena, and Gregory XI, on January 17, rode into Rome on a white mule.

Catherine, now thirty, almost transparent from her fasting and already sick, visited Florence again in December. The town was still under an interdict, so she was not accompanied by any priests. There were hopes of peace, when suddenly Pope Gregory XI died, on March 27. On April 18 Urban VI was elected. The Guelphs in Florence so enraged the guilds that a rebellion there broke out under Salvestro de Medici, himself a Guelph. The rebels declared that they would catch the Sienese witch (Catherine) and burn her alive. They came on Catherine in a Florentine garden, with words and clubs in their hands. She met them: "I am Catherine. Do whatever God allows you to do, but do not touch my companions." (Ibid., p. 213) The attackers fled. Catherine remained, to write to Urban VI and ask him to have mercy on the Florentines, and to beg him to proclaim a crusade. Peace was finally signed, on July 28, between Florence and the Pope: the interdict was withdrawn, and the Florentines, reconciled with the Pope, remained loyal to him during the subsequent Clementine schism.

Catherine now kept three secretaries at work, and spent the last years of her life rooting for Urban VI, whose election had been questioned by the French cardinals, who wanted a French Pope and were supported by the king of France. Three cardinals at Fondi elected Robert of Geneva as a rival Pope. He took the name of Clement VII and his followers were called Clementines.

Catherine meanwhile dictated her spiritual legacy, a book called *The Dialogues*, which is one of the chief glories of early Italian literature, besides being one of the most important Christian documents extant. The book ends with a prayer to the Trinity: "O eternal Trinity, you are a bottomless ocean. The more I throw myself into the ocean, the more I find you, and the more I find you, the more will I search. I can never say of you, it is enough. As the hart pants for cooling brooks, so my soul longs to escape from the prison of my body to see you in truth. For in the light with which you have illuminated my intellect I have seen and tasted your bottomless depths, O eternal Trinity, the beauty of all that is created." (Ibid., p. 238) The book was finished on October 13, 1378. Catherine now asked the Pope (Urban VI) for a written order requiring her presence in Rome, and authorizing her to leave Siena, since the Sisters of Penitence, with whom she lodged, did not approve her constant traveling, and her fellow townspeople did not wish her to leave Siena. Urban VI sent the required written order, and was delighted to see her, making her speak to the assembled cardinals. He told them this *"piccola donzella"* (little woman) was strong and calm, and that she proved that Christ is stronger than the whole world, and that He cannot fail His Church. Catherine remained in Rome until Urban

VI's death, while her dear confessor, Raymond of Capua was sent to France as papal envoy. They never met again. Raymond became master general of the Dominicans after Catherine's death, and wrote her life wonderfully well.

On Holy Saturday, 1380, Catherine's thirty-third birthday, she appeared to be dying, but rallied to offer her life for the peace of the Church at Communion on Easter Sunday. She lingered until April 29 of that year, the Sunday before the Ascension. She died about noon, with Lapa at her side and many of the *Caterinati* around her. Her last words were, "Father, into thy hands I commend my spirit." She was canonized in 1461 by Aeneas Silvius Piccolomini, of Siena, who had become Pope Pius II. What has this willful, extravagant, enormously politically minded young woman to teach us today? Surely the first thing is that saints can surface anywhere: that no country is safe from their interference if one does, and that to become a saint is (usually) very disagreeable for the saint's family: recently, in France, the head of the de Montfort family told his relatives, after the canonization of one of them: "Don't any of you ever *dare* to become a saint again. It's too expensive and too unsettling for the family." Bridget of Sweden's king-nephew, and no doubt Catherine of Siena's mother Lapa, would have surely agreed!

St. Thomas More (1477–1535)

The most probable date for Thomas More's birth is February 7, 1477, though this has been disputed by many of his biographers, some of whom have opted for February 6, 1478. His father was Sir John More, a barrister (lawyer), and his mother was the daughter of Thomas Granger, elected sheriff of London in 1503. Thomas had in all three stepmothers and was a model son to them all, and to his father. Holbein drew a family portrait of the happy More family, as well as painting fine portraits of Sir John and Sir Thomas More.

Thomas was brought up in the Latin tongue at St. Anthony's in London. At the age of twelve he was received into the house of Cardinal Morton, where he waited at table; the cardinal prophesied: "This child here waiting at the table will prove a marvelous man." Children were often thus placed in the households of people of higher rank, a survival of the training given by great men to pages in the days of chivalry. Foreigners marveled then—as they still do— that the English "put out" their children "at the age of seven or nine years at the utmost," which argued "the want of affection towards their children," as an Italian diplomat wrote at that time.

After two years, Cardinal Morton sent the fourteen-year-old Thomas More, "for his better furtherance in learning," to Oxford, where he entered Canterbury College, which later became part of Cardinal Wolsey's Christ Church. At sixteen he returned to London to study law first at New Inn; then, just after his eighteenth birthday, he was admitted to Lincoln's Inn. And there, when he was about twenty-one he met Erasmus, who was then about thirty and already famous. They met at the Lord Mayor's table, and without having been introduced were so delighted each with the other's wit that Erasmus exclaimed (in Latin): "You must be More or no one," and More replied, "You must be Erasmus or the devil!" More quickly brought Erasmus face to face with the future Henry VIII, then a handsome boy of nine, who asked Erasmus for something from his pen. Erasmus finished a poem in three days in praise of King Henry VII and his children. Erasmus and More became friends for life, and twenty years later Erasmus described More:

> He seems born and made for friendship, and is a most faithful and enduring friend. He so delights in the company and conversation of those whom he likes and trusts, that in this he finds the principal charm of life. . . . Though he is rather too negligent of his own interests, no one is more diligent in those of his friends. . . . He is so kind, so sweet-mannered, that he cheers the dullest spirit and lightens every misfortune. Since his boyhood he has so delighted in merriment that he seems to have been born to make jokes, yet he never carries this to the point of vulgarity, nor has he ever liked bitter pleasantries. If a retort is made against himself, even if it is ill-grounded, he likes it, from the pleasure he finds in witty repartees. He extracts enjoyment from everything, even from things that are most serious. If he converses with the learned and wise he delights in their talent; if with the ignorant and foolish, he enjoys their stupidity! With wonderful dexterity he accommodates himself to every disposition. His face is in harmony with his character, being always expressive of a pleasant and friendly cheerfulness and ready to break into smiles. To speak candidly, he is better adapted to merriment than to gravity or dignity, but he is never in the least

degree tactless or coarse. (Erasmus to Erich von Hutten, July 23, 1519 in *The Essential Erasmus* [New York: New American Library, 1964], p. 99)

What did young Thomas More look like? He was of medium height with a bright and clear complexion, auburn hair, and blue-gray speckled eyes. His expression was "sweet and intelligent"; he had rather coarse hands; his voice was penetrating but not musical. When More died—thirty-six years after he and Erasmus had first met—the latter wrote that "his soul was more pure than any snow, whose genius was such as England never had," and added, "in More's death I seem to have died myself; we had but one soul between us."

Both Erasmus and More looked up to John Colet, the dean of St. Paul's and founder of St. Paul's School. For four years, More hesitated over whether to give himself to the law or to holy orders. He "gave himself to devotion and prayer in the Charterhouse of London." He shared the life of the monks but without vow. His friends —John Colet, Grocyn, Linacre, and Erasmus—were all in orders. More studied Greek, "the key to the new religious learning, just as it was of the new scientific teaching." More, by wearing a hair shirt and sleeping on planks with a log for a pillow, managed to sleep only four or five hours a night. He chose John Colet as his spiritual director. England, at that time, was in the first flush of the Renaissance: Greek was flourishing at Oxford, and Erasmus thought England superior to Italy. He wrote:

> But how do you like our England? you will ask. Believe me, dear Robert, when I answer that I never liked anything so much before. I have met with so much kindness and so much learning —not superficial either, but intelligent and accurate—both Latin and Greek, that but for the curiosity of seeing it, I do not now so much care for Italy. When I hear my Colet, I seem to be listening to Plato himself. In Grocyn, who does not marvel at such perfection of learning? What can be more acute, profound and delicate than the judgement of Linacre? What has nature ever created more sweet, more endearing, more happy than the genius of Thomas More? It is marvellous how general and abundant is the harvest of ancient learning in this country. (December 5, 1499, to Robert Fisher, op. cit.)

Sir John More, however was not partial either to Greek or to philosophy, and cut off Thomas' allowance. "Being himself skilled in English law, he almost disowned his son, because he seemed to be deserting his father's profession," complained Erasmus.

While at Oxford, the sixteen-year-old More had fallen in love with a fourteen-year-old girl, but:

> Then the duenna and the guarded door
> Baffled the stars and bade us meet no more

as More wrote in *Philomorus*. What prevented More from becoming a priest was his fear that he would not be a good one, though he felt sure he could be a good husband, being uxoriously inclined.

In 1504 More was elected to Parliament, where he argued so eloquently against the king's demands for money for his daughter's marriage that the "king's demands were clean overthrown." When the king was told that "a beardless boy had disappointed all his purpose," he put poor Sir John in the Tower, and kept him there until he had paid a fine of one hundred pounds. Thomas More was already lecturing in Furnival's Inn and in St. Lawrence Jewry; in the latter he gave a course on St. Augustine's *City of God*. He, also at this time, translated into English the life of Pico della Mirandola, whose great cry, "How beauteous mankind is!" was the epitome of all that was best in the Renaissance.

More was also courting, having at this point decided to remain in the world. Toward the end of 1504, he "paid frequent visits" to a house called Netherhall, in Essex, the home of John Colt and his wife, Elizabeth, who had three daughters. The following is from William Roper's *Life* of his father-in-law (Roper married Thomas More's favorite daughter, Margaret), which R. W. Chambers has called "in seventy pages," probably the most perfect little biography in the English language.

> He resorted to the house of one Master Colte, a gentleman of Essex, that had oft invited him thither, having three daughters whose honest conversation and virtuous education provoked him there specially to set his affection. And albeit his mind most served him to the second daughter, for that he thought her the fairest and best favoured, yet when he considered that it would be both great grief and some shame also to the eldest to see her younger sister preferred before her in marriage, he then of a certain pity, framed his fancy toward her and soon after married her.
>
> "She was very young," said Erasmus, who stayed with More soon after his marriage, "of good family, with a mind somewhat uncultivated, having always resided in the country with her par-

ents and sisters, but she was all the more apt to be moulded according to his habits. He took care to have her instructed in learning, and especially in all musical accomplishments, and had made her such that he could willingly have passed his whole life with her, but her premature death separated them." (The Camelot Series: *Sir Thomas More: The Utopia and The History of Edward V by Sir Thomas More, with Roper's Life* [London: Walter Scott, 1890], p. 4)

Thomas More and Jane Colt were married early in 1505. She was just sixteen, and More took her home to Bucklersbury, near Wallbrook, where he had taken a house to be near his father. They had six happy years, in which four children were born: Margaret, Elizabeth, Cecily, and John. In 1507 More visited his sister, Elizabeth Rastell, at Coventry, and about a year later he went to the Continent for the first time, visiting the universities of Louvain and Paris. Roper suggests he was still so much in dutch with King Henry VII over his opposition to the king in Parliament, that "had not the King soon after died, he [More] was determined to go over the sea, thinking that being in the King's indignation, he could not live in England without great danger." (Roper, p. 8, op. cit.)

But the accession of the eighteen-year-old Henry VIII changed all that. Henry was very handsome, with blue eyes and a gay laugh, immense physical strength, courage, and great quickness of mind. He was interested in everything; a good linguist and a more than competent musician, he was well read in theology, literature, and science. Erasmus came hurrying back to England to join in the general rejoicing, and staying with More, wrote the *Praise of Folly,* "making the camel frisk." In his preface, Erasmus describes how he came to the title, and the book: "To beguile the tediousness of travel, I chose to amuse myself with the Praise of Folly. What put the idea into your head? you will say. Well, the first thing was your name of More, which is as near the name of Folly (Moria) as *you* are far from the thing. Next, I surmised that this playful production would please you, disposed as you are to enjoy jests of this kind, and to play in society the part of a sort of Democritus. Some critics may complain that these trifles are too frivolous for a theologian and too aggressive for a Christian, but when we allow every department of life to have its amusements, how unfair it would be to deny to study any relaxation at all." (*The Essential Erasmus,* p. 101, *supra*)

In 1510 More became under-sheriff of London, a post he held until 1518. Those were his happiest years: he loved to keep open house, entertaining, besides Erasmus, (Bishop) John Fisher of Rochester, Latimer, Grocyn, Linacre, and also Reginald Pole (who was to become archbishop of Canterbury), Miles Coverdale, and many others. More liked salt beef and coarse bread, eggs, milk, and fruit: he drank only water or very light ale, but would use a pewter cup so his guests would not be aware of his temperance.

In 1511 his young, "very good-natured wife" died: More wrote her epitaph: "Dear Jane lies here, the little wife of Thomas More." More was left with four children, the eldest five, the youngest barely two. He married again within a few months: he was thirty-four, his new wife, a widow, Alice Middleton, several years older. She was not popular with More's friends: "aged, blunt, rude and barren," wrote one: "harsh and worldly," wrote another; More himself said she was "neither a pearl nor a girl." Others were more frank: Ammonio, Latin secretary to Henry VII, stayed in More's house, and when he moved was not happy, although he "no longer saw the hooked beak of the harpy" (Alice More). She had had a daughter, Alice, who was absorbed into More's household, and one of More's biographers, Nicolas Harpsfield, declares More "so framed and fashioned her by his dexterity that he lived a sweet and pleasant life with her."

Erasmus wrote:

> He lives with his wife on as sweet and pleasant terms as if she had all the charms of youth. You will scarcely find a husband who by authority or severity has gained such compliance as More by playful flattery. What indeed would he not obtain, when he has prevailed on a woman already elderly, by no means of a pliable disposition and intent on domestic affairs, to learn to play the harp, the viol, the monochord, and the lute, and by the appointment of her husband to devote to this task a fixed time every day?

> With the same address he guides his whole household, in which there are no disturbances or quarrels. If any such arise, he immediately appeases it and sets all right again, never conceiving enmity himself nor making an enemy. Indeed there seems to be a kind of fateful happiness in this house, so that no-one has lived in it without rising to higher fortune; no member of it has ever incurred any stain on his reputation. (Erasmus to Hutten, ✳999 The Camelot Series: *Sir Thomas More: The Utopia and The History of Edward V by Sir Thomas More, with Roper's Life* [London: Walter Scott, 1890], Introduction by Maurice Adams, p. xxix)

More even wrote on his tombstone—his second wife still being alive—that he hoped they might all three (he, Jane, and Alice) live united in Heaven, a happiness not allowed them on earth.

More's son-in-law, William Roper, who lived sixteen years in More's house (and remained a widower for thirty-four years after his wife's death) declared he had never seen More even once "in a fume" (temper). But Erasmus complained to a friend that "I am tired of England, and More's wife is tired of me." As Erasmus never learned a word of English, and Alice More knew no Latin, there may indeed have been some failure of communication.

Now the humanists were scattered by the war that for twenty years England, under her young king, waged as the Pope directed. "England made war, England made peace, as it suited the papal interest. . . . English interests were recklessly sacrificed to the interests of the small and not very reputable Italian state ruled by the Pope." (R. W. Chambers, *Sir Thomas More* [Westminster, Md., 1949], p. 112) Only Archbishop Warham dared protest, declaring, as he opened Parliament in 1512, that God permitted war only because of the sins of kings and people.

Thomas More was just thirty-five when his most famous book, *Utopia*, was printed, in Louvain, Paris, and Basel. It has become a socialist textbook, converting William Morris, among others. The land of Utopia's government is based upon the four cardinal virtues —Wisdom, Fortitude, Temperance, and Justice—upon which Plato had already based his *Republic*. Utopia, a pagan country, shows up the vices of Christian Europe—Sallust had already done a model for this when he praised the barbarians over the effete Romans. The Utopians had freedom of thought, but not freedom of speech. *Utopia* is a protest against enclosures of public land and is a plea for communal life in all its aspects. The Utopian may himself possess nothing. All must wear the same clothes (as in a monastery, as in China today); they may play only worthwhile, instructive games; they must all eat together in a refectory; girls below eighteen and men below twenty-two serve, and do not speak at, meals unless spoken to. War is forbidden, except to secure colonies when the population overflows: here More almost joins with his great contemporary Machiavelli, whose *The Prince* was published in 1513, although it is, as it were, the antithesis of *Utopia*. Utopia was squarely based on the work of all, however different from the sixteenth-century commonwealths which, More makes Raphael declare, "are nothing but a conspiracy of rich men procuring their own commodities under the name and title of the commonwealth."

In 1517 More was sent on his first diplomatic mission, to negotiate with French merchants. He did not care for the assignment, as he wrote:

> You will be glad to hear that our embassy was pretty successful, except that it dragged on much longer than I expected or wished. When I left home I thought I should be away for a couple of months, whereas I spent six in the legation. However, if the delay was long, the result was satisfactory; so when I saw the business for which I had come concluded, and that other affairs were likely to arise, I wrote to the Cardinal and obtained leave to return home. I managed this by the help of my friends, and especially of Pace, who had not then left England. While I was returning I met him unexpectedly at Gravelines, but he was hurrying on so fast that we had barely time to salute each other. Tunstall has lately returned to England, but after scarcely ten days' interval, not spent in rest, but most tediously and anxiously, in giving a report of his mission, he is now forced upon another embassy, to his great regret, but he might not decline it.
>
> The office of ambassador never much pleased me. It does not seem so suitable to us laymen as to you priests, who have no wives or children to leave at home—or who find them wherever you go! When *we* have been a short time away, our hearts are drawn back by the longing for our families. Besides, when a priest is sent out, he can take his whole household with him, and maintain them at the King's expense, but when *I* am away, I must provide for a double household, one at home, the other abroad. A liberal allowance was granted me by the King for the servants I took with me, but no account was taken of those whom I was obliged to leave at home. You know what a kind husband I am, what an indulgent father and considerate master, yet I have never been able to induce my family to go without food during my absence, even for a short time! (To Erasmus)

Because of the pressure of work, More found it hard to finish *Utopia*—he describes under what conditions he did finish it in a letter to Peter Giles used as a preface:

Even to carry through this simple task, my other tasks left me practically no leisure at all. While I am constantly engaged in legal business, either pleading or hearing, or giving an award in arbitration, or deciding a matter as judge; while I am paying a friendly visit to one man, or going on business to another; while I devote almost the whole day to other men's affairs and what remains of it, to my family at home, I leave to myself, that is, to writing, nothing at all.

For when I have returned home, I must converse with my wife, chat with my children, and talk to my servants. All this I count as business, for it has to be done—and it is quite necessary unless you want to be a stranger in your own home. And one must take care to be as agreeable as possible to those whom nature has provided, or chance made, or you yourself have chosen, to be companions of your life, provided you do not spoil them by kindness or through indulgence make them your masters instead of your servants.

In these occupations that I have named, the day, the month, the year, slip away. When then can I find time to write? Nor have I yet said anything about sleep, nor even of meals, which for many take up as much time as sleep, and that takes up almost half a man's life. So I only get for myself the time I can filch from sleep and food. Slowly, therefore, because this is but little, yet at last, as it is something, I have finished *Utopia* and send it to you, dear Peter, to read, and remind me of anything that has escaped me. (*The Utopia, supra,* p. 73; The Camelot Series: *Sir Thomas More: The Utopia and The History of Edward V by Sir Thomas More, with Roper's Life* [London: Walter Scott, 1890], pp. 123–24 [abridged])

Utopia was an instant best seller. It went into four editions in two years and was translated into French, Italian, and Flemish; one senator at Antwerp learned it by heart! It was considered a major literary achievement and a courageous denunciation of current political ills.

In 1518 More gave up his job in, and for, the City of London, and entered the king's service. Wolsey and Henry had persuaded him, and he resigned on July 23, 1518, as under-sheriff. The king, wrote Erasmus, "could not rest until he dragged More to his court— dragged is the word." The king delighted in More's company and it "pleased the King and Queen, after the Council had supped, for their pleasure, commonly to call for him to be merry with them." To such an extent "that he could not once a month get leave to go home to his wife and children, whose company he most desired." The king would also take More up on his roof, "there to consider with him the diversities, courses, motion and other operations of the stars and planets." Nor would the king leave More alone even at home: as Roper wrote how he "suddenly would come home to his house in Chelsea to be merry with him. Whither, on a time unlooked for he came to dinner, and, after dinner, in a fair garden of his, walked with him for the space of an hour, holding his arm about his neck" (Ibid., p. 8). Roper told Sir Thomas More how happy he was whom the king had so familiarly entertained. More replied, "I thanked our Lord, son, I find his grace my very good lord indeed. . . . Howbeit, son Roper, I may tell thee I have no cause to be proud thereof, for if my head could win him a castle in France, it should not ail to go." (Roper, op. cit., pp. 21–22)

In Utopia, there were no distinctions of sex in education. And More, who himself took care of what was a whole school in his own household, practiced what he preached. Besides his own four children, he himself took care of the instruction also of his stepdaughter, Alice Middleton, and his three wards, Margaret Giggs, Anne Cresacre, and Giles Heron. Eleven grandchildren were later additions, and other children were sent him, as he had been sent to Cardinal Morton. Probably John Heywood, who later married Joan Rastell, was among them. John Clement, lecturer at Oxford in Greek, was one of the tutors More hired to help him with his "school." John Clement married Margaret Giggs in 1526. The "school" had an impressive curriculum: Latin of course, also Greek, logic, philosophy, theology, mathematics, and astronomy. More could not bear to see the children weep, and in a poem, written on horseback when he was soaked with rain, reminds them how he rewarded them with cakes, apples, and pears, and when he whipped them, used a "birch of peacock's feathers." More followed his students even when they were grown up, urging Margaret Giggs to surpass her husband in study: "I give you full leave to strive to get before him in the knowledge of the celestial system." As a result, his daughters became prodigies of learning, as Richard Hyrde's translation of *The Instruction of a Christian Woman* makes clear:

. . . the daughters of Sir Thomas More, whom their father, not content only to have them good and chaste, would also that they should be well learned. . . . Wherein neither that great, wise man is deceived, nor none other that are of the same opinion.

Here, indeed, More was a tremendous innovator, and is a model for our own time.

More was unique in that he educated his three daughters, choosing for them "the best available teachers in divinity, classics, astronomy, and music." Margaret, his eldest daughter, was the most prestigious member of More's school, though married to William Roper at sixteen. When More had to stay at the court or go abroad, he wrote often to his children and expected them to write to him daily. As he told his "dearest children," nothing

can come from your workshop, however rough and unfinished, that will not give me more pleasure than the most accurate thing anyone else can write, so much does my affection for you recommend whatever you write to me. Indeed, without any recommendation, your letters are capable of pleasing by their own merits, their wit and pure Latinity.

There was not one of your letters that did not please me extremely; but to confess frankly what I feel, the letter of my son John pleased me most, both because it was longer than the others, and because he seems to have given to it more labour and study. For he not only put out his matter prettily, and composed in fairly polished language, but he plays with me both pleasantly and cleverly, and turns my own jokes on myself wittily enough. And this he does not only merrily, but with due moderation, showing that he does not forget that he is joking with his father, and that he is careful not to give offense at the same time that he is eager to give delight.

Now I expect from each of you a letter almost every day. I will not admit excuses—John makes none—such as want of time, the sudden departure of the letter-carrier, or want of something to write about. No one hinders you from writing, but on the contrary, all are urging you to do it. And that you may not keep the letter-carrier waiting, why not anticipate his coming, and have your letters written and sealed, ready for anyone to take? How can a subject be wanting when you write to me, since I am glad to hear of your studies or of your games, and you will please me most if, when there is nothing to write about, you write about that nothing at great length! This must be easy for you, especially for the girls, who, to be sure, are born chatterboxes, and who have always a world to say about Nothing!

One thing however I admonish you; whether you write serious matters or the merest trifles, it is my wish that you write everything diligently and thoughtfully. It will be no harm if you first write the whole in English, for then you will not have much trouble in turning it into Latin; not having to look for the matter, your mind will be intent only on the language. That, however, I leave to your own choice, whereas I strictly enjoin you, that whatever you have composed, you carefully examine before writing it out clean, and in this examination first scrutinise the whole sentence, and then each part of it. Thus, if any solecisms have escaped you, you will easily detect them. Correct these, write out the whole letter again, and even then examine it once more, for sometimes, in re-writing, faults slip in again that one had expunged. By this diligence your little trifles will become serious matters, for while there is nothing so neat and witty that may not be made insipid by silly and inconsiderate chatter, so also there is nothing in itself so insipid, that you cannot season it with grace and wit if you give a little thought to it.

Farewell, my dear children. (*The Correspondence of Sir Thomas More* [Princeton, N.J.: Princeton University Press, 1947], pp. 255ff.)

In a letter to one of his children's tutors, William Gunnell, More discusses female education most pertinently:

I have received your letters, my dear Gunnell, elegant as your letters always are, and full of affection.

From your letters I perceive your love for my children, and their diligence I see in their own. Every one of their letters delighted me, but I was particularly pleased to observe that Elizabeth shows as much gentleness and self-command in her mother's absence, as would be possible were she present. Let her understand that this pleases me more than all possible letters from anyone!

Though I esteem learning joined to virtue more than all the treasures of kings, yet renown for learning, when it is not united with a good life, is no more than distinguished infamy. This would be especially the case in a woman; since learning in women is a new thing and a reproach to the slothfulness of men, many will be ready to attack it, and will impute to learning what is really the fault of nature, thinking that the vices of the learned will allow their own ignorance to be esteemed as virtue. . . . Among all the benefits bestowed by learning, I count this first, that we are taught by the study of books to value that study, not for the sake of gaining praise, but for its own true usefulness.

I have said the more, dear Gunnell, on this matter, because of the opinion you express, that the lofty quality of my Margaret's mind should not be depressed.

I do agree with you in this judgment, but it seems to me, and no doubt to you also, that he who accustoms a generous mind to admire what is vain and low, depresses it, and on the other hand, he who rises to virtue and true good, elevates it.

I have often begged you, and not only you, my dearest Gunnell, who would do it of your own accord out of affection for my children, and my wife, who is sufficiently urged to it by her motherly love for them, which has been proved to me in so many ways—but also all my friends, to warn my children to avoid the precipices of pride and to walk in the pleasant meadows of modesty; not to be dazzled by the sight of gold, not to sigh for those things which they mistakenly admire in others; not to think more of themselves for the possession of gaudy trappings, nor less for the want of them; not to spoil by neglect the beauty that nature has given them, nor to heighten it by artifice. Let them put virtue in the first place, learning in the second, and esteem most in their studies whatever teaches them piety towards God, charity to all, and Christian humility in themselves. So will they receive from God the reward of an innocent life, and in this expectation, they will not dread death. . . . The harvest will not be affected, whether it be a man or a woman who sows the seed. Both are reasonable beings, distinguished in this from the beasts; both therefore are suited equally for those studies by which reason is cultivated, and like a ploughed field, becomes fruitful when the seed of good precepts is sown.

If it be true that the soil of a woman's brain is naturally poor, and "more apt to bear bracken than corn"—(a saying by which

many keep women from study) then so much the more, for that
reason, should a woman's mind be diligently cultivated, so that
the defect of nature may be redressed by industry. This was the
opinion of the ancients, of those who were the wisest and most
holy. . . .

Do you then, my most learned Gunnell, of your goodness
make it your care that my girls learn well the works of those
holy men. . . .

I fancy I hear you object that these precepts, though true, are
beyond the capacity of my young children, since you will
scarcely find a man, however old and advanced, who is not
stirred sometimes with the desire of glory. But, dear Gunnell,
the more I see the difficulty of getting rid of this pest of pride,
the more do I see the necessity of getting to work at it from
childhood. For I find no other reason why this evil clings to our
hearts so closely, than because almost as soon as we are born, it
is sown in the tender minds of children by their nurses, it is cultivated by their teachers and brought to its full growth by their
parents, no one teaching what is good, without at the same time
awakening the expectation of praise as of the proper reward of
virtue.

That this plague of vain glory be banished far from my children, I do desire that you, dear Gunnell, and their mother and
all their friends, would sing this song to them, and repeat it and
knock it into their heads, that vain glory is a despicable thing,
and that there is nothing more sublime than the humble modesty so often praised by Christ. This your prudent love will so
enforce as to teach virtue rather than reprove vice, and make
them love good advice instead of hating it. (Quoted in Staple-
ton, *Tres Thomae* [1588] pp. 225–26; English version, *Life of Sir
Thomas More*, translated by Msgr. P. E. Hallet [1928] London:
English Text Society)

For More, in public as in private life peace was his passion. Peace
in his huge household, which he succeeded most marvelously in
keeping; peace between princes, which he strove for with all his intelligence; and peace in the Church, which was to be disastrously
broken by Luther's nailing of his ninety-five theses to the church
door at Wittenberg in 1517. More's beloved son-in-law Roper was
for a time a Lutheran, and More himself was very displeased with
the king's defense of the Papacy, pointing out to him as a lawyer

that the Statute of Praemunire limited the Pope's power in England. Henry replied that "we are so much bounden unto the see of Rome that we cannot do too much honor unto it." (Roper, *supra*, p. 68) Among More's and Henry's popes was a particularly bad one: Alexander VI. Henry insisted that More reply to Luther's reply to Henry's defense of the Papacy, which More reluctantly did. The resulting bitterness did neither credit: More had for once forgotten his manners, Luther never had any.

In 1521 More became undertreasurer and was knighted; and in July 1525 he became chancellor of the Duchy of Lancaster; his salary was 173.6.8 pounds—even if multiplied by fifteen to equate it with present-day values, not a large sum. In 1523 he was elected Speaker by the Commons, and in the negotiations that resulted in the peace of Cambrai he acquitted himself so well that "for his good service in that voyage the King, when he after made him Lord Chancellor, caused the Duke of Norfolk to declare unto the people how much all England was bound to him." (Roper, pp. 36–37) This peace was to last thirteen years, the longest interval of peace in the reign of Henry VIII.

Erasmus, writing to Ulrich von Hutten, described More, soon to be the greatest man in the kingdom after the king:

> Whatever influence he has acquired by his dignity, whatever favour he enjoys with his powerful Sovereign, he uses for the good of the State and for the assistance of his friends. He was ever desirous of conferring benefits and wonderfully prone to compassion. This disposition has grown with his power of indulging it. Some he assists with money, others he protects by his authority, others he advances by his recommendation. If he can help in no other way, he does it by his counsels; he sends no one away dejected. You would say that he had been appointed the public guardian of all those in need.

> He counts it a great gain to himself, if he has relieved some oppressed person. . . . No man more readily confers a benefit, no man expects less in return—and, successful as he is in many ways, I have never seen any mortal more free from self-conceit.

> In serious matters no man's advice is more prized, while, if the king wishes to recreate himself, no man's conversation is gayer. Often there are deep and intricate matters that demand a

grave and prudent judge. More unravels them in such a way that he satisfies both sides. No one, however, has ever prevailed on him to receive a gift for his decision. His elevation has brought with it no pride. Amidst all the weight of State affairs he remembers the humble friends of old, and from time to time returns to his beloved literature.

In 1529 the "King's great matter"—the question of his divorce from Catherine of Aragon, the niece of Emperor Charles V—came to a head, when the Pope, "unwilling to offend Henry, but not daring to oppose the Emperor, cited the marital case to Rome." (R. W. Chambers, *Sir Thomas More* [Westminster, Md., 1949]) The Pope had no sympathy for Catherine and, through Wolsey, implored her to retire to a convent, which she refused to do, whereupon the Pope "wished her in her grave," fearing her obstinacy would "lose all England for the Spirituality," which, indeed, is just what it did. It also undid Wolsey: Henry deprived him of his office of Lord Chancellor, and Wolsey was condemned in the Court of King's Bench for illegally using his authority as papal legate. He was allowed to retire to the Palace of Esher. Henry, refusing to appoint another cleric, gave the Great Seal, on October 25, to Sir Thomas More, who, on the twenty-sixth, took the oath as Lord Chancellor: the first layman to hold the office. More's comment on his predecessor was "Glorious was he very far above all measure, and that was a great pity, for it did him harm and made him abuse many great gifts that God had given him." Wolsey's last words were as much an antithesis of More's as his life style had been. Wolsey said: "Had I but served my God as I have served my king, he would not have abandoned me in my last hour." Wolsey enriched himself: his avarice was counterbalanced only by his arrogance and extravagance. More's integrity was such that he even scolded his son-in-law for requiring preferential treatment: "Were it my father stood on one side and the devil on the other," wrote More, "his cause being good the devil should have right."

More's attendance on affairs of state had destroyed his private practice and he was entirely dependent on his official salary and allowances.

More's contemporaries admired him, almost without exception. But, today, objections have been made because "as Chancellor, he never attempted to introduce into the country the reforms which he had sketched as a younger man." (Joyce Dramel Hertzler, *The History of Utopian Thought* [New York: Cooper Square, 1923], p. 127)

Is this true? He was chancellor for only two years and seven months. During this time, as Dr. Scarisbrick has argued, "More continued to press for his ideals." Dr. Scarisbrick found in the London Public Records Office an undated packet of legislative proposals once ascribed to Thomas Cromwell but actually the work of More. This document contains "measures to curb the influence of the clergy, a proposal for translating the Bible into English and programs to aid the poor." Dr. Scarisbrick thinks this document was a "crisis agenda" for a 1530 session of Parliament, which never took place. The idea, declared Dr. Scarisbrick, speaking at Fordham University in 1977, "was to defuse anticlericalism by removing the causes of friction between Parliament and Church."

On May 16, 1532, More resigned as chancellor, declaring it was for reasons of health. Actually, as everyone at the time was aware, it was because he foresaw that the submission of the clergy, who agreed that all Church legislation be subordinated to the "pleasure of the Crown," would lead to further royal arbitrary measures. More surrendered the Great Seal the day after this "submission of the Clergy" had occurred, and wrote to Erasmus to explain what he had done:

> I saw that I must either lay down my office or fail in the performance of its duties. I could not carry out all the tasks imposed by my position without endangering my life, and if I were to die, I should have to give up my office as well as my life. So I determined to give up one rather than both!
>
> Wherefore for the benefit of public business and my own health, I humbly appealed, and not in vain, to the goodness of my noble and excellent Prince. . . .
>
> I am good for nothing when I am ill. We are not all Erasmuses! Here are you, in a condition which would break the spirit of a vigorous youth, still bringing out book after book, for the instruction and admiration of the world. What matter the attacks upon you? No great writer ever escaped malignity. But the stone which these slanderers have been rolling so many years is like the stone of Sisyphus, and will recoil on their own heads, and you will stand out more grandly than ever. You allow frankly that if you could have foreseen these pestilent heresies you would have been less outspoken on certain points. Doubtless the Fathers, had they expected such times as ours, would have been more cautious in their utterances. They had their own disorders to attend to, and did not think of the future. . . .
> The bishops and the king try to check these new doctrines, but

they spread wonderfully. The teachers of them retreat into the Low Countries, as into a safe harbour, and send over their works written in English. Our people read them, partly in thoughtlessness, partly from a malicious disposition. They enjoy them, not because they think them true, but because they wish them to be true. Such persons are past mending, but I try to help those who do not go wrong from bad will, but are led astray by clever rogues. (A *Key to the Colloquies of Erasmus* [Cambridge, 1927])

More had been unable, and unwilling, as "the king's good servant," to oppose Henry while holding office under him. With what was left to him of life he would, by his writing as a free man, defend what he believed even against the king's majesty. His religious writings are no better and no worse than other polemical writings of the same date: what is to his immense credit is that during the time he held power, for twelve whole years, no heretic was burned or tortured in the whole of England.

In March 1534 the Act of Succession was passed, which required all Henry's subjects who "arrived at full age" to "make a corporal oath" to "observe and maintain the whole effects and contents of the Act." More was given due warning by the duke of Norfolk: "As they chanced to fall in familiar talk together, the duke said unto him: "By the Mass, Master More, it is perilous striving with princes; therefore I would wish you somewhat to incline to the King's pleasure; for by Gods body, Master More, *Indignatio principis mors est.*"

"Is that all, my Lord?" quoth he; "then in good faith the difference between your grace and me is but this, that I shall die today and you to-morrow." (Roper, pp. 68–69)

"More knew, and humanly feared, what was coming to him: "I found myself (I cry God mercy) very sensual and my flesh much more shrinking from pain and death than methought it the part of a faithful Christian man." (Sir Thomas More to Margaret Roper, from *The Correspondence of Sir Thomas More, supra*, p. 540)

And in another letter, to his daughter Margaret, he wrote: "That you fear of your own frailty, Margaret, nothing misliketh me. God give us both twain grace to despair of ourselves and wholly to hang upon the strength of God. . . . Surely Meg, a fainter heart than thy frail father hath, thou canst not have. And yet I verily trust in the great mercy of God that he shall of his goodness so stay me with his holy Hand that he shall not finally suffer me to fall wretchedly from his favour." (Roper, p. 149)

On Low Sunday, April 12, 1534, More was cited to appear before the commissioners at Lambeth. He was shown the Act of Succession, and was willing to swear to that, but would not accept that he must obey the king in all matters. Thomas Cranmer, archbishop of Canterbury, tried to persuade him to sign, saying that "so long as More did not condemn the consciences of those that swore the oath, he was then bound, for himself, to accept the orders of the State." More refused to accept this line of reasoning, and was shocked that Cranmer, the archbishop of Canterbury and thus the successor of Thomas Becket, should argue in this fashion. For four days, More was confided to the custody of the abbot of Westminster; then, on April 17, he was committed to the Tower.

At first he was allowed his own servant, John a Wood. The lieutenant of the Tower, Sir Edmund Walsingham, apologized for not offering him better cheer; an Italian friend, Antonio Bonvisi, sent him a warm gown and meat and wine. Lady More had to pay fifteen shillings a week for More's prison fare, and five shillings for that of his servant. More was indignant, as a lawyer, because his imprisonment was illegal; that he was right in his objections was proved by the fact that "an act of Parliament had to be passed to legalize *retroactively* the oath for refusing which he was imprisoned." (26 Henry VII, cap. 2, Second Act of Succession) His daughter Margaret was allowed to visit him; later his wife came, and grumbled at him that "You have always been hitherto taken for so wise a man, will now so play the fool to lie here in this close filthy prison and be content to be shut up among mice and rats, when you might be abroad at your liberty and with the favor and goodwill both of the King and his Council, if you would but do as all the Bishops and best learned of this realm have done." (Roper, pp. 78–79) "Her persuasions moved him but a little." As the months went by, More's family and friends grew more and more worried. More himself wrote to Meg, showing his own anxiety:

> Now have I heard since, that some say that this obstinate manner of mine, in still refusing the oath, shall peradventure force and drive the king's grace to make a further law for me. . . . But I am very sure that if I died by such a law, I should die for that point innocent before God. . . . And I thank our Lord (Meg) since I am come hither, I set by death every day less than other. . . . Nor never longed I since I came hither, to set my foot in mine own house, for any desire of or pleasure of my house; but gladly would I sometime somewhat

talk with my friends, and specially my wife and you that pertain
to my charge. But sith that God otherwise disposeth, I commit
you all wholly to his goodness, and take daily great comfort, in
that I perceive that you live together so charitably, and so
quietly: I beseech our Lord continue it: And take no thought
for me . . . whatsoever you shall hap to hear, but be merry in
God. (*The Correspondence of Sir Thomas More, supra,* pp.
542–44)

Dame Alice's daughter Alice, now Lady Alington, who loved her
stepfather dearly, also tried to help. As she wrote Margaret:

Sister Roper, with all my heart I recommend me to you,
thanking you for all your kindness. The cause of my writing at
this time is, to show you that at my coming home, within two
hours after, my Lord Chancellor did come to take a course at a
buck in our park, the which was to my husband a great comfort,
that it would please him to do so. Then when he had taken his
pleasure and killed his deer, he went to Sir Thomas Barneston's
to bed: where I was the next day with him at his desire, the
which I could not say nay to, for methought he did bid me
heartily: and most especially, because I would speak to him for
my father. And when I saw my time, I did desire him as humbly
as I could, that he would (as I have heard say that he hath
been) be still good lord unto my father. First he answered me,
that he would be as glad to do for him as for his father, and
that (he said) appeared very well, when the matter of the nun
was laid to his charge. And as for this other matter, he mar-
velled that my father is so obstinate in his own conceit. . . ."
(Ibid., p. 512)

In November 1534, Parliament, which had been opened by
More in 1529, met again to pass the Act of Supremacy, by which the
king was affirmed to be "the only supreme head in earth of the
Church of England." It was administered all through the realm, and
only the Franciscan Observants of Richmond and Greenwich, the
Carthusians of London, and the brethren of Sion refused to sign.
More's lands were forfeited, and during the winter his health failed
and his family appealed to the king and to Thomas Cromwell to
release him because of this; in vain. Early in May 1535, More was ex-
amined in the Tower by the King's Council, presided over by
Thomas Cromwell. More wrote his daughter what he had said:
"I am the King's true faithful subject and daily bedesman, and

. . . I do nobody no harm, I say none harm, I think none harm, but wish everybody good. . . . My poor body is at the King's pleasure. Would God my death would do him good." On May 4 he saw the three Carthusian priors and Dr. Richard Reynolds go from the Tower to be hanged, drawn, and quartered. Soon after, Cromwell interviewed More again, and threatened to torture him. More wrote to William Ledes, a priest, and said, "If ever I should mishap to receive the oath you can be sure it was expressed and extorted by duresse and hard handling." (Ibid., p. 553)

On June 22, John Fisher, old and ill, the saintly bishop of Rochester, was beheaded. On July 1, More was taken to stand trial at the Court of King's Bench.

He was charged with treason, "traitorously and maliciously attempting to deprive the King of his title of Supreme head of the Church of England." (R. W. Chambers, *supra*) Richard Rich, the solicitor general, had declared that More had said that Parliament could not make the king supreme head of the Church, which was perjury: what More *had* said was that the Parliament could make Rich king, and he, More, would then accept him as such. When More asked Rich in turn if Parliament "could make a law that God should not be God, would you then, Master Rich, say that God were not God?" "No, sir," Rich replied, "that I would not, for no Parliament may make any such law." More had evaded Rich's "clumsy trap," though Rich swore to the contrary. More declared to Rich, "I am sorrier for your perjury than for my own peril."

More, aged only fifty-eight, looked ill after fifteen months in the Tower. He leaned on a stick and had gray hair and a long gray beard. He was given a chair. In answer to Cromwell's taunt, "What, More, you wish to be considered better, wiser, and of better conscience than all the bishops and nobles of the realm?" he replied: "My lord, for one bishop of your opinion, I have a hundred saints of mine, and for one Parliament of yours I have all the General Councils for a thousand years, and for one kingdom I have France and all the kingdoms of Christendom." Sentence of death was then pronounced.

More was taken back to the Tower. He sent his "shirt of hair, not willing to have it seen," to his daughter Margaret Roper, with a touching letter, the last part of which, unfinished, was as follows:

I cumber you good Margaret much, but I would be sorry, if it should be any longer than to-morrow. For it is Saint Thomas even, and the octave of Saint Peter: and therefore to-morrow long I to go to God: it were a day very meet and convenient for me. I never liked your manner toward me better, than when you kissed me last: for I love when daughterly love and dear charity, hath no leisure to look to worldly courtesy. Farewell my dear child, and pray for me, and I shall for you and all your friends, that we may merrily meet in heaven. I thank you for your great cost. I send now my good daughter Clement her algorism stone, and I send her and my godson and all hers, God's blessing and mine. I pray you at time convenient recommend me to my good son John More. I liked well his natural fashion. Our Lord bless him and his good wife my loving daughter, to whom I pray him to be good as he hath great cause: and that if the land of mine come to his hand, he break not my will concerning his sister Daunce. And our Lord bless Thomas and Austin and all that they shall have—— (*Correspondence, supra*)

Next day, July 6, he was told he was to die before 9 A.M. The traitor's sentence (hanging, drawing, and quartering) had been commuted to beheading. More thanked Sir Thomas Pope, the bearer of the news, and spoke of his gratitude to the king "for many past benefits and honors, and yet more bounden am I to his grace for putting me into this place, where I have had convenient time to have remembrance of my end. And most of all am I bounden to his highness that it pleaseth him so shortly to rid me out of the miseries of this wretched world."

On the scaffold, so weak that it seemed about to collapse, he said "merrily" to Sir Edmund Walsingham, "I pray you, see me safe up, and for my coming down, let me shift for myself." His last words to the people were, "I call you to witness, brothers, that I die in and for the faith of the Catholic Church, the King's loyal servant, but God's first." He then said to the executioner, "Pluck up your spirits man, and be not afraid to do thy office; my neck is very short, take heed therefore thou strike not awry, for saving of thy honesty." He bound his own eyes, and removed his long beard from the block so it should not be cut, "for at least it hath committed no treason."

When the king was told of More's death, he was playing dice with Anne Boleyn. "You, *you* are the cause of that man's death," he exclaimed, and left the room. (R. W. Chambers, *supra*)

As Al-Ghazali had commented some five hundred years earlier, "The fall of one who comes between a king and his wife is a fall from which there is no rising, and an unspeakable slip."

Robert Whittington had written in 1520, "More is a man of angel's wit and singular learning. I know not his fellow. For where is the man of that gentleness, lowliness and affability? A man of marvellous mirth and pastimes, and sometimes of as sad gravity. A man for all seasons."

Thomas More's relevance today is in many fields. His pioneering work in the field of female education has already been noted. His "extended family" is also an inspiration in these days of the "nuclear family" when here in the United States so few people are aware of grandparents, cousins, and in-laws: Margaret Mead is only one anthropologist who has pointed out that children *need* three generations to develop real security in themselves. His sense of humor is another bond with us, and his imagination, which in his own time was sometimes considered "a great blemish to his gravity." And his absolute financial integrity in an age as corrupt as ours is both marvel and model for us all.

But it is as a political thinker that he is unique among the saints. Not since the earliest Christians has private ownership been as denigrated as it was in the *Utopia:* the socialist theory that "property is theft" can lean on the *Utopia,* as William Morris did. Indeed, England's Fabians regarded the *Utopia* as almost a blueprint for the reforms they advocated, which, by 1945, were being legislated in London.

Still more important is his significance in the history of nationalism and in the demarcation of the limits of loyalty. It is both simplistic and untrue, and bad history to boot, to regard St. Thomas More as reiterating the position of St. Thomas Becket (1117–70) four hundred years earlier. Becket was archbishop of Canterbury, and his allegiance was therefore to the Pope; Thomas More was a layman, and, as such, was "the king's good servant." But, in the nine words of his supreme statement, he declared his final allegiance was "God's first." He took full responsibility for his actions, unlike the Nazis who pleaded that their oath to Hitler exempted them from the moral law, or the Vietnam veterans who had taken prisoners up in airplanes and dropped them, with the excuse they were obeying orders. (Both Clausewitz and Hitler declared *no* soldier should obey an order he thought morally wrong!)

More was aware of the moral danger of an oath: when Henry VIII
and Anne Boleyn were married, he told Roper, "God give grace son,
that these matters within a while be not confirmed with oaths"
(Roper, p. 57) and, of course, refused to take the oath when his
worst fears were confirmed.

But, in the end, it is not as an early feminist, not as a "major English author" (as C. S. Lewis called him, placing him as the writer of
the best specimen of the Platonic dialogue ever produced in English
—the *Dialogue* of 1528), not as a great patriot, not even as the
supreme example of a devoted husband and father, but quite simply
as a Christian, that More shines most brightly for us.

In his last letter to his wife, written after he was condemned to
death (a far more horrible death than More's, as he was hung on a
meathook and his dying jerks filmed), Helmuth James, Count von
Moltke, wrote on January 11, 1945: "Your husband stood before
Freisler not as a Protestant, not as a landed proprietor, not as a
nobleman, not as a Prussian, not as a German—but as a Christian
and as nothing else." For Freisler had told him: "Christianity and
we National Socialists have one thing in common, and one thing
only: we claim the whole man."

For, as Lord Acton wrote, "it was Christianity which introduced
the novel concept of a conscience immune from political interference, a sanctuary of liberty. When Christ said: 'Render unto
Caesar the things that are Caesar's, and unto God the things that
are God's,' he gave the State a legitimacy it had never before acknowledged. And Christ not only delivered the precept, he also
forged the instrument to execute it. The limit of the power of the
State ceased to be the hope of patient ineffectual philosophers and
became the perpetual charge of a universal church." (*Essay on Freedom and Power*, by John Emerich Edward Dalberg-Acton [Boston:
The Beacon Press, 1949], p. 57)

For the Church, whose unworthy Supreme Pontiff in More's day
was an example of how not to be or to behave, Saint Thomas More
lived and died. He was an example to von Moltke and is to us all,
today, tomorrow, and forever.

St. Francis Xavier (1506–52)

꧁✽꧂

Since World War II we have seen such a proliferation of "wise men from the East" coming over to convert us from our materialism, to teach us to meditate, to bring us the values of asceticism, of communal living, of detachment, whether these teachers come from India, Tibet, Japan, or, more recently, from South Korea, that it is hard to remember that in the sixteenth century it was we Christians who were sending missionaries to the East, to bring the light of the gospel, and the benefits of Christian ethics, to the East. The thousands baptized by Xavier are today paralleled here by the millions who follow Maharishi, or Zen Buddhism, or the Tibetan monk Trumpa, or the Reverend Moon. And one must remember, in both cases, the context of the missionary journeys. If South Korea is unbelievably corrupt, Portugal, from which St. Francis Xavier sailed to India, and in the context of whose trading ports in the East he worked, was at least as corrupt, and even as cruel: the Christian record in the East is as nasty as the behavior of the South Koreans; Christianity was as cruel in the sixteenth century as the Japanese were in Sumatra and Borneo in the twentieth. The difference is between individuals: between such missionaries as Francis, who never drank wine, who never accepted money, who ate only just enough to keep himself alive, who spent all his time in the hospitals and lazar houses comforting the sick, and such missionaries as the Maharishi, with big cars, rich followers, at least one wife, and enormous money-making devices.

The sixteenth century was a century in almost as horrid a turmoil as the twentieth. The Church was itself corrupt, though a few holy men were trying to reform it; the Reformation and the wars of religion, the discovery of the Americas as well as the plundering of the East, were going on throughout the whole century. It was a time that, in its turn, paralleled to some extent the breakup of the Roman Empire in the fourth century: just as the emperor Julian the Apostate was at Athens with Basil, Gregory of Nyssa, and Gregory of Nazianzus, so Ignatius Loyola and Francis Xavier were at Paris with John Calvin and George Buchanan.

Yet, as Thomas Traherne wrote, "the most tempestuous weather is ever the best seedtimes." The great century of cross-pollination

that the sixteenth turned out to be started in Spain with the legacy
of the Moors: Spain was, indeed, the main channel through which
Oriental mysticism penetrated into the Church. So, though Spain
was fiercely Catholic, it was so in a very different way from, say, either France or Italy. In Spain, Christianity had been for seven hundred years under the domination of Muslim rulers, so, when Fer-
dinand and Isabella finally drove these out, the Christianity of the
people had a frontier quality about it, a freedom of expression and a
vigor lacking to Christians who had lived for centuries under corrupt
popes and venal clergy, of kings who alternately backed up the
Church and opposed it. Spain never could have produced either a
Thomas Becket or a Thomas More; on the other hand, Dominic or
Ignatius Loyola or Francis Xavier could not have originated in any
other country than Spain.

Francis was born on Thursday in Holy Week of 1506 at Xavier, a
castle brought her husband, Don Juan de Jasso, by Doña María de
Apilcueta as part of her dowry when she was married, at fourteen.
She was better-born than her husband, though he, too, was of noble
birth, a distinguished man, a doctor of law from Bologna, who became counselor and treasurer to the king of Navarre. As a child,
Francis probably spoke Basque, and when he lay dying, he reverted
to that language. When young, Francis was a splendid athlete, playing pelota and enjoying the wolf hunting, fishing, and rock climbing
afforded by his native mountains. His family was pious, and daily
Mass was said in the chapel, also Vespers; the Salve Regina was sung
every evening. It was a happy and united family; Francis had two
older brothers and three much older sisters. His father died when he
was nine. When he was ten, Navarre rose against the king of Spain,
but the rebellion was put down: the government of Spain ordered
the fortifications of Xavier demolished, and Francis and his mother
watched the smashing of the outer walls, the drawbridge, and the
battlements, leaving the garden a desert of charred beams and spilled
stones. His brothers refused to surrender and were condemned to
death but were not caught; finally they were pardoned, coming home
to find their mother and younger brother poor indeed. Francis was
now eighteen. In October 1528 he found himself, in Paris, a nine-
teen-year-old student.

Francis took the arts course, leading to theological studies. His
first four years, he first took an examination in Greek, history, gram-
mar, and writing Latin verse. The next two years were mostly
devoted to logic, then a licenciate exam. The students "rose at four,
lecture at five, followed by Mass, and a roll for breakfast. Lecture

from eight to ten; at eleven, master and students dined together, while the Bible or Lives of the Saints were read aloud. Then, for recreation, the reading of poetry and questions on the preceding lesson. Another class from three to five; at six, supper, repetition, benediction of the Blessed Sacrament, to bed." (*Monumenta Historiae Societatis Jesu, Rome 1944–45; Monumenta Xavieriana, Madrid, 1899–1914,* Vol. 1., p. 285) Francis was at Ste. Barbe's College, whose principal was a Portuguese. It had a high reputation and many of the best French and Scottish students. Francis' closest friend at college was Peter Faber, a shepherd boy from Savoy, who wrote of his college days: "I went to the college of Ste. Barbe in the year 1525. I was nineteen. . . . I put among the foremost of my mercies . . . that I found in the room of this college in which I was installed such good companionship: I speak above all of Master Francis Xavier, who is of the Company of Jesus." (P. Faber, *Fr. Fabri Monumenta, Memoriale,* Madrid, p. 493) George Buchanan was also at Ste. Barbe's, and Erasmus had only recently departed: "I carried nothing away from Paris," he wrote, "but a body infested with disease, and a plentiful supply of vermin." And he adds: "The beds were so hard, the food so meagre, the labors so exacting, that many youths of splendid promise, after the first years of their sojourn, became mad or blind or leprous, if they did not die. Some of the bedrooms, because they were close to the lavatories, were so dirty and infected that none of those who lodged there came away alive, or without the germ of some grave disease. . . . O, how many rotten eggs I ate there, and how much mouldy wine I drank." (Doumergue, *Vie de Jean Calvin* [Lausanne, 1899], Vol. 1, p. 69)

At this time, Francis met Ignatius Loyola. Ignatius was thirty-three, lame, and poor—he came to Paris on foot, driving a donkey laden with his books; his leg had been shot at the battle of Pamplona, possibly by one of Francis' brothers, who were on the opposite side. But Ignatius, like Francis, was, in spite of appearances, a nobleman. Francis, Faber, and Loyola shared a room in Ste. Barbe. Francis was by now lecturing in Greek in the college of Beauvais. In 1530, Xavier got his degree. His mother had died; his elder sister, abbess of Gandía, too. Francis had been eight years in Paris, and had never gone home once.

Peter Faber, however, now went home to Savoy to say good-by to his father and friends: he had decided to join Ignatius for his whole life. During the seven months he was away, Francis was alone with Ignatius, and when Faber returned, Francis had made the same decision as his friend. Francis' devoted servant, Miguel, was jealous of Ignatius, and went one night to murder him with a dagger. But, instead, he fell at Ignatius' bedside, confessed his intention, and begged forgiveness. One day, Francis, Faber, and four others found themselves together with Ignatius and discovered they were all of one mind. They took together the triple vow of poverty, chastity, and pilgrimage to Jerusalem. But Ignatius bade them finish their theological studies. Then they walked, black-robed, to Notre Dame de Montmartre and there vowed to depart on January 25, 1537, for Jerusalem. They made the same journey and repeated the same vow on the two following years, 1535 and 1536 Faber, the only priest among them as yet, said Mass.

Among the books Ignatius had brought on his donkey to Paris was the manuscript of his "Spiritual Exercises." These he now "gave" to Francis, who emerged from them a changed man: "As a result he even, remembering his great delight in his early athletic prowess, macerated his body, carried away with his fervour, with too little prudence. With hard and tightly-bound strings he tied his arms and his legs so that the flesh swelled and broke, and almost entirely covered the cords. It seemed impossible to cut them. . . . He endured two days of terrible suffering. We feared that his arms, which were the worst, would have to be amputated. But, by a singular providence of God, they healed completely."

Then they set off, as Tursellinus describes (the following is from the English version of 1632):

> Therefore upon the thirteenth day of November, a most unseasonable time of the year, having according to their vows given all they had to the poor, except their writings and some little thing to help them on the journey, he, together with his other company, setteth forth on the way. Their manner of travelling was this: they were clothed in coarse and old habits, every one with a staff in his hand, and a short leather mantle upon his shoulder like poor pilgrims: about their necks they hung their beads to be known for Catholics as they travelled among heretics, their writings they carried at their back in a little bag.
>
> They used every day to communicate, being the only comfort of all their labours, thereby both to renew their forces, and to revive their spirits, being wearied with painful travail. When they departed from their lodging, they always commended themselves to God, and when they came into it they gave Him thanks. Being upon the way, they first spent some time upon meditating upon heavenly matters: then they used some pious

discourse together, and now and then they lightened the labour and weariness of their journey with singing of hymns, psalms, and spiritual canticles.

In this manner, for the most part taking his way through Lorraine and Germany, to avoid the troubles of the war, he endured the autumn showers of France, and the winter colds of Germany, and though he was not accustomed to travel on foot, yet he cheerfully undertook and performed this long and tedious journey, being loaden with his writings, and this in the dead of winter, and through most foul ways many times encumbered over with snow and frozen up with ice, especially as he passed the Alps.

And Francis:

. . . throughout the whole journey (as he was always before wont to do) applied himself with such diligence and alacrity in helping and serving his companions as was wonderful. For as they all strove to the uttermost—this being the one emulation among them—to excel one another in courtesy, he, either out of fervour of spirit, or natural civility, far outwent the rest. And this care and desire of his was no greater to help his companions than to procure the salvation of others. Whensoever occasion was given him of helping his neighbours, either with counsel, advice, or example, he with great zeal made his commodity thereof, and enhanced the same as opportunity served. And herein his labours were not in vain, for many Catholics were thereby reclaimed to a good life, and some heretics also reduced to the wholesome way of truth. Which way soever they passed they left behind them tokens of sanctity, for all to behold, and Catholics to imitate. And so it happened oftentimes that even heretics themselves, taken with admiration at their sanctity, would courteously show them their way, tell them what difficulties they were to pass, and when need was, would themselves freely conduct them on their journey. Francis, therefore, waded through all the incommodities and dangers of the way and upon the tenth of January of the following year, arrived safe with his companions in Venice. There he found Ignatius Loyola. (Tursellinus, *Life of S. Francis Xavier* [Antwerp, 1596], Book I, Chap. IV)

In Venice, they found Ignatius lodging in the Incurable Hospital, where Francis inured himself "to sights and smells he could hardly

bear." Barely recovered from their fifty days of walking from Paris to
Venice across the Alps in winter, they set off for Rome. It was now
Lent, and they ate only what food they could beg. In whatever town
they stayed, Francis, his gown "kilted up to the knee, asked the merchants in the market for a vegetable, or a little fruit." When they
got to Rome, the Pope gave them permission to go abroad, and they
returned to Venice. On June 24, Francis was ordained, and then
spent, forty days in a deserted, roofless cottage in the Euganean
Hills, after which they began preaching and teaching in the villages.

> And this was Francis manner of preaching. Remembering that
> Christ was wont to preach in the fields, upon mountains, and on
> the sea-shores, whenever he saw any hope of doing good, there
> he would put himself among assemblies of people to preach,
> and especially would he teach such as never used to come to ser-
> mons, . . . gathering together people in crossways and streets,
> and borrowing a stool out of some shop, standing thereon he
> would speak of virtuous and godly life with more fervour of
> spirit than flourish of words, to such as either stood there idle,
> or else were in their plays or pastimes; insomuch as some who
> came to his sermon only to get something to laugh at, being
> moved by the weight of his speech, and the divine force where-
> with he spoke, instead of laughing, went away weeping. Nothing
> caused him to be more admired, or helped on his business bet-
> ter, than refusing to take money, a token of sanctity most pleas-
> ing to all men. For when all saw that he neither asked anything
> of the people about him, nor would take anything which was
> offered him, they could not but think that he sought the salva-
> tion of others more than his own commodity. (Tursellinus, *Life*,
> p. 31)

The companions still could not go to Jerusalem, since Venice and
Turkey were at war, and now Francis fell ill. As Rodríguez, one of
his companions, described it, they were admitted together to the hospital, where they had to share a single bed, "and that was an occasion of great discomfort to us. For when one was shivering and wish-
ing a dozen blankets, the other was burning with fever and wished
none at all. We both profited by this affair in the practice of patience and charity. Further, the room where we lay was open to all
the winds of heaven."

"When they recovered and returned to Ignatius, they 'wondered
what name would be best.' They remembered that they knew no

name but Jesus Christ and that they served him alone. And so it appeared to them that they might take the name of their Leader and that they should call themselves the Company of Jesus." (Rodríguez, *Commentarium de origine et progressu Soc. Jesus* [Lisbon, 1777])

Francis then was sent to Bologna with one of the original companions of Ignatius, called Bobadilla, and there Francis contracted another violent fever. In March 1538, Francis joined the rest of the Company in Rome. He looked, and was, so ill that he could not go out preaching, but he was able to help formulate the document presented to Pope Paul III on June 24, 1539. The Pope, on reading it, is supposed to have cried out, "*Hic digitus Dei est*" (this is the finger of God), but the document had to be approved by three cardinals as well as the Pope, two of whom welcomed the new order while the third, Cardinal Gia, was sticky but finally agreed to the "official formation of the Company." For the next six months, Loyola kept Francis with him as his private secretary.

The Portuguese were clamoring for missionaries to go to India. Ignatius, sick in bed, called Francis to help him, and said that Bobadilla was too ill to go. The Portuguese ambassador could not wait until he recovered. Francis, "with great joy and promptitude," replied, "Well, then, forward! Here I am." He left Rome the next morning. In his bag he had three or four worn garments, and two books, one his breviary. He was to travel in state with the Portuguese ambassador, and:

> In his journey he gave no less sign of modesty than of sanctity. For although he were given to the contemplation of heavenly things, yet being not altogether unmindful of human, he showed himself so courteous unto all, that when he came to the Inn he would leave the best chambers and beds to other of his company, contenting himself with the worst things. And when the servants neglected to look unto their master's horses, or discharge other inferior servile offices, he would himself do them all, showing himself therein rather a servant indeed, than a companion. Yet none was more pleasant in conversation than himself, nor more ready in all kinds of courtesies. . . . But, which is hardest of all, he kept such a mean in these things, that, tempering courtesy with gravity, both his actions and words savoured all of sanctity. (Tursellinus, *Life*, p. 48)

He had said good-by to Ignatius and never saw him again.

Francis hoped to see Peter Faber in Parma, but they missed each other and never met again. On this journey a young man was converted by Francis and gave this account of his experience:

> I was an *hidalgo*, young and rich, and I was out to see the world. I visited France, Germany, Italy, and finally I reached Rome in 1540. I visited Don Pedro Mascarenhas, the ambassador of John III., and he asked me to accompany him on his return voyage to Portugal. I had many things on my conscience, as often happens when a rich youth roams at large in strange countries, free from all surveillance. On the way, I made the acquaintance of Master Francis, and he showed great kindness to me. He sought out my company, and warmed my heart by his honest gaiety, as side by side we travelled onwards. Gradually, he came to speak of general confession, and persuaded me to make it. I made it to Francis himself, and with great satisfaction, in a church which we passed by the way. From that time I became, thanks to God, another man. It is true that Master Francis had a notable gift for impressing the fear of God on men's souls: I felt this fear grow within me even as I confessed. It was then, for the first time in my life, that I understood what it was to be a Christian." (Quoted by J. M. Cros, *Vie de S. François Xavier* [Toulouse, 1899], Vol. I, p. 161)

Tursellinus describes how Francis saved the physical life of one of his fellow travelers:

> Afterwards they travelled over the Alps where, not being able to take sure footing by reason of the driving of the snow, and the craggy rocks and paths, their horses being tired, with no small danger to their masters, the ambassador's secretary fell by chance from his horse, and was suddenly swallowed up in a huge mass of snow. The place was upon a slippery and steep rock, under which ran a swift torrent. The greatness of the danger stroke all his companions into such a fear that none durst undertake to assist him . . . so they, being all amazed, stood still looking upon one another. As they thus stood, on cometh Xavier, and regarding another's life more than his own, leapt presently from his horse and by main strength drew him up out of the snow and delivered him from manifest danger with no small peril to his own life. (Tursellinus, *Life*, p. 51)

They then crossed the South of France, and passed nearby the castle of Xavier. The ambassador offered Francis a chance to visit his relatives, but Francis refused to "turn aside a little from the road to see them." His mother was dead, and the old home had been broken up. So they reached Portugal.

In Lisbon, Francis found Simon Rodríguez, one of the companions who had walked with him up to Montmartre, who was sickening with ague. But "my coming was such a joy to him, and seeing him was such a joy to me, that the two joys added expelled the fever. That is a month ago, and it has not come back since." Writing to Ignatius, Francis describes Lisbon: "There are many good persons here, who long to serve our Lord if there were anyone to help them, and to give them some Spiritual Exercises to help them to put into practice the good which day to day they put off doing. This full knowledge, given by the Exercises, helps many to awake, and keeps them from finding peace where it is not, chiefly those, who, against all reason, try to lead our Lord whither they desire, and do not wish to go whither our Lord calls them. Towards such, one must have compassion." He goes on to say the King sent for them, and received them kindly: "he was alone with the Queen and they talked for an hour. . . . A number of people here are trying to keep us from going to India." A few days later, on July 26, 1540, Francis again wrote to Ignatius: "We are always at it to find companions, and I believe that they will not be wanting, as they keep on turning up. If we stay here we shall found some houses and it will be easier to find men who will stay here than go."

Offered rooms at court, Francis and Rodríguez lodged at the hospital. They began by begging food in the streets, but they soon did this only twice a week, as it took so much time. The other days, they accepted what the king sent, ate a small portion, and gave the rest to the patients at the hospital.

At last they were off. The king had promised to found a college and a house for the Society of Jesus, and recommended Francis and two others to the viceroy (Sousa—actually only governor) with whom they would travel: "We go in his ship, and he shows us much love, so much so that he does not wish anybody but himself to be concerned with our embarkation and the things needed at sea, and he has taken charge of providing everything, even to having us at his table." (*Life and Letters of St. Francis Xavier*, by Henry James Coleridge [London: Burns & Oates, 1881], p. 89)

Francis was pleased with the result of his visit to Lisbon:

Let me tell you that this court is greatly reformed. So much so that it is more like a religious house than a court. It is a matter for thanks and praise to God that so many make their confession and take communion every week without fail. We are so engaged with confessions, that if our numbers were doubled, there would still be penitents. We are engaged the whole day and part of the night, and this with courtiers alone without others. When we were in Almerin those who came to do business at the Court were astonished to see the multitude who communicated every Sunday and feast day. Seeing the good example of the courtiers they did the same. So that if there were many of us, there would be no one with business who would not search to do business with God before doing it with the King. We have no time for preaching on account of the number of confessions, as we judge it a better service to our Lord to be taken up with confessing than with preaching. There are plenty of preachers in this Court, so we have given it up.

There is nothing else to tell you but when we are to embark. (Ibid., p. 92)

The following is the account of Francis' departure from Lisbon as given by Gonçalvez (quoted by J. M. Cros, *Vie de S. François Xavier* [Toulouse, 1899]):

When the time of departure was near John III. commanded Don Antonio de Ataide, the Count of Castanheira, to find out from Master Francis the things which he would need during the voyage, and procure them for him. All that the Count could do was to get the Father to accept, for himself and his companions, a rug of coarse wool, as a protection against the cold weather at the Cape of Good Hope, and several religious books which were not obtainable in India. He would accept no provisions of food. Still less would he accept a servant which Don Antonio offered him. "Your position demands it," the Count said to him, "you can't wash your own linen, nor busy yourself over the stock-pot." To this, with a grave and modest air, Francis made answer, "Sir, this care for an imaginary dignity, this anxiety to fulfil unreal obligations, has put Christianity into the deplorable state in which we now see it. As for me, I mean to wash my own clothes, and watch my own soup-pot, and look after other people's as well, and by doing these things I hope I shall not lose any authority."

The Count remained much struck with these words; often later on he recalled them, and would add, "Entrusted with providing for the passengers on those ships who were in the service of the King, my great trouble was usually with those who asked too much, or even took more than they were given, but the hardest task I ever had was with Father Francis, when I tried to persuade him not to refuse absolutely everything, but to consent to accept some small gift from the King."

The sea route to India had been explored by Europeans for less than fifty years when Francis set sail. Hitherto the Arabs had been almost the only navigators across the Indian Ocean. They never attempted to colonize the coasts, as the Portuguese did at once. Vasco da Gama had landed near Calicut and been received by Zamorin, who called himself the emperor of the twelve rajahs of Malabar. The second Portuguese expedition, a fleet of thirteen ships of which only six arrived in India, left in 1500. In 1502 Da Gama set out again, and with superior artillery established Portuguese power all along the western coast of India. In 1510 Albuquerque, governor of India, captured Goa, and made it the capital of the new colonies. He was a man with a great personal sense of duty—he never shut his door, save for a short time while he took his siesta. But his government depended on plunder, prize ships, or conquering the local Muslims: little money was forthcoming from Portugal, and the ships and cargoes that came from Lisbon suffered enormous losses, while the local officials had to be paid their salaries, and their extravagances were monumental. Colossal raiding expeditions were constant, blessed by the bishop; Indian temples were desecrated and despoiled, and their priests slaughtered, in Christ's name. Albuquerque cut off the noses of Arab women, and tortured the Brahmins to make them give up gold they did not have. He encouraged the colonists to marry native women, with the result that the Portuguese harem became a commonplace, and Francis found "a large and pitiful population of half-castes, many of them slaves, all ignorant and uncared for." As Correa wrote in his *Lendas,* in 1556:

The present evils are caused by cruelty and cupidity; the prosperity of the early days has turned to public calamity. . . . I hoped that my work would have a happy conclusion. It seemed to me that some of the ills which I saw growing up would disappear in the face of punishment. But . . . here murderers go back to the kingdom without the least fear that justice, either human or divine, will punish their crimes or their robbery of Christians, Moors, natives, and foreigners. How many offences against God and incredible crimes have I seen! The guilty ones would appear before the king, but there was no punishment. . . . The evil is that the governors live with nothing to fear; also captains of fortresses, judges, administrators . . . are reckless and go to great excesses. . . . I have seen those who are deep in guilt and clearly condemned arriving in Portugal and being honoured there because they came back with great wealth. . . . As for the robbers, they give the judges part of the stolen money and keep the rest and triumph and have the favours of the court just like honest men.

Rewards are due to those who conquered India at the beginning. . . . They have never received anything. They have grown old and gone to die in the hospital.

Francis and his companions left Lisbon on April 7; they reached Mozambique on September 3. They had to winter there, and Francis almost died, being three days delirious. At the end of February he sailed for Goa, which he reached in a little over two months, on May 6, 1542, when he was thirty-six. Four months after his arrival he wrote, "It [Goa] is a city wholly of Christians, a sight for sore eyes." At once he began his evangelistic work, carrying a little bell to gather his sheep together:

He went up and down the streets, a little bell in his hand, crying "Faithful Christians, send your boys and girls and slaves to the *Santa doctrina,* for the love of God!" At this summons, a crowd of people of all sorts would gather round, and he would put them in rows, and lead them to the Church of the Rosary. There all that he did delighted his hearers and the onlookers. As he raised his eyes to heaven, he seemed to raise their souls. Making the sign of the Cross, he spoke to them in a loud voice, with such devotion that the people, and, above all, the children, fell into complete sympathy with him. To these he taught hymns which contained the holy doctrine, and thus he fixed the teaching on their minds. Then, with outstretched arms, he intoned a kind of Litany, of which each verse held very briefly one point of the teaching of the Church, and that was followed by a chanted response, explaining an act of faith. Master Francis finished the service by an explanation of an article of the Creed, or one of the Commandments. In this explanation Master

Francis suited his words to the intelligence of the least of his listeners, using a kind of Portuguese patois, the only language which these folk understood. (J. M. Cros, *Vie de S. François Xavier*, Vol. I, p. 216)

Francis wrote to Ignatius on September 20, 1542:

Here in Goa I have lodged in the hospital. I confessed and communicated the sick who were there. So many came to be confessed that if I had been in ten places I should have had to confess in them all. After I finished the sick I confessed in the morning the sound folk who came to seek me, and after noon I went to the jail to confess the prisoners. . . . I took a hermitage of Our Lady which was near the hospital, and there I began to teach the prayers, Creed and Commandments to the boys. Well over three hundred often came to the Christian teaching. The Lord Bishop ordered that the same should be done in the other churches, and so it goes on now, and in this way the service which is done to God is greater than many think. . . . On Sundays and feast days after dinner I preached in that hermitage of Our Lady on an article of the faith to the native Christians. So many came that they could not get into the hermitage. After preaching I taught the Paternoster, Ave Maria, Creed and Commandments. On Sundays I went out of the city to say mass to the sick of St. Lazarus evil. . . .

Now the Governor is sending me to a district where everyone says many Christians ought to be made. I am taking three natives with me, two are in deacons' orders. They know Portuguese very well. . . . I believe that much work has got to be done there for God. . . . The district which I am going is called the Cape of Comorin. Please God our Lord that with the favour and help of your devout prayers (God our Lord not looking at my infinite sin), He will give me His most holy grace so that there I may serve Him well.

On October 28, he wrote to Ignatius from Tuticorin:

If the labours of so long a voyage, the case of so many spiritual illnesses, this life in a land so subject to sins of idolatry, and because of the great heat so hard to live in—if all this is undertaken for Whom it ought to be undertaken, it brings great refreshment, and many and great comforts. I believe that for those who delight in the Cross of Christ our Lord such labours are rest, and the ending of them, or the fleeing from them, death. What death is so great as after having known Christ to leave Him, and go on living in the pursuit of one's own opinions and likings! There is no toil like that! But what a rest to live dying every day by going against our own will, *seeking not our own but the things which are Christ's*. By the love and service of God our Lord, I pray you, dearest *brothers*, write at great length about all of the Company, for now I do not hope in this life to see you any more *face to face*, but, *at least, darkly, that is, by letter*. Do not deny me this grace, tho' I am unworthy of it. Remember that God our Lord made you worthy, so that I, through your great merit and refreshment, may hope and attain.

On our way here we came through some villages where the people had become Christians eight years ago. There are no Portuguese living there now, as the country is extremely sterile and very poor. As they have no one to teach them our faith, the Christians of these villages know no more of it than to say that they are Christians. They have no one to say Mass, still less to teach them the Creed, *Pater noster*, *Ave Maria*, or the Commandments. When I arrived in these places I baptized all the children who were not baptized, so that I baptized a great multitude of infants *who could not distinguish between their right hand and their left*. When I came to these places the children would not let me read my office nor eat nor sleep, but made me teach them some prayers. I began to understand then that *of such is the kingdom of heaven*. As I could not refuse such a holy petition, I taught them, beginning with the confession of the Father, Son and Holy Spirit, with the Creed, *Pater noster*, *Ave Maria*. I recognised great gifts in them, and if there were anyone to teach them the holy faith, I am very sure that they would be good Christians. (*Monumenta Historiae Societatis Jesu— Monumenta Xavieriana*, Vol. I, p. 273, as quoted in *Life and Letters of St. Francis Xavier*)

He traveled continually, on foot, drinking only a little sour milk— he never took wine—and had only one meal a day. He slept but two or three hours a night, spending the rest of the time in prayer, eating whatever he was given, a bowl of soup, a little rice. He talked with the Brahmins (he calls them Bragmens) and in one case at least seems to have arrived at some understanding of Hinduism. He wrote:

I came across a solitary Bragmen in a village on this coast who had some education, and I was told he had studied in some famous places of learning. I tried to see him, and took advantage of an opportunity of meeting him. He told me as a great secret that the first thing those who teach in those places of learning do is to take an oath from the pupils never to tell certain secrets which they are taught. Because of some friendship he had for me this Bragmen told me those secrets as a grand secret. One was this: never to tell that there is but one God, creator of heaven and earth, and that this God should be adored, and not idols, who are devils. They have some scriptures, in which they have the commandments. The language taught in these places of learning is like what Latin is among us. He told me the commandments very well, each one with a good exposition. Those who are learned keep the Lord's days—an incredible thing. The only prayer they say on the Lord's day is this, and they say it very often, *Oncerii naraina noma,* which means *I adore Thee, O God, with Thy grace and help for ever.* They say this prayer very slowly and quietly, so as not to break their oath. . . .

This Bragmen . . . wanted me to tell him the principal tenets of the Christian religion and promised me to make them known to no one. I said to him that I should not tell him if he did not first promise to me not to keep those principal tenets hidden. So he promised me to publish them. Then I said and expounded, much to my delight, these important words of our religion, *who believes and is baptized shall be saved.* He wrote them in his language with their exposition, and I told him all the creed. He told me that one night he had dreamed with great delight that he had to become a Christian and be my companion and go with me. He asked me to make him a Christian secretly, and moreover with certain conditions. As these were not honourable and permissible, I refused to do it. I hope in God that he will have to be a Christian without any of them. I bade him teach the simple folk to adore one God. . . . He was not willing to do it because of his oath, and for fear lest the devil should kill him. (Ibid., p. 161)

In November 1544 Francis walked to Travancore, at the invitation of the rajah, attended by three natives. When he got there, in the rainy season, he baptized ten thousand people in a month, giving to each a new name, written on a piece of paper. This became a kind of passport, proving the bearer could claim Portuguese protection. He caused about forty-five churches to be built along the coast, and, as a contemporary Portuguese, João Vaz, wrote of him, "He speaks the language of the country very well. Followed in that flat countryside by two, three, or four thousand people, he would climb up a tree and preach from there."

Francisco Mansilhas was one of the Portuguese who came to India with Francis, and Francis wrote to him while they were both traveling up and down the coast. Some of these letters follow, as they show Francis' day-to-day problems.

Very dear Brother,

I am greatly pleased with your news and with your letter, and to see the fruit you are gaining. God give you force always to persevere from good to better.

I cannot stop feeling within my soul the injuries which heathen and Portuguese alike are doing to the Christians, and no wonder. I am already so accustomed to see the wrongs done to the Christians, and yet not be able to help that is a bruise, which I have always with me. I have already written to the Vicar of Coulam, and to the Vicar of Cochin about the slaves whom the Portuguese stole at Punicale . . . that they may learn by means of the great excommunications who the thieves were. I sent this message three days ago, as soon as I got the headman's letter.

Give Matthew everything necessary for his clothing. Be hospitable to him that he may not leave you, now that he is freed. Treat him very lovingly, for so I did when he was with me, that he might not leave me.

In the Creed, when you say *enquevenum,* instead of -*venum* say -*vichuam,* for *venu* means *I will,* and *vichuam* means *I believe.* It is better to say *I believe in God* than to say *I will in God* (*quero* in Portuguese means I will, I desire, love, like). Do not say *vao pinale,* because it means by force, and Christ suffered voluntarily, and not by force.

When you come from Piscaria, visit the sick, making some of the children say the prayers, as in the Memorandum I gave you. And finish up by reading part of a Gospel yourself. Always deal very lovingly with your people, and do your best that they may love you. I should be greatly pleased to know that they do not drink arrack, nor make pagodas (or images), and come every Sunday to the prayers. If at the time they became Christians there had been anyone to teach them, as you now teach them, they would have been better Christians than they are.

27th March, 1544

(Ibid., pp. 196–97)

Very dear Brother,

I was greatly pleased with your coming to visit the Christian villages, as I told you, and I am more pleased with the great fruit which everybody tells me you gained. I expect to-day or to-morrow a message from the Governor. If it is as I expect, I will not fail to arrive. I will direct myself toward you, for I am most anxious to see you, though I see you always in spirit.

João d'Artiaga goes, dismissed by me, full of temptations without knowing them. He does not take the road to know them. He says he will go to Combuturé to teach that village, so as to be near you. I believe little in his plans, for, as you know well, he is very fickle. If he comes near you, don't waste much time with him.

I have written already to the Captain to provide you with what is necessary. I also told Manoel da Cruz to lend you money as often as you have need, and he has promised me to do so, with very good will.

Take good care of your health, since with it you serve the Lord God so well. Tell Matthew from me to serve you well. If you are content with him, he has in me father and mother. If he is not very obedient to you, I don't wish to see him nor watch over him. Give him what is necessary for his clothing.

In the villages where you go, make the men meet one day in one place, and the women another day in another place. And make them say the prayers in every house. Baptize those who are not baptized, children and adults alike.

Our Lord help and guard you always.

Manapar, 8th April, 1544.

(Ibid., p. 199)

Very dear Brother in Christ,

God always with you [sic]. I was very pleased with part of your letter. I was pleased to see the comfort you had in your visitation. But I was very sorry about your tribulation. I shall be sorry till the Lord God frees you to us. Tribulations are not lacking to us. Praised be God.

I have sent word to the Father [one of the auxiliary priests] to launch the boats in the sea, all through these villages, and to embark before it is too late. For it seems to me certain that they [the Badages, locals very hostile to the missionaries and to all Christians] must surprise you and capture the Christians, as we are told that they will certainly come to the shore. I got this news from a judge who is friendly to the Christians. I sent a man to this judge, who is a favourite of the king Iniquitibirim, with a letter to the king. I wrote that since he was friendly with the Governor he should not allow the Badages to do us harm, for the Governor would be very displeased if any harm came to the Christians. The judge, who is my friend, and who loves me because I am so friendly to the Christians of the coast, came to see and help me, as he has a lot of Christian relatives. I wrote to him that he might advise me as to what was happening, and let me know when they come to the shore, that we might have time to withdraw together to the sea.

I have written already to the Captain to send a small warship to guard your people and you. Make your people keep a strong watch on the mainland. The Badages come at night, on horseback, and take us before we have time to embark. Look carefully after the people, for they have so little sense that to save two *fanoens* they would give up setting a watch. Make them launch all the ships at once, and put their goods into them. And make the women and children say the prayers, now more than ever, for we have none to help us but God.

Send me the paper which remains in the box. I have nothing to write on. Send this to me at once by a coolie. Let me know any news; if the boats are launched, and the goods placed in them, and how they get on with this. Tell Antonio Fernandez the Fat from me to watch carefully for the people, if he wishes to be my friend. These people [Badages] do not make the poor wretches prisoners, except those who can be ransomed. Above all, make them keep good watch at night, and have their spies on the mainland. I have great fear that with this moonlight they

may come by night to this shore and rob the Christians. Therefore command them to watch carefully at night. Our Lord be
your guard.

Manapar, 3rd Aug., 1544.
(Ibid., pp. 217–18)

The next letter tells how the rajah of Jafnapatam, near Ceylon
(now Jaffna, in Ceylon) had invited Francis to come there:

Here I am going alone among this people without interpreter.
So you see the life I am leading and the sort of exhortations I
can make. They do not understand me. I understand them less.
I baptize the new-born babies, and others whom I find ready for
baptism. There is no need of an interpreter for this. The poor
make me understand their needs without an interpreter, and I
by seeing them understand without an interpreter.

And again to Francisco Mansilhas, he wrote:

Very dear Brother,

God be with you always, Amen. By the saying of the Lord,
He who is not with me is against me, you can see how many
friends we have in these parts who help us to make this people
Christian! Let us not despair. God gives to each his pay at last.
If He please, He can be served by few as by many. For those
who are against God I have rather pity than any desire for their
punishment, for at the last God punishes His enemies heavily,
as we can see by those who are in hell. This Brahmin goes with
a dispatch from the Badages to king Betibumal. For the love of
God order a boat at once to take him to Tuticorin. Let me have
the news of Tuticorin, of the Captain and the Portuguese and
the Christians, for I am very anxious. Commend me much to
João d'Artiaga and to Manoel da Cruz. Tell Matthew not to
weary, that he is not working in vain, that I will do better for
him than he thinks. Our Lord be always with you. Amen.

Manapar, 20th Aug., 1544.

For the love of God, help this Brahmin with everything for
his journey, and say to the Captain, at least to do him honour.

Your very dear brother in Christ.
(Ibid., p. 223)

The king of Jafnapatam ruled also the island of Manar, and asked
Francis to send a priest there. He sent a native priest, who made six

hundred converts. But now the king of Jafnapatam was afraid that
"open dealings with the Portuguese would spoil his secret dealings
with the Portuguese," and so he offered the new converts the choice
between a return to idolatry and martyrdom. None of the 600 had
heard of Christianity before, yet they all chose martyrdom: their
teacher died with them. Francis, told the story by the brother of the
king, was given full authority to bring the murderer to death by
Sousa, the Portuguese governor. Francis set off, hoping the prayers of
the six hundred martyrs would bring the murderous king to penitence. Meanwhile, he wrote to Ignatius:

> Men who have no talent for confessing, preaching, or doing the
> like for the Company could, after having completed their Exer-
> cises and having served some months in humble duties, do
> much service in these parts, if they had bodily strength as well
> as spiritual. For in these heathen districts learning is not neces-
> sary, except to teach the prayers and visit and baptize the chil-
> dren. . . . I say that they must have bodily strength because
> this district is very troublesome on account of the great heat and
> the lack of good water. There is little for bodily sustenance; in-
> deed, only rice, fish, and fowls. . . . They (the men who come
> out) must be healthy and not delicate, able to stand the con-
> stant labours of baptizing, teaching, walking from place to place
> . . . but they must go through dangers, remembering they were
> born to die for their Redeemer and Lord, and therefore they
> must have spiritual strength. And because I have not, and walk
> where I have much need of it, I pray you to have special
> remembrance of me. And those who have talent either for
> confessing or for giving the Exercises, though they have not the
> physique to bear other troubles, you should send too, as they
> can go to Goa, where they can do much service to God. (Ibid.,
> p. 271)

However, the rajah of Jafnapatam was not taken; on the contrary,
he seized a Portuguese ship that had run aground, and kept the
cargo, so the governor was more concerned with getting the ship
back than with the six hundred martyrs. Francis went to Moro,
where there were many Christians, abandoned long since, and on to
Malacca, and wrote to Ignatius on May 10, 1546:

> The people of these islands are very barbarous and full of
> treachery. They are baser than the black tribes—an utterly
> thankless people. There are islands here in which men eat one

another. This is those who are killed in battle when there is war, and not otherwise. The hands and heels of those who die naturally are eaten at a great banquet. The people are such barbarians that in some islands a man who wishes to have a great feast will ask his neighbour for the loan of his father, if he is very old, for eating, and promises to give his own father when he is old and the neighbour wants to have a banquet. I hope within a month to go to an island where those killed in war are eaten, and in it also men lend their fathers when they are old for banquets. The inhabitants wish to be Christians, and this is why I am going there. There are abominable fleshly sins among them that you could not believe, nor do I dare to write.

The islands are temperate, with great and thick woods and plenty of rain. They are so mountainous and difficult to travel that in war the people go up them for defence, so that they are their forts. There are no horses, nor could riding be possible. Land and sea often quake. When the sea quakes those who are sailing think the ship has struck a rock. To see the earth quake is frightful, and still more the sea. Many of the islands cast out fire with a greater noise than any discharge of artillery, however heavy. In the places where the fire comes out, very large stones are carried with it by the great impetus with which it comes. For lack of anyone to preach in these islands the torments of hell, God permits hell to open for the confusion of the infidels and their abominable sins.

Each of these islands has a language of its own, and there is an island where nearly every village has a different language. The Malay language, which is spoken in Malacca, is very general here. When I was in Malacca, I translated with great labour into this language the Creed, with an exposition of the articles, the General Confession, *Paternoster, Ave Maria, Salve Regina,* and the Commandments, so that they may understand when I speak to them of matters of importance. There is one great lack in all these islands: they have no writings, and very few can write. They write in Malay, and the letters are Arabic, which the Moorish *cacizes* (priests) taught, and teach at present. Before they became Moors (Mohammedans) they could not write. . . . (Ibid., pp. 381–82)

In this letter he first mentions China: "I met a Portuguese merchant in Malacca, who was coming from a busy country called

China." It was in Malacca too that Francis first heard of Japan, writing as follows:

> When I was in the city of Malacca some Portuguese merchants gave me great news. They are trustworthy men. Some very large islands were discovered, a little time ago, called the islands of Japon. There, according to the Portuguese, much fruit might be gained for the increase of our holy faith, more than in any other parts of the Indies, for they are a people most extremely desirous of knowledge, which the Indian heathen are not. A Japon, called Yajiro, came with these merchants to look for me, as the Portuguese who went there from Malacca had talked so much about me. . . . He had told the Portuguese of certain sins done in his youth, and had asked them how God might pardon him. The Portuguese advised him to come with them to see me. He did so, coming to Malacca with them. When he came I had left for Malacca. When he found out that I had gone there, he embarked again to go to his own country of Japon. When within sight of the islands of Japon they were surprised by such a storm of wind that they were like to perish. Then the ship returned again to Malacca, where he found me, and was delighted. He came to seek me with a great desire to know about our religion (*ley* in the Spanish). He can speak Portuguese pretty well, so he understood all I told him, and I what he said to me.
>
> If all the Japanese are like this, so eager to learn as Yajiro, I think they are the most inquiring people in all the lands hitherto discovered. This Yajiro wrote down the (teaching on the) articles of faith which I have made, when he came to the class. He went very often to the church to pray. He asked me numerous questions. He is a man who is very anxious to know, and that is the mark of a man who will profit greatly, and will quickly come to a knowledge of the truth.
>
> . . . I asked Yajiro whether the Japanese would become Christians if I went with him to his land. He answered that his countrymen would not become Christians straight away. First, they would ask many questions, and would see what I answered and what I knew, and, above all, whether I lived in accordance with what I said. If I did these two things—spoke well, satisfying their questions, and lived without their finding anything to blame me, then half a year after they knew me the king, the

nobility, and all the other people of discretion would become Christians. He tells me they are a people who rule themselves only by reason. (Mon. Xav. Vol. I., p. 433)

. . . I think by what I am feeling within my soul that I or some one of the Company will go to Japon within two years, although it is a very dangerous voyage, both because of great tempests and of Chinese thieves who sail that sea to rob. Many ships are lost there. (Ibid., pp. 417–18)

On January 12, 1548, Francis was back in India and wrote to the king of Portugal. It was "the fault of the governors that so few Christians are being made in India." Francis suggests that the king punish the unjust governors by forfeiting their estates; then, "If the Governor understands as a certainty that you mean what you say, . . . the whole of Ceylon will be Christian in a year, but so long as the governors have not this fear before them of being dishonored and punished, you need not count on any increase of our holy faith. . . . I, Sire, am not quite determined to go to Japon, but I am thinking that I will, for I quite despair of any real chance in India for the increase of our holy faith." Francis kept continually on the move, going up and down the coast, to and from Goa, and wrote to Ignatius on January 12, 1549:

By the principal letters which all we the least of your sons in India wrote by Master Simon, your holy Charity will be informed of the fruit and service which, with the help of God our Lord and of your devout and holy sacrifices and prayers, is done in these parts of India, and will be done in future. By this letter I will give you details of some affairs of this land so remote from Rome. First, the native Indians, so far as I have seen, and speaking generally, are barbarians. We of the Company are carrying on a great deal of work with those who are and daily become Christians. It is necessary that your Charity should have special care for all your sons in India in commending them to God our Lord continually, for you know what a great toil it is to have to do with people who through their very habitual evil living neither know God nor obey reason.

The great heat in summer, and the winds and rains in winter, make life in these lands very troublesome. There is little to maintain the body either in the Moluccas, Socotra or Cape Comorin. The spiritual and bodily toil is marvellously great when one has to deal with such people. Their languages are hard to get hold of. . . . All the Indians whom we have seen up to now, both Mohammedan and heathen, are very ignorant. Those who have to live among these unbelievers and in the work of converting them need many virtues: obedience, humility, perseverance, patience, neighbourly love, and great chastity. For there are many opportunities for sinning. They need too, sound judgment and strong bodies to carry on the work. I give your Charity this account because of the need there is, in my opinion, of testing the spirits of those you are going to send to this country. . . .

The man whom you, my Father, will have to send to take charge of the College of Santa Fé at Goa, and of the native students and of the Companions, will need, not to speak of all the other things necessary to a man who has to rule and command, these two qualities: first, great obedience, so as to make himself beloved, both by all our greater ecclesiastics and by the laymen who rule the district, so that they may not be conscious of his pride, but rather of his great humility . . . second, to be affable and calm in dealing with others, and not strict, using every means he can to make himself loved, firstly by those whom he has to command, both natives and those of the Company who are here and are to come, so that they may not feel that he wishes to make himself obeyed by strictness or servile fear. (Ibid., Vol. III, pp. 67-68)

Before leaving India for Japan, Francis wrote again to the king of Portugal:

It is almost a kind of martyrdom to look with patience on the destruction of what one has gained with so much labour.

And again:

At last experience has taught me that your Highness is not powerful in India for the increase of Christ's faith, and is powerful for carrying off and keeping all the temporal riches of India. (*Mon. Xavieriana*, Vol. I, p. 508)

And again:

I, Sire, because I know what goes on here, have no hope that commands or prescripts sent in favour of Christianity will be fulfilled in India; and therefore I am almost fleeing to Japon, not to waste any more time. (Ibid., Vol. I, p. 513)

Be prepared, for kingdoms and lordships finish and have end. A new thing it will be, and something that never happened to your Highness before, to find yourself dispossessed at the hour of your death of your kingdom and lordships, and to have to enter into others, where this new thing must happen to you, to be sent, may God forbid it! out of Paradise. (Ibid., Vol. II, pp. 82–83)

To Ignatius, Francis wrote that he and his companions had decided to become vegetarians, so as not to give scandal to the Japanese, who, he wrote, never ate meat. Francis left Malacca on June 24, 1549, and arrived at Kogoshima on August 15. His letters from Japan "were the earliest first-hand reports of that country to come to Europe." Francis had eight companions, three of whom were Jesuits. Kogoshima was the home town of Yajiro, whom Francis had baptized and called Paul of the Holy Faith, and his native city gave Yajiro and his mentors a great welcome. No one objected to Yajiro's having become a Christian; rather, it added to the interest of his return. The governor of the town was kind, and after six weeks there, the *daimio* of the province sent for the missionaries and lent them a house, where Francis studied Japanese, and also studied the people. He wrote on November 5, "The people with whom we have conversed so far are the best yet discovered. In my opinion no people superior to the Japanese will be found among unbelievers. They are of good behaviour, and good generally, and not malicious, marvelously honorable. They esteem honor more than anything. They are mostly poor, and neither the nobles nor those who are not esteem poverty as a reproach. They are abstemious in eating, though they drink a good deal. They drink rice wine, as there are no vines in these parts. They never gamble. . . . They have not more than one wife. It is a land of few thieves. A great part of the people can read and write."

The country was at war, and overrun with soldiers. In spite of warnings, Francis wanted to get to the "principal city of Japon," Kyoto, and walked there in the winter. "There are no beds in Japanese inns. We did very well if they lent us a straw mat, or a wooden pillow. Sometimes when we arrived in the evening, frozen with cold and famished, there was no kind of shelter for us. . . ." So wrote Juan Fernández, one of Francis' companions. (*Mon. Xav.*, Vol. I, p. 123)

When they arrived at Kyoto, Francis wrote, "We tried for some days to get speech with the King [the Mikado] but we could not get speech with him. This city of Kyoto was once very great, now it is much ruined with wars. They say there were more than 180,000 houses, at present there are not more than 100,000." (Ibid., Vol I., p. 336) The return journey was even worse: "It was February, the time of the greatest cold, snow, frost and wind and for us there was neither shelter nor succor."

Francis had found the Japanese would not listen to him when he was poorly and strangely clad, so he put on a handsome Japanese gown, and carried presents for the daimio of Yamaguchi—European books, a musical instrument, three crystal vases, a decorated clock, and a Portuguese dress. The daimio was delighted, gave them permission to preach, and lent them an empty monastery. Francis wrote:

> While we stayed in this monastery many came to hear the sermons. Generally there was preaching twice daily. At the end of the sermon there were discussions, which lasted a long time. We were continually taken up with answering questions and preaching. Numbers of bonzes, nuns, gentlemen, and crowds of other people came to the sermon, so that the house was almost always as full as it could hold. The questions they put to us were such that by our replies they knew that their laws and the saints in which they believed were false, and the law of God true. They kept up the discussions for many days, and then they began to become Christians. Many of them were gentlemen. After having become Christians, they grew more friendly than can be told.
>
> Those who became Christians showed us very faithfully all the things the heathen have in their religions. . . . After getting correct information about their religions, we began to seek reasons for proving them false. So every day we smashed up some points of their laws, and put before them arguments which neither the bonzes nor monks nor wizards nor any of the people who abhorred the law of God could answer.
>
> When the Christians saw that the bonzes could not answer, they were greatly delighted, and became confirmed more every day in the faith of God our Lord. The heathen present at the discussions lost belief in their former sects and errors. . . .
>
> The Japanese are full of curious questions, with a keen desire for knowledge. So much is this the case that they never stop discussing with others about the questions they put to us, and the answers we give them. They are very inquisitive, especially about religions. They say that before we came here they were al-

ways discussing which of their religions was the best. . . . It is a wonderful thing to see, in a city so large as this, people speaking of the law of God in every street and house. . . .

The Japanese regard the Chinese as very wise, both about religions and the other world, and about the government of the commonwealth. So one of the questions they put to us . . . was, How did the Chinese not know, if these things were so? . . . In the space of two months more than 500 Christians have been made, and so it goes on every day. . . . It is wonderful how truly friendly the Christians are. They are always coming to visit us, and to see if we want anything. The whole nation in general is much given to compliments and courtesies, and the Christians seem to give all the greater care and attention to this, especially with us, for the great love they have to us. (*Mon. Xav.*, Vol. I, pp. 662–63)

Francis stayed six months in Yamaguchi; then, in November 1551, left Japan. From Cochin he wrote to Ignatius that he hoped in 1552 to go to China. He arrived back in India in January 1552. Once more in Goa, he met Teixeira, his earliest biographer, who thus described the saint: "The Father Master Francisco was tall rather than small in stature, his face well proportioned, white and ruddy, happy and very attractive, the eyes black, the brow high, the hair and beard black. He wore poor and clean clothes."

In April, on Maundy Thursday, Francis said his last mass in Goa, and left for Malacca, which he reached at the end of May. He left Malacca about July 15, telling his friends there to "take care that we meet each other in heaven, for here we shall meet no more." In August his ship arrived at Sanchian, a barren island west of Hong Kong. In November he wrote that he had at last arranged with a Chinese merchant to take him on to Canton, but the nineteenth of December, the day the junk was to come, came and went, and no junk. Francis fell ill. He had no shelter, for the Portuguese did not dare set any up on Sanchian, and no food was to be obtained except by rowing out to the ship that had brought them. This Francis did on December 22, with his companion Antonio. Francis had a high fever, the ship was cold, the waves high. In the morning, Francis and Antonio rowed back to land. Arrived at the shore of Sanchian, Francis could barely stand. A kindly Portuguese gave him shelter in his tiny cabin, and bled Francis, but Francis fainted. Next day, he was bled again, and again fainted. He could not eat, and had a high fever and nausea. On the twenty-fourth he became delirious, speaking in a language Antonio did not know (Basque). On Christmas Day, Antonio heard him quote from the psalms: *Tu autem meorum peccatorum et delictorum miserere.* They were his last words. He died on December 27, a Sunday.

It would seem his life, however holy, had been a total failure. Yet, centuries later, there are many devoutly Christian descendants of the Indians he baptized (Father Jerome D'Souza, of the Society of Jesus, who was India's representative to the United Nations, is but one example) and when Japan was finally opened to Western commerce and ships, in the nineteenth century, there were still Christians there, descended from Francis Xavier's converts. Above all, Francis Xavier showed that in an almost totally corrupt, brutal, bestial, and materialistic Christian society, such as was the Portugal of his time, it is enough for one man to be what the rest profess, to make a permanent impact not only on that society but on the world. It was necessary, we are told in Scripture, that one man die for the people; it is enough that one man live wholly for God and his neighbor, since "He that sanctifieth and they that are sanctified are all of one." Or may by God's grace become so.

St. Francis de Sales (1567–1622)

ᢌᢦᢍᢂᢎᢌᢦ

Most races and peoples, like most human beings, are a mixture of good and bad. Yet recently anthropologists have met with primitive peoples, relics of stone-age cultures, who seem wholly good, like the gentle Tasaday, who do not even have a word for evil, or wholly bad, like the venomous Ik, who show no good qualities at all. Some saints have become saints by struggling with natural evil tendencies; their sanctity, however admirable, is obviously the result of long, even if unseen, warfare. Others seemed bathed in grace from their childhood, loving and beloved, their soul's climate sunlit. Of such was Francis de Sales.

His father, a great Savoyard landowner, was thirty when, in 1560, he married a little girl of seven. She did not come to live with him in his rather austere mountain-circled castle until she was thirteen, and when she came, she brought as her dowry the rich lands of Boisy

with her. She was at least as well-born as her husband: one of her kin
on her mother's side had been Pope in the year 1000, and little
Francis was also descended from Charlemagne. At thirteen, she had
a busy life: she had to manage the kitchen, the wine cellar, the dairy,
the herb garden, the vegetable and flower gardens, and the linen
closets, and to watch over a household of some forty people. Her
husband had many other properties and had to travel between them
often: he employed lawyers, notaries, bailiffs, and land agents, and
spent a lot of time doing the paperwork his properties entailed.
When, around 1560, the de Sales castle fell into ruins, about fifty
thousand title deeds were removed from it. To this aristocratic couple a son was born, two months prematurely, on Thursday, August
21, 1567. The baby's mother, who was very devout, had, a year
earlier, kneeling before the Holy Shroud, promised that, if she had a
son, she would raise him for God alone. The baby was "very small,
thin and delicate." The room in which he was born was already
called St. Francis' room, as there was on the wall a big picture of St.
Francis of Assisi surrounded by birds, beasts, and fishes, to which he
was preaching.

The baby's father had himself also been born in the same room.
At the christening, the baby was called Francis Bonaventura, and his
father kept open house that whole day from dawn to dusk, giving
charity to all who came. Francis' mother could not feed him, and his
wet nurse, Petramande Puthod, would wheel him to church. On the
way, the baby would give candy to any beggars they met. One day,
he had given all his candy away, so Petramande, seeing his sad face,
offered her breast to the next beggar, which delighted Francis.

Later, after he was weaned—aged about three—his mother would
take him walking with her and would teach him to repeat prayers:
back home, he loved making little altars in the bays of the big win-
dows, silently. But one day a visitor came from Geneva, a Calvinist.
Francis had heard plenty about the wicked city of Geneva, which
had expelled all the priests and broken all the crucifixes, and while
the visitor was chatting with his father, Francis, now five, chased the
hens in the courtyard outside, crying out, "Run, run, you heretics."

At five he was given a tutor, M. Déage, an intelligent man but
harsh. At six, he was sent as a boarder to the Roche school, about six
miles from Sales, lodging with one of the masters. His father visited
him once a week, and sometimes took him back to Sales for a day or
two. But Sales was on the land of the duke of Nemours, who wished
to "borrow" the castle of Brens in order to lay siege to the town of

Geneva. Francis' father did not dare remain at Sales, and himself occupied Brens, putting his son, now aged eight, into the college of Annecy, which was nearer Brens than Roche. For the holidays, Francis rode some fifteen miles on horseback to Brens.

Aged ten, he made his first communion and was confirmed the same day. He had long, fair hair, gray-blue eyes, regular features, and a charming voice. At eleven he wished to become a priest, and asked to be tonsured. His father had quite other plans for him, but thought Francis would grow out of the idea, so allowed him to have his hair cut, in church: Francis was surprised, as his fine head of curling hair fell around him, to realize he minded losing it quite a bit. Year by year, when he came home, he would find new brothers born in his absence: they doted on this big, gentle brother, and his mother, who almost venerated her eldest son, told the little ones to do whatever he bade them.

When Francis was fifteen, his father sent him off to Paris, where already there were more than fifty colleges. His father had opted for the college of Navarre, the most "with it" and elegant, but Francis enlisted his mother to persuade his father to send him instead to Clermont College, run by the Jesuits. Francis traveled with his sour tutor, M. Déage, and a valet, on horseback. They carried their money in their belts and their spare clothes in a leather case behind the saddle. Once arrived, Francis took rooms at the White Rose Inn, and went daily to Clermont. There he learned Latin so well he could speak it fluently; he also learned Greek, Hebrew, philosophy, and theology.

He was also obliged by M. Déage to learn fencing and dancing. Francis was tall, well made, handsome: to oblige his father, he paid visits to the various duchesses and princesses to whom he was related. But he fasted Wednesdays, Fridays, and Saturdays; he wore a hair shirt, spent as much time as he could in church, and received communion every week. Yet, at eighteen, he had a spiritual crisis. He thought that if he were tempted, he would fall, and would be separated for all eternity from the love of God. So he prayed: "My God, at least may I love you always in this life, if I may not love you in eternity."

The crisis went on for a month, and Francis was terribly cast down. Then, one day, he found himself in front of a statue of Our Lady, and there found the prayer, "Remember, O most holy Virgin," and weeping read it through. Then he made a vow of perpetual chastity, at the same time begging God to take pity on him. Instantly, peace flooded his soul.

Thereafter he grew in optimism and became the sovereign exponent of gentle confidence in the love of God. And this at a time when Europe was rent asunder by religious and dynastic strife. Francis lived in the Europe of the Medicis, of the Massacre of St. Bartholomew, of the counterpoint in England between the fires of Smithfield and the tortures of Tyburn.

When the young de Sales left Paris and returned briefly home to Savoie, he had not seen his family for six years. "The whole household came to meet him joyfully. His mother embraced him with tears; his father was delighted to see him: both hung upon his every word for whole days at a time." This in the fall of 1588. His father wished him to become a magistrate, and it was decided Francis should go to Italy, to Padua, to study law. So, still accompanied by the ubiquitous M. Déage, Francis settled down there, spending four hours daily attending the lectures of Guy Pancirole, a famous law professor, and a further four hours daily studying theology with the Jesuit Father Poissevin.

Francis' piety exasperated some of his noisier fellow students. Once, some set on him in the twilight, fully armed, expecting him to flee: they were surprised when he drew his sword and defended himself so well that it was they who fled. They then tried to inveigle him into sin. Pretexting that a famous jurist had arrived in town, they persuaded Francis to go with them to meet him. Instead, they took him to a brothel. The lady of the house, pretending to be the jurist's wife, apologized for his delay in joining them. The others slipped away, the lady became insistent, Francis fled, pursued by the lady. Thereafter, Francis redoubled his fasts, his hair shirts, his long vigils, and "grew so pale and thin that he looked more like a skeleton than a living man."

He fell ill of a fever. Told he was dying, he still was gentle and charming to his doctors. M. Déage, moved at last by his charge's plight, asked what he wished for a funeral. The young man replied, "My dear master, I leave such things to you. I only ask that when I am dead, you should give my poor body to the doctors to be used for their anatomy courses: it would be a comfort to me to know that I will be of some use dead, since I was of none during my lifetime."

(*St. Francis de Sales and His Friends,* by Maxwell Scott [London: Soinds & Co., 1913], p. 38)

At that time, the medical students in Padua were detested by everyone, because, since they needed corpses for their studies, and there were not enough executed criminals for their purposes, they dug up at night the newly buried in the cemeteries, which led to bloody fights, since the relatives of the newly buried came armed to prevent their graves being robbed. As the students were also armed, there were fights, which added corpses to the newly interred; Francis wished to help put a stop to such unseemly scenes.

Surprisingly, Francis recovered. And drew up for himself a schedule, which he carried in his prayer book in his pocket. In the morning, to preview the day's engagements in order to prepare his line of conduct. At least once a day to practice what he called "spiritual sleep"; that is, mental prayer.

His rules for societal life followed: "At a meeting, I must speak little and well, so that whoever I meet leaves my company with appetite for more rather than with boredom. If the encounter is brief, and someone is already speaking, I shall do nothing more than salute the company and keep silence with an agreeable expression. In conversation, I must show what is exquisite to some, what is good to others, what is indifferent to yet others, but to no one what is evil. And, moreover, what point is there in unveiling imperfections? Are they not obvious enough? With the great and powerful, I must be continually on my guard, for with them one must be as with fire: it's good to draw near it sometimes, but never too near. Great lords like to be loved and respected; love engenders liberty so there's no harm in being a bit free in their company, so long as the respect is greater than the free speech." (*Vie de Saint François de Sales,* by G. Hamon [Paris, 1909])

After two years the great jurist Guy Pancirole gathered forty-eight doctors for Francis' graduation ceremony, when he received what would now be a doctor-of-laws degree. Pancirole praised his incomparable student, and solemnly crowned him; Francis blushed.

Francis' proud father offered him a postdoctoral trip, and Francis and his tutor went to see the Holy House of Loreto, where Francis had an ecstasy much admired by the grumpy Déage. They went on to Rome, thence to Ancona, where they were to take ship for Venice. They found a boat, and were seated in it, when a grand lady with a big suite arrived and threw them out, though Francis politely asked her to let them have just a small corner. So they retired and watched the boat leave and, before their eyes, barely outside the harbor, sink with all on board. Francis was horrified, even more so, when they got on the next boat, and everyone was chatting and singing. They soon got into very rough weather, and the boatman said it was the fault of Francis and Déage for reading their breviaries. When the storm was calmed, Francis quietly suggested to the boatman that since "the sea has no king but God alone" it was foolish to be rude to those who were trying to be His friends.

Next day, Francis lost his hat overboard, and Déage scolded him roundly. Francis put on a nightcap against the blazing sun, and was all smiles though everyone on board was laughing at him. When they put in to Chiosa to dine, Francis thought his tutor would buy him a new hat, but Déage refused crossly, and said he would only do so when they got to Venice. Francis, aged twenty-four, calmly went on wearing the nightcap.

When Francis got home, he found his parents at La Thuile, another of their castles, on the edge of the Lake of Annecy. His father sent him to visit the local magnate, Claude de Granier, prince bishop of Geneva, who, chased from his see by the Calvinists, was sheltering in exile at Annecy. As it happened, the day Francis called to pay his respects, a group of theologians were arguing, and the bishop asked the handsome young man to settle a disputed point. Francis demurred, but was overruled, and to this group of priests and learned men, spoke so intelligently, so wisely, that all deferred to him. The bishop, from that moment, thought of this young genius as his successor. Not so Francis' father, who told him his family was rich in land and in ancestors, but "as for revenue in that we are minimal. This is where you can help. You must become a senator." Obediently, Francis went to Chambéry, the capital of Savoy, and was immediately appointed "advocate of the supreme Senate."

On his way home, however, his horse threw him, and his sword and scabbard fell in the shape of a cross. Taking no notice, he picked both up, and remounted. Next, the horse fell, and the sword and scabbard again fell into a cross. Still Francis didn't pay much attention, but when it happened a third time, he said to Déage: "God does not want me to embrace the life for which my father destines me."

Déage was too scared of Francis' father to say anything, so Francis told his mother of his decision. She, remembering her long-ago vow, promised her help, and began sewing priest's clothes for him, while a cousin, a canon, Louis de Sales, said, "I'll do what I can to influence my uncle." Now Francis' father tried to marry him off to a well-born, modest, and devout girl, but Francis was chilly to her when they met. Then Francis was offered the title of senator, but refused. His father began to suspect. That winter, the provost of Geneva, the first canon of the cathedral, asked Bishop Granier to write to Rome to nominate Francis as his provost, which Monsignor de Granier did, and Rome agreed. When his father was faced with this *fait accompli*, he grumbled a bit but gave his consent. Next morning, in the village church, Francis put on the soutane his mother had made, and after a month's retreat was made subdeacon, on June 12, 1593. On December 18, he became a priest and was installed as provost of the cathedral chapter of Annecy at Christmas.

From the first, he enjoyed preaching, as he felt he thus could reach people. He was delighted when there was a line outside his confessional. One man calmly confessed to many infamous acts but stopped when he saw Francis in tears. "Why are you weeping?" he asked him. "I'm weeping for the things for which you are not weeping," was the reply.

And then, in 1594, Francis accepted the post of missionary in the Chablais. This district had become completely Calvinist: the Catholic churches had all been burnt, the castles of the Catholic nobility also. Priests and laity had fled into Savoy; the convents were all closed, Mass was forbidden under pain of death, and in one generation the whole Chablais—an extensive area along the borders of the Lake of Geneva—was lost to the Catholic Church. But, in 1593, Henry IV, abjuring Protestantism to become King of France ("Paris is worth a Mass"), threw his weight behind Charles Emmanuel, duke of Savoy. The latter reconquered the Chablais. He begged Monsignor de Granier to send priests there, which much embarrassed the poor bishop. For sixty years the country had been wholly Calvinist: what could he do? He decided to send his new, young, brilliant provost. When he heard of this, Francis' father was in despair: he thought his son would certainly be killed, and complained that he had allowed his son to become a priest but would not have him a martyr. Francis bade his bishop stand firm against his father, bade the latter a tearful farewell, and set off, taking with him only his cousin, Louis de Sales.

Francis' father had refused them a servant; they carried their own baggage, they had no money either from the de Sales or the duke of

Savoy. There were thirty thousand people in the Chablais, and not a hundred Catholics. Francis and his cousin settled in the castle of Allinges, whose owner was Catholic though the village was entirely Calvinist. Each day, they left the castle and walked or rode around. It was a very hard winter. Francis had chilblains, and his swollen feet bled from the cold. Sometimes, unable to walk, he crawled back up the hill to Allinges on his hands and knees. The local Calvinists hired men to kill Francis, but they were overcome by his courtesy and his gentleness. Francis spent four years in the Chablais. The winters were so fierce that, crossing the great St. Bernard Pass on a visit to Turin, the two de Sales almost perished from the cold, but were saved by monks from the monastery founded there six centuries earlier by St. Bernard, a great-great uncle of Francis' mother. One night, the two cousins were refused shelter by everyone in a remote village: they spent the night huddled in an old stove. Another night, Francis found himself alone in a wood where wolves were howling: he climbed a tree and tied himself to a branch with his belt, lest he fall off in his sleep: next morning some woodcutters saw him, half frozen, and took him to thaw out in front of their fire.

The second winter, Francis' cousin left him, unable to afford to stay, since neither the bishop, the duke, nor Francis' parents provided any money. Francis' mother was, however, able to persuade his father to let George Rolland, a valet of his who was fond of Francis, accompany him, but George kept writing scare letters to Francis' father about the dangers they continually ran from hostile Calvinists, wolves, etc. Francis' father wrote to the bishop to withdraw Francis from such a dangerous assignment: Francis wrote to his father that, were George Rolland his son instead of his servant, he would not be so cowardly!

Francis even ventured into Geneva, to try to convert one Théodore de Bèze, a Calvinist divine. He failed, after three visits, each time taking his life in his hands: had he been discovered, he would have been killed. One lady, whom he had almost won back to the Church, objected, after several talks, to the celibacy of the clergy. Francis told her, "My dear good woman, how do you think I would have had time for all the long discussions I have had with you, had I a wife and children to provide for?"

Meanwhile, sporadic fighting continued between the king of France and the duke of Savoy.

Another time, coming out of church, where he had been preaching on Jesus' command "If someone strikes you on the right cheek, offer him the other," a local Calvinist asked him, "If I gave you a blow on one cheek now, would you turn the other for me to strike it also?" Francis replied, "My friend, I know what I *should* do, but I don't know what I *would* do, as I am full of misery. But you can always try and see!"

Meanwhile, during all the four years Francis labored in the Chablais, sporadic fighting occurred between the king of France, the duke of Savoy, and the citizens of Geneva. But, after four years of unremitting toil, Francis, in a gathering that lasted eleven days, "reconciled" twenty-three hundred families with the Church: never had one man reaped such a harvest.

In 1601, Francis' father, then almost eighty, fell ill. He died on April 5, leaving eight children, whom he asked not to divide their inheritance. Francis, about to preach at Annecy when they brought him the news, gave his sermon, on the death of Lazarus and Jesus' tears. When he had finished, he asked his congregation to pray for his father, and left the pulpit, weeping. His mother stayed on at Sales, and her children never ever quarreled with each other.

In 1602, Monsignor de Granier sent Francis to Paris to obtain peace terms for Gex, part of the Geneva diocese, which had abolished the Catholic faith and stripped the Church of lands and rent. Now, by the Treaty of Lyons, Gex became French and Catholicism was restored. Francis was sent to Paris to see Henry IV about the change-over. He took nineteen days to reach Paris, where he found the Jesuits had been expelled, following the attempt on the king's life by one of their former students, Châtel. Lent was approaching, and the Duchess of Longueville, whose job was to find a preacher for the queen's chapel, chose Francis, a protégé of her cousin the duchess of Mercoeur. Francis' father had been the duchess' grandfather's page! On Ash Wednesday, 1602, Francis began his sermons, and immediately had an immense success. Without ever saying a word against the Calvinists, he managed to convert many. At Easter, Francis finally got to see the king, who said of him, "A rare bird indeed; devout, learned, and a gentleman into the bargain. . . . He does not know the art of flattery, his mind is too sincere for that. He is gentle, good and humble, deeply pious but without useless scruples." Francis did not only please his sovereign: during the six months he remained in Paris, he preached over a hundred times, and also directed a number of ardent souls, among them Mde. Acarie (better known by the name she was called after her death, as the Blessed Mary of the Incarnation), who levitated, which alarmed her greatly: she thought it might be a diabolical illusion. Francis, hearing her confession, reassured her: he admired enormously the absolute purity of her soul, and was obliged to make her recall teen-age faults, for since then she had never committed the shadow of a sin.

Francis obtained for the jurisdiction of Geneva only three parishes in the whole Gex country; a poor political result, but he was lucky not to have got involved with local criminals: the duke de Biron and the baron de Lux, who had plotted against Henry IV and came to sticky ends. Francis returned home to Savoy to learn that Monsignor de Granier had died ten days previously, and he, Francis de Sales, was now bishop of Geneva, with no possibility of even entering the chief city of his see. While Francis was in Paris, Henry IV had offered him far better sees, to which Francis had politely replied, "Sire, I am married to a poor wife; I do not want to leave her for a richer."

His enthronement was splendid: Francis could do nothing to prevent the local enthusiasm in Annecy, but, the inaugural ceremonies over, he lived simply. He had to. He had given up his share of his patrimony to his brothers, and his see's revenues were meager. He had to keep eight persons in his establishment, and also to be host to every passing priest and monk. He was, besides, the sole support of two convents of Capuchins and Poor Clares, and twice a week he gave alms to all who came to the episcopal residence to ask them.

He taught the catechism himself, not only to the children: even his mother came, which embarrassed him. "You distract me," he told her, "when I see you at catechism among the children, for it is yourself who taught it me." Vinegary M. Déage, now elevated by Francis to the rank of canon, complained that the bishop was too popular with the young: they would flock around him every time he went out on the streets and grab his hand and tag after him. "Undignified," said Déage.

At Dijon, dining with the archbishop of Bourges, Francis met Madame de Chantal, with whom his name would be forever linked. She was a young widow who had been extraordinarily happy in her marriage, but her husband had been killed by a friend in a hunting accident. His widow was desolated, but turned to piety, and after she had met Francis, brought her four young children to him so he could bless them. She already had a director (absent at the time), and the bishop did not wish to interfere. But he wrote to her, and after four months, they met again, he accompanied by his mother, she by an abbess and by the wife of President Brulard, of the Savoy Senate, on August 24, 1604. Francis was thirty-seven. He told Madame de Chantal he would take charge of her spiritual life. That same morning, he heard her confession. Six months later, she came for a week to stay with his mother at Sales; Francis told Madame de Chantal then that someday he would strip her of all earthly ties and give her wholly to God.

In October 1605, Francis began a six-month visit to his whole diocese: each day, he visited a parish or two. His feet bled when he walked the steep mountains, but when he got on a horse he could barely stay on it, his legs were so swollen and sore. Horrid Canon Déage said Francis had kept him waiting, to which Francis replied, "Dear friend, we go along as best we can."

In the fall, he inaugurated an academy, of letters, arithmetic, cosmography, and music. Thirty years before the foundation of the Académie Francaise, this academy had forty members; it was called La Florimontaine, and lasted only three years, after which the bishop was too busy to attend meetings, and the members gradually dispersed.

Francis had been for some time mulling over the idea of an entirely new type of religious congregation. The great orders had, at this time, all become relaxed. Francis, after a visit to those in his diocese, had written to the Pope in 1606 that "their wine was changed into venom." He excepted the Poor Clares and the Chartreux from his strictures, but he envisaged an altogether different type of religious life. No heavy penances: even old women, even people whose health was not too good, could enter and lead spiritual lives. Obedience, gentleness, mutual support, and kindness were to be the virtues stressed.

The really innovative idea was, however, that the sisters should leave their convent regularly to visit and to nurse the sick poor. This was unheard of hitherto. The time had now come, Francis thought, to discuss his plan with Madame de Chantal. He was too busy to go to Sales, but his mother moved into his house at Annecy to receive the guest. Francis had not seen Jeanne-Françoise for two years, and at first he was too busy celebrating Pentecost and the funeral of the duke of Savoy's mother, Anne d'Este, to talk with her. Finally, on Whitmonday, he was able to tell her what he had in mind.

"Well, my daughter," he told her, "I have decided what I want to do with you." "And I, your Excellency and my Father, I am resolved to obey you," she replied. First he told her to join the Poor Clares.

"I am ready," she replied. Then, "No, you are not strong enough; you should be a hospital sister," he said. "Whatever you wish," she responded. When he had tried her thus for a while, to assure himself that she had no preferences, he described to her the congregation he wished to found. She was absolutely delighted. But both foresaw many difficulties. He insisted that the congregation should be founded at Annecy so he could visit the nuns daily. But Annecy was a small town, without many resources: already it housed Capuchins, Poor Clares, and Dominicans; the bishop's revenues were all sequestered by the Genevese. Jeanne-Françoise de Chantal was rich, but she had four children, and Francis would not allow her ever to use any of their patrimony for his sake.

Francis had confided his favorite sibling, his only sister, eight years old, to Madame de Chantal; in the summer of 1607 the child complained of violent headaches and died in a few days. Madame de Chantal was in despair: she had offered her own life, or that of any of her own three daughters to God instead of the little Jeanne de Sales; Francis scolded her for not accepting the will of God. However, she still felt remorse, and offered one of her daughters to the de Sales. Marie-Aimée was only ten; Francis' brother Bernard, to whom she was now affianced, was twenty-four, and Madame de Chantal took her, for the Lent of 1609, on a visit to her future mother-in-law.

Francis' second book, the *Introduction to the Devout Life,* had just been published. Ten years before, he had published a *Defense of the Standard of the Holy Cross,* in answer to a Protestant who accused the Catholics of worshiping the Cross. It was a dull book, stuffed with facts and arguments. The second, very different book, had been written by Francis for a brilliant and beautiful cousin by marriage, Louise de Vidomme, née de Chastel. She was from Normandy, and her husband brought her to a dour Savoyard castle, Feuillet, where the contrast between the roaring of a river and the cowbells, and the music of the Paris court, where she had been lady in waiting to the duchess of Guise, made the young woman melancholy. She put herself under Francis' direction in 1607, and his counsels to her were shown by her to others, who begged Francis to publish them, which he did.

With this little, unpretentious book, Francis brought spirituality down out of the high theological airs and made it appetizing, indeed enchanting, for all Christians. It was an instant best seller, reprinted forty times during his lifetime; to date there have been more than one thousand printings. The *Introduction to the Devout Life* was read, and is still, by every kind of Protestant hardly less avidly than by Catholics. Indeed, in the far north of Scotland, in the bitterest Convenanter times, small groups of Calvinists met to read and comment on it—favorably!

Francis took his success in stride: only the comment of the Carthusian general, that he should never write anything again, as he could never again write so well, slightly piqued him—which proves that even the holy are not wholly immune from the venial sin of vanity!

Francis made friends, that summer of 1609, with his neighbor the new bishop of Belley, Jean-Pierre Camus, then aged only twenty-five. This young man was an exuberant Parisian who published books by the dozen and admired Francis so much that he made a hole in the wall of the room he kept only for his guest at Belley, to watch Francis at prayer. He later wrote a charming account of his sainted brother bishop: *The Spirit of the Blessed Francis de Sales.*

That same summer, of 1609, Francis was ordered by Henry IV to go to Gex, where several parishes were being returned to the Roman obedience. The Rhône was so swollen that the local fords were impassable. The only bridge was at Geneva. Francis decided to go into the town, in his soutane. He knew he was risking imprisonment and death by doing this; yet when he got there the drawbridge was let down for him and he traversed the whole town on horseback, unmolested. When he reached the gate leading out to Gex, it was closed, and he had to wait until the Sunday services were finished, to have it opened for him. So he sat in a hotel for an hour.

Later, the Genevese were appalled to think they had let the greatest enemy of the Reformation, the "so-called Bishop of Geneva," slip through their fingers. Francis told his friend the bishop of Belley, "I don't know what has become of the virtue of prudence: I have difficulty loving it." "Well, if the worse had come to the worst, it might have been the best for you: you would have been martyred," said Camus. "Don't be so sure that," said Francis, "I know what I should do under such circumstances, but St. Peter was just as sure of what he should do, and looked what happened to him."

That same year, the marriage of Francis' brother to Jeanne-Françoise de Chantal's daughter was celebrated and, after the wedding, Madame de Chantal again sought, and this time obtained, permission from her father to leave the world. All her late husband's debts were paid; his estates were flourishing, their only son was about to go to Paris to become a courtier; one daughter was married; she and her sister would go with their mother to the convent until they were completely grown up.

But before the projected convent could become a reality, Jeanne-Françoise lost her youngest daughter, Charlotte, and Francis lost his mother. The latter died of a stroke the first days of Lent; Francis was able to give her the last rites, "to close her eyes and mouth and give her the last kiss, after which," Francis admitted, "I cried more than I ever had since I became a priest." That same summer, Jeanne-Françoise de Chantal left her family to enter religion at Annecy. Her fourteen-year-old son, wild with grief, begged her not to go: she tore herself from his arms and moved to the door. He threw himself on the ground, across the threshold, and said, "At least it will be said that you trampled on your son." Without hesitation, she stepped over him. His tutor asked her: "Can the tears of a young man shake your resolution?" She managed a smile. "In no way," she replied, "but you must realize I am a mother." Her father came up to her. A long embrace, more tears, she asked his blessing, and left quickly. He never saw her again.

They were three, who became the first members of the Visitation order: Jeanne-Françoise de Chantal, thirty-eight; a spinster friend of hers, Charlotte de Brechard, thirty; and the lovely, eighteen-year-old daughter of the president of the Annecy tribunal, Jacqueline Favre, with whom Francis' brother Louis, aged twenty-eight, had fallen in love. But Jacqueline had already decided on her vocation, and the charming child joined her two elders while waiting for a house in which the young congregation could be lodged. At that moment, Henry IV was assassinated.

On Trinity Sunday, June 6, 1610, the three ladies supped with the bishop and the de Sales family. Then, after being blessed by Francis, the three went on foot to a little gloomy house in the suburbs the bishop had bought. No one had any money: Francis had insisted Jeanne-Françoise keep none but give all to her children; Charlotte de Brechard's father refused to give her a cent; and Jacqueline Favre had ten brothers and sisters, so her father couldn't give her a thing. Next morning, at 5 A.M., they rose and put on their new costume: a black dress with white collar, and a black veil. There was nothing to eat in the house. At eight, the bishop came and said Mass, followed by a crowd of curious fellow citizens. At 10 A.M., still nothing to eat, so Jacqueline Coste, the very holy maid Francis had confessed on his first visit to Geneva, years before, and who had followed him to Annecy and now waited on the three ladies, begged some milk from a neighbor and picked some herbs in the garden. As she was serving this drink, there was a knock on the door, and outside were bread, meat, and a barrel of wine, left by President Favre. This barrel lasted the ladies for over a year.

After they had been living the life Francis had chosen for them for twelve months, in June 1611 they made their final vows to Francis, then lay face down on the ground and were covered with a winding sheet. The bishop sprinkled them with holy water as though they were already corpses, while the De Profundis was sung. But when they rose, there were hymns of joy.

Now Madame de Chantal fell ill, and remained for several years afflicted with "perpetual indisposition." Canon Déage finally died, and Francis mourned him, though few others had liked him. President Favre died too. Also, the duke of Savoy was annoyed with Francis, who had to cross the Alps on horseback to visit him in Turin.

On January 1, 1612, after nineteen months of a wholly cloistered life, the Visitation nuns began to nurse the sick. By this time, the congregation had grown considerably; yet only two sisters at a time were chosen each month to go daily to the miserable local hospital and help out there.

In 1616 Annecy was besieged. Savoy had been at war with Spain for three years, but nothing had happened on Savoyard soil. Then, in July 1616, three French companies came to Annecy, which shut its gates and refused to let them in. The citizens were terrified, but Francis told them there was no danger, and after three days the French went away. Twenty days later, the prince of Savoy's son, aged twenty-nine, came in triumph and stayed with the bishop, whom he greatly appreciated. Francis had just published the Treatise on the Love of God, not a book for beginners in the spiritual life like his Introduction to the Devout Life, though it has always stayed in print and is an early glory of French prose.

In 1617 Marie-Aimée, blissfully married to Francis' brother Bernard, came to visit her mother at the Visitation convent while Bernard went to war. She was afraid something would happen to her beloved, and it did: he died two weeks later of a fever. Marie-Aimée was pregnant; she wished to become a nun, like her mother, but died shortly after giving birth to a boy who lived only long enough to be baptized by his grandmother. Marie-Aimée was nineteen, and her mother was so miserable after her daughter's death that she, too, fell ill.

In 1618 the cardinal prince of Savoy went to Paris to attend the marriage of the prince of Piedmont to Princess Christine of France. He took Francis with him, and being only twenty-five at the time, loved rowing. Part of the trip was made in boats on the Loire: the prince cardinal made Francis row with him, and was delighted the latter did it so well! They arrived at the Louvre to find the seventeen-year-old king, Louis XIII, with his sixteen-year-old queen and his twelve-year-old sister. Francis became such a popular preacher that people crowded around him in the street to touch him. His valet gave away Francis' hairs when he clipped his hair or shaved him, and he was given objects to stuff into Francis' pockets each evening which the pious owners would fetch next morning.

Francis was kept a whole year in Paris, as the royal marriage of his suzerain ran into delays. During that time, he became the confessor of Angélique Arnauld, who at the age of eleven had become the abbess of Port-Royal. The child had begun by being amused with her grand position; then, at eighteen, wanted to get married and quit, but her father had many daughters, and having provided for Angélique, refused to allow her to change her state. Francis found her difficult; later she was to become famous as a leader of the Jansenists —a marginal group of heretics who permeated French spirituality, and French life and letters, and whose influence spread far and wide in the Church and continues to this day.

When Francis finally was able to go back to Savoy, he felt exhausted, drained by his flock, who expected so much of him. He tried to train one of his brothers to succeed him, but the brother was a crosspatch and had the same mean disposition as Déage or Francis' old valet Rolland. Francis always liked termagant types, perhaps as an antidote to his own consummate gentleness. At this point he longed to retire to a hermitage, and write quietly and pray. He found a perfect site, the chapel of St. Germain, over a thousand feet above the Abbey of Talloires. But he had strong feeling he would never enjoy such peace here on earth, and when he returned to Annecy, it was with the conviction his end was near.

During the winter of 1621–22 his health grew more and more precarious, and though his friends begged him to do less, he had been ordered by the Pope to reform various monasteries in and around his diocese, and he spent himself tirelessly working to bring clashing factions together; when he was asked to spare himself, he replied his time was short and he must do whatever good he could.

As Francis had thirty-two quarterings,* he was cousin to all the Savoyard noble families; many of them came to him with their squabbles and domestic problems, and he made himself available to all. In November of 1621 he set off for Lyons, where Madame de Chantal was awaiting him. They had not met for three years, during which time eleven new convents of the Visitation order had been founded.

On December 12, 1622, Francis and Jeanne-Françoise met for the last time. That Christmas, he knew he was dying, and after horrible sufferings caused by the doctors, who burned his flesh with red-hot irons and put cantharides plasters on his head, he died very "gently and quietly," on the feast of the Holy Innocents, December 28, 1622. His body was brought back to Annecy, after a journey of four days from Lyons, and he was buried in the Visitation convent, where Madame de Chantal received the coffin.

What has the gentle Francis to teach us today?

Above all, that there is only one way to win people to one's way of thinking, and that is by one's own being. Not by arguing, but by loving; not by preaching, but by producing in oneself the qualities one wishes others to have, is it possible to convince. For example, at the international level, the Marshall Plan succeeded, whereas the Christmas bombing of Cambodia failed; at the human level, Mahatma Gandhi succeeded in freeing a whole subcontinent, while Roger Casement failed to liberate a small island. The only way out is the way in; and perhaps Francis is the saint who can help us most today, at all levels. Above all, he had a delicious sense of humor—very rare in any of us, rarest of all in the saints. He is also, as the patron of journalists, a blissful reminder that scribes and scribblers can also be saved and that the intellect can be as supernaturally irradiated by holiness as the emotions.

* That is to say, every one of his thirty-two great-great-great-grandparents had a coat of arms (armorial bearings). Everyone, male or female, who has the right to a coat of arms halves them for his or her children, quarters them for grandchildren, etc. No one can be listed in the Almanach de Gotha, for example, without sixteen quarterings.

St. Martin de Porres (1579–1639)

ᠵᢤᢢᡬᢤᡬ

"There are no sad saints," Clare Boothe Luce wrote. But some seem gladder than others. And one of the most extraordinarily cheerful and delightful of all is surely Martin of Porres.

He would seem to have had little enough to be cheerful about. He was born on December 9, 1579, in Lima, Peru. His father, Juan de Porres, was a noble Spaniard; his mother, Ana Velázquez, a free Negro. When his father saw that his son was black, he did not wish to acknowledge him, so the baptismal entry carries his name, Martin, "of unknown father." Two years later, Juan de Porres had a daughter, Juana, by the same mother, and acknowledged them both but did not support them. Martin's mother, as soon as he could navigate alone, sent little Martin to market with money and a shopping basket. Often he came back with no money and nothing in the basket—he had given what he had to the many poor. Then he would stop to pray in any church he passed, and when he returned home, his mother would reproach him because neither she nor Martin nor Juana had anything to eat.

The neighbors began to notice how bright and helpful Martin was, and to comment adversely on the fact that Juan de Porres, rich as he was, did not support them. Juan de Porres was at that time working in Ecuador. After a visit to Lima, he took the two children back with him, and took proper care of them. One day, out walking with the two, he met one of his uncles, Juan de Miranda, who asked him who they were. He told the truth. "They are mine, by Ana Velázquez. I am seeing to their education." Martin was eight, Juana six. He later entrusted Juana to Juan de Miranda, as he left to become governor of Panama, but Martin was returned to his mother.

When he was twelve, Martin had to find himself a trade. He chose to be a barber. Barbers then not only cut hair but did many things later done by doctors, such as letting blood, treating cuts, wounds, and fractures, and even prescribing medicines. Martin seems to have been quite extraordinarily bright, and soon his boss, when he had to leave, left him in charge of the first-aid section of his shop.

Martin now served several masses every morning, then went to his barbershop (he was always on time), and at night, begging candle stubs from a neighbor, he would spend the night in reading and in prayer. The neighbor, intrigued by his request for candle stubs, peered through the keyhole to find the teen-age boy on his knees, motionless, his arms stretched out in a cross. She called the neighbors, who would peer in night after night, while Martin was unaware of their indiscretion.

Then, one morning, when there was already a line in the barbershop of clients waiting to be bled, to get a poultice, to be shaved, they were told Martin was leaving to enter the Dominican monastery. He requested the habit of a *donado*, or lay helper, at the Monastery of the Holy Rosary. He was then around fifteen years old, and was accepted in spite of his illegitimate birth. His father was shocked: why didn't Martin at least ask to be a lay *brother?* But Martin refused: "I have chosen to be abject," he declared. He was given the job of sweeping the cloisters and corridors—a broom was so much his distinguishing mark, that tiny brooms are still given the faithful in Peru as a sign of devotion to Martin.

But he still also worked as a barber (now he had three hundred clients) and surgeon: he was entrusted with the care of the monastery sick. He was an example of humility, never sitting down in the presence of a priest, and particularly devoted to anyone who called him names such as "mulatto dog." One day the prior, having to pay some debts for the community, went off to sell some valuable objects. Martin ran after him, as the prior was making his way to the merchants' quarter, and suggested that the prior sell him—he was a young and strong mulatto and would fetch a good price. The prior was much moved. "Go back to the monastery," he told Martin. "You are not for sale."

Already he had the gift of bilocation. He would be praying in Limatambo, an estate belonging to the monastery, and be seen there wrapped in prayer. But in the evening he would be visibly back in Lima, doing chores generally done by the Negroes, such as feeding monastery animals. And at night, he would be seen in the chapter room, raised above the ground in the form of a cross "the height of the great crucifix above the ground." He would scourge himself three times every night, in penance for the sins of others—and Lima at that time was a place of much sin. He wore a hair shirt and an iron chain around his waist and fasted continuously: only on Easter Monday would he eat some bread stew (no meat). The rest of the year he lived on bread and water, except for Easter Sunday, when he ate some sweet potatoes.

Surprisingly, considering the prejudices of the time, his superiors, having tested Martin's humility to their own satisfaction, began to appreciate him. Even the master of the novices, Father Andrés de Lisón, would tell them, "This mulatto is a saint." And after Martin had spent nine years as a *donado* he was accepted to make his solemn profession, as his superiors wished. He was thought the most edifying of lay brothers, manifesting constantly the virtues of humility, perfect obedience, poverty, and chastity. Father Andrés Martínez testified that Martin never evaded "any command, but did everything he was told."

He slept only on planks. One day when he had a bad attack of malaria, the prior ordered him to make up a bed for himself like the others, with a mattress, sheets, and blankets. Martin obeyed but slipped under the sheets wearing his habit and hair shirt. The prior gave him a good scolding for disobedience, but Martin said, "Father, how could a poor mulatto slave like myself have, here in a monastery, a luxurious bed such as I never had in my own home? You cannot have intended it—how could I believe it?" The prior smiled and told the person who had informed him of Brother Martin's "disobedience" that Martin was a "good master of mystical theology, and understands the laws of obedience very well."

Another time, Martin was told to go to the archbishop of Mexico, who was sick, and to do whatever he told Martin, and not return until the archbishop was well. Martin went without any medicaments, and was ushered into the presence of the archbishop, who began to scold him for not coming more quickly. Martin fell on his knees beside the archbishop's bed. Then the archbishop commanded Martin to give him his hand. Martin objected that so great a prelate should take the hand of a poor mulatto. The archbishop insisted Martin had been told to obey him. "Then, put your hand here," the archbishop ordered. Martin put his hand where the archbishop told him, on the side of his chest, where he was suffering terrible pain, and had been, day and night. The pain vanished. Martin blushed, and tried to withdraw his hand. "Isn't that enough, my lord?" he asked. "Leave your hand where it is," commanded the archbishop. In a short while, not only was the pain gone but the fever as well. Martin rushed back to the monastery, and was found cleaning out some latrines. One of the fathers asked him, "Were you not better employed at the archbishop's?" But Martin replied that he had chosen to be abject and added, "I think one moment spent in doing what I am doing now, is better than days spent in the house of the archbishop."

It was in the care of the sick that Martin most showed his charity.

If anyone was seriously ill, Martin would remain at the bedside until the person either recovered or died; often he would bilocate to his other tasks, fulfilling them all; often, too, when the monastery doors were shut and locked, he would go through them on his way out of the monastery, or to come back in. No one of his fellow Dominicans was a bit surprised at these powers; they just regarded them as Brother Martin's little ways. If someone complained Martin was neglecting him, Martin told him, "Don't worry; if I am rarely at a bedside, it means the illness is not dangerous."

Because of Martin's reputation, he was able to beg many things for the monastery that they were without. Sheets for the sick, for example. He had managed to collect quite a good quantity of sheets when he discovered that they were being eaten by mice. The mice "seemed to delight in gnawing the best and newest sheets." The head infirmarian proposed to spread poison around. Martin was horrified. "Poor little beasts," he said. "They don't find their meals ready for them daily in the refectory as we do." So he managed to catch a mouse in his hands. He spoke to the terrified creature, explaining that the mouse and its friends were doing grave harm to the sick. "You must assemble all your friends and lead them to the end of the garden, and I'll bring you food every day so long as you leave the sheets alone." The mouse grew quite calm and quiet in Martin's hands, and he let it go. It disappeared. At once "a great rustling began . . . from under the wardrobes, from the joists of the ceilings, from cracks in the floor, the mice emerged. Who would have thought one room would hold so many? When they were all assembled, they all moved towards the garden. Martin's long stride accompanied the tiny scurrying steps of the mice. They went to the far corner of the garden, where there was a fine hedge and bushes and enough open ground for all the mice to dig holes, and they took possession of it all. Every day, after he had served dinner to the sick, to the servants, and to the poor, Martin went out to bring the mice their meal. It was a service to the mice, but also to the community. He knew if he kept his word, the mice would respect the pact. From that time on no mouse ever set paw in the wardrobe, or tooth into the monastery linen." (*Positio super dubio an constet de fama* [Rome, 1669], p. 45; English transl. in *Martin de Porres*, by J. C. Kerns [New York: Kenedy, 1977])

Every day at the dinner hour, Martin grew restless, because at that hour the poor began to gather at the monastery door. With a cup and kettle, Martin went around the refectory to gather all the leftovers he could find. As he ate only bread and water, his portion went into the kettle first. Then he went into the kitchen of the infirmary, where his clients had gathered: Spaniards, Negroes, Indians, mulattoes, even dogs and cats, and a row of bowls belonging to the local poor who could not walk but got their friends to deposit their bowls. Martin never minded how many came, and though there was never enough in the kettle for more than four, or at the outside, six, people, there was always enough soup for everyone, even the dogs and cats: he fed up to two hundred people a day.

Martin would bring in the sick from the streets and lodge them in the supply room. One brother complained, and soon Martin was told the sick must be cleared out of the supply room. Martin asked his sister, married and with children of her own, if he could set up his "hospital" in her house. She agreed, and Martin visited them every day, walking about a mile and a half from the monastery.

Martin was much worried about the abandoned children and orphans who roamed the streets. He himself, he declared, had he not had a loving mother, might have been one of these. So he began to gather these children together, though his monastery could do nothing for them because of restricted means. What is so amazing about this venture of Martin de Porres is how excellently it was organized. From a small orphanage that grew into a school, arose the Collegio de Santa Cruz, which still exists and shelters children in Lima today, more than three hundred years after Martin's death. Martin chose the best available teachers and gave them good salaries: the boys and girls all got a good education, and the girls got dowries.

How did he do this, with no money at all? He enlisted such men as the viceroy of the king of Spain, the count of Chinchón, who gave him one hundred thousand pesos a month. And the governor of Lima, Juan de Figueroa, who brought him generous offerings every Monday. Indeed, as Father Gutiérrez, an early biographer, noted, "It was considered a constant marvel by the religious, to see that a poor lay brother, dressed in ragged clothing, had the means of helping as many poor as came to him, so it seemed that alms rained down on him."

Martin also never neglected to work at producing wealth. Early on, he had planted a whole grove of olive trees for his monastery; and whenever he was called out of Lima he planted rows of fruit trees along the way, which produced food that grew on public land, so the poor were saved from the temptation of climbing the hedges to steal from the orchards. He also, at Limatambo, planted a herb garden, which included all the herbs used in the medicine of his day and helped him run his clinic without cost to the monastery.

Martin was just as good to sick dogs and cats as to people: the animals came to him. Even a mean dog that bit all the other religious was quiet while Martin bound him up, and a cat whose head had been half crushed by a stone was sewed up by Martin, who made a little cap for her and sewed it on. He told the cat to come back next day, and it was found waiting outside his door. A wounded turkey came daily also to be treated, and on one occasion, when Martin fed a bandaged cat and dog together, he scolded them when they growled at each other. "Don't fight, or I must send you away," he told them. On another occasion, a dog and a cat had litters in the cellar under the infirmary, so Martin gave them one bowl of good soup daily for the two. One day, a mouse came and joined them, and "the other two continued to lap up the soup" without bothering about the mouse.

Martin began to suffer badly from headaches, and his doctor ordered a poultice made with the blood of freshly killed roosters. Martin asked that such a prescription not be carried out, as it would be useless—he knew himself to be in his last illness. Dr. Navarro then admitted that there was nothing to be done. Martin died in great pain, with all the community around him. Everyone loved him, and everyone had his own special reason to be grateful to Martin, from the viceroy on down.

The viceroy came to visit the dying man, but, finding him rapt in ecstasy, asked that he not be disturbed. He wanted till Martin returned to consciousness, then came into Martin's cell, and fell on his knees, kissed Martin's hand, and asked him to pray God, when he was admitted to the beatific vision, to grant Peru peace, and that he, the viceroy, might have a happy death. Martin assured him he would not fail to remember him in his prayers. The archbishop of Mexico, and Don Pedro de Ortega, who later became bishop of Cuzco, came too. Martin's agony took a long time, during which he asked pardon of all the community for what he called "his bad example." He died during the recital of the Nicene Creed, at the words *Et homo factus est*, on November 3, 1639, at about 8:30 P.M., aged sixty. He had been in the Dominican order forty-five years, a professed religious for thirty-six.

He was beatified in 1837, canonized in 1962, three hundred and twenty-three years after his death. He was named Patron of Social Justice by Pius XII in 1945, and is, in a very special way, the patron of all Negroes.

In his lifetime he was especially beloved for the cures he wrought, and for his miraculous faculties, such as bilocation, the power of reading hearts and minds, the ability to move through solid walls, etc.

For us, he is an early example of a man who, like Albert Schweitzer, realized the sanctity of all life. A lifelong vegetarian, Martin was devoted to animals and plants, and his healing powers were exercised on all living beings, not merely on his fellow humans. His total inability, also, to take account of any class distinctions or race differences in others is something that was unique in his time and rightly is passionately admired in ours.

Martin de Porres also "speaks to our condition" today, because he never let anything bother him—neither his mixed blood, his illegitimate birth, nor his abject poverty. Today, criminals are constantly excused rape, murder, and the nastier forms of cruelty because of one or other of such impediments; Martin blithely ignored them completely, thus giving our psychiatrists as well as our legislators and our do-gooders the lie direct.

He was also very contemporary in his perception that what the sick need most is affection and concern. And to be told the truth—not cosseted with lies.

Also, his delight in the "prayer of quiet" is something that brings him close to a generation that is finding TM, meditation, and silence not merely more rewarding, but also more agreeable, than drugs and drink.

St. Thérèse of Lisieux (1873–97)

Joseph, Mary, pray for all
The proper and conventional
Of whom this world approves. . . .
O pray for our salvation
Who take the prudent way
Believing we shall be exempted

From the general condemnation
Because our self-respect is tempted
To incest, not adultery:
O pray for us, the bourgeoisie.

from "For the Time Being" by W. H. Auden

The "saint of the antimacassars" or "of the lace curtains" (depending which side of the Atlantic one was born on) is one of the most absolutely astonishing of all the great company of the saints in light. Thérèse Martin was born to pious parents—each had tried to enter the religious life (Louis-Joseph-Stanislas Martin, the Cistercians at the Great Saint Bernard; Marie-Zelie Guérin, the order of St. Vincent de Paul) and been rejected. He for lack of Latin, she simply because the prioress said it was not God's will.

They both lived in Alençon, and their families did not know each other; they did not even live in the same parish. Like Dante and Beatrice, they first saw each other on a bridge, the Pont St. Léonard, over the river Sarthe; he stood aside to let her pass. They were married in July 1858; he was thirty-five, she twenty-eight. He was a watchmaker and jeweler; she was a lacemaker. She had wanted many children. On their wedding night, he told her they should live together as brother and sister. They did so for many months. Then they had nine children. First four girls, then a boy who died at five months, then another boy, who died at nine months. Then came a second batch of girls: one of each of the two batches of girls died. Madame Martin was left with four girls.

A ninth child, also a girl, was born on January 2, 1873. Madame Martin had no milk; waiting for it to "come in" (this often takes forty-eight hours), she walked out of Alençon on foot to a village nearby, where lived Rose Taillé, a peasant with whom Madame Martin's family had made friends. Rose walked back with Madame Martin, and they found the baby apparently dying. But Marie-Françoise-Thérèse began to suck, and Rose took her to her village, Semalle. Thérèse grew strong. She lived with Rose for fifteen months, pushed in a wheelbarrow full of hay, taken into Alençon when Rose went in to sell butter. Thérèse's father was fifty when she was born, and he idolized this last child. When she was returned to her family, she was enchantingly pretty and very self-willed: she would creep into her next sister's bed and tell the maid, "Leave us alone, don't you see we're like two little white chickens, you can't separate us?" Thérèse would climb the stairs, at every step calling "*Maman*" and refusing to proceed until her mother responded. The mother's lacemaking was so successful that in 1870 her husband had given up his own shop to help her with her business. The two elder girls went to school at Le Mans, where an aunt was prioress.

Thérèse was pious from her earliest words. She would never leave out a word in a prayer and at the end would say she had also to pray for grace. "Dear little mother," she said, "I wish you would die, because then you'd go to Heaven." Her wish came true when Thérèse was four and a half: her mother, aged forty-six, died in agony of cancer of the breast. She had tried Lourdes, in vain, and Thérèse remembered the administration of extreme unction to her mother all her life, and also how, alone in the corridor outside her mother's bedroom, she saw the waiting coffin, propped upright. She knew instantly what it was, though she was so small she could only see the whole of it by tilting her head back.

Thérèse's father was now left with five young girls. He decided to move from Alençon to Lisieux, where he could count on the help of his late wife's brother and sister-in-law. M. Guérin was a chemist. The Guérins found the Martins a house, Les Buissonets (The Shrubbery), in the suburbs of the small town. The house was topped by a belvedere with good views. There M. Martin made his study; only his youngest, his "Benjamin, his little queen," as he called her, dared interrupt him there. As she wrote:

> I loved still the belvedere
> Drenched in light
> Received my father's kisses there
> Caressed his snowy hair
> Now white.

(*The Eagle and the Dove*, by V. Sackville-West [London: Michael Joseph, 1943], p. 108)

Thérèse loved, too, the new house: standing in its own grounds, it was far more agreeable to her than living on a street. She would go fishing in the nearby streams with her father, and made a little altar in Les Buissonnets with her own flower vases and with tapers for candles—sometimes the maid would give her real candle ends, but rarely.

When she went to make her first confession, she knew exactly what to do and say, but her head did not reach the ledge, and the priest, looking for his penitent, could not see her. The first word she learned to read was *ciel* (heaven). Her autobiography is a model of simple awareness: she tells how she and her sister would walk along the street hand in hand with shut eyes, pretending to be blind. Once, they fell over a pile of empty boxes outside a store, and the storekeeper ran out in a rage and scolded them.

She was immensely sure of herself. Her mother had once offered her a penny if she would kiss the ground. "I would rather go without the penny," she told her. And one winter's night, walking home with her father, she thought she saw a T in the constellation of Orion. "Look, Papa," she said, "my name is written in the sky." She was so delighted she asked her father to lead her home by the arm, "as I don't want to look at the horrid old world any more," and again kept her eyes shut. As Henri Gheon pointed out in his *Secrets of the Saints* (New York: Sheed & Ward, 1949, p. 165), "Holiness can be grafted onto pride, just as grace is grafted onto nature." And how sound Thérèse's instincts were is shown by the fact that she once hurt a poor man's feelings by offering him a penny as though he were a beggar, however, realizing her tactlessness, she wanted to offer him a cake she was about to eat but feared another refusal. She remembered that what one asks for in prayer on the day of one's first communion is always granted: she would pray for him that day, she resolved. Six years later, aged eleven, she remembered to do so. Yet when she and her sister Céline were playing with dolls, and another sister, Léonie, came up, offering with her own doll a basket of doll's clothes, bits of nice stuff, saying to her two younger sisters, "Here you are, choose," Céline took a ball of braid, but, Thérèse relates, "I considered for a moment, then exclaiming 'I'll take the lot,' I snatched basket and doll and everything." Comment fifteen years later, Thérèse said about her "way" to holiness: "As in my childhood's days, I said, 'O God, I choose them all.' " "Them" was all the many degrees of self-sacrifice.

For Thérèse's sanctity, like Seurat's painting, was made up of an infinity of minute dots—each a sacrifice. After her mother's death she had chosen her sister Pauline to be her "little mother," and she would daily ask her, "Have I been a good girl today?" If she was told no, she would sob herself to sleep. When she was eight and a half she began to go daily to school at Notre Dame du Pré, in a working-class quarter. She did not care for school, though she loved her cousin Marie Guérin, who went with her. Soon Pauline told her she was going to enter Carmel. Thérèse thought she would die of grief, but when Pauline explained the cloistered life to her, she decided she, too, would enter Carmel. She got Pauline to take her to Mother Mary of Gonzaga, the Carmelite prioress. The prioress pretended to believe in Thérèse's vocation—the child was only nine—but said she must wait until she was sixteen. Before she left, the prioress told her, "When you join us, dear child, you shall be called Teresa of the Child Jesus."

On October 2, 1882, Pauline entered Carmel, and thereafter Thérèse could only see her for a few minutes in the convent parlor, on special days. She hated these visits, with the convent grating and curtains, and did not eat or sleep, making herself quite ill. She had ghastly headaches, and also mysterious seizures. "Her condition seemed desperate, and it was feared her mind would be permanently deranged." Her illness ended when it seemed to her that, in her own words, a statue of Our Lady on a bracket near her bed came alive. "Our Lady came to me still smiling. How happy I am, I thought, but I won't say a word to anyone, as then my happiness would go away." (Sackville-West, *The Eagle and the Dove*, p. 111) Her sister Mary, watching by Thérèse with Léonie and Céline, saw the reflection of Our Lady's smile in Thérèse's eyes, and guessed she was healed. But when Thérèse confessed to her, Céline told the nuns at Carmel, and because the nuns fussed over Thérèse, she would only say, "Our Lady was very beautiful," and began to doubt her own vision. "Many years were to pass before she recovered from what she regarded as a betrayal and humiliation," writes V. Sackville-West (*The Eagle and the Dove*, p. 112), and Thérèse upbraided herself, "If only I had kept my secret to myself I would also have kept my joy."

She also had a terrifying vision of her handsome father old and ill —a vision that came true before her own death. Her childhood ended when, aged fourteen, coming home from midnight Mass on Christmas Eve, she was prepared to find her shoes beside the chimney filled, as always, with presents. Going up the stairs before her annual moment of delight, she heard her father say, "This is too babyish a surprise for Thérèse; I hope this will be the last year of it." Céline warned Thérèse not to go down at once: "You will cry too much." (Ibid., p. 115) But Thérèse ran down, made for the shoes, pulled out everything: Papa was now laughing, and Thérèse notes she herself "had recovered for always her strength of soul, which she had lost at the time of her mother's death."

She now accompanied her father on several "country-house visits" to old friends of his near Alençon, since she was not considered strong enough to return to school. Thérèse wore pretty clothes, and being enchantingly pretty herself, was much petted and feted. During the summer, her aunt took her to the seaside for two weeks, and Thérèse worried lest donkey rides and shrimping were too frivolous pursuits. Pauline was now fully professed, and Marie followed her into Carmel; Céline was waiting to follow. On the Whitsunday before Thérèse was fifteen, she told her father, after Vespers, of her own vocation. Her father burst into tears but made no other protest. The prioress of Carmel was told and agreed to receive her. But the ecclesiastical superior of the Carmelites, Canon Delatroëtte, declared unequivocally that no girl could join them until she was twenty-one, unless she had a dispensation from the bishop.

On October 31, Thérèse went, her hair up for the first time, to ask permission of the bishop of Bayeux. The bishop was impressed and promised he would take the matter up himself with the canon. Meanwhile, three days later, M. Martin, with Thérèse and Céline, set out for Rome with a party of pilgrims shepherded by the vicar-general of Bayeux, Monsignor Révérony. When the pilgrims gathered for a papal audience, having been told they must not speak to the Pope, Thérèse addressed Leo XIII directly: "Most holy Father, I have a great favor to ask." No reply. She went on, "In honor of your jubilee, let me go into Carmel when I'm fifteen." The vicar-general interposed, "The superiors have the matter in hand, your Holiness." "Very well, do as the superiors decide," said the Pope. Thérèse replied, "If only you say yes, holy Father, nobody will raise any difficulty." The Pope looked at Thérèse. "You will enter if it is God's will," he said and gave her his hand to kiss.

When Thérèse got back to Lisieux, she found the prioress still willing, and the vicar-general had come over to her side. Then the bishop yielded too, leaving the matter to the discretion of the prioress, who told Thérèse she might enter the following feast day, April 8, when she would be fifteen years and three months old. M. Delatroëtte was still cross: "I trust this child will not disappoint your hopes, but I remind you, if it turns out otherwise, the responsibility is yours alone," he told the prioress. Nine months later, Thérèse took the habit. Her father, recovering from a second stroke, walked Thérèse into the chapel on his arm. Dressed in white velvet with swansdown and lace, a sheaf of white lilies on her arm, her curling hair loose down her back, Thérèse was just sixteen, and lovely. Led away to have her hair cut short, she was then dressed in the brown Carmelite tunic and white veil. Sandals were put on her feet; a black belt, a scapular, and a great white cloak were put on. Then Thérèse prostrated herself on the ground, her arms spread out in a cross.

Her father, later brought again to the convent, "muttering incoherently and almost unrecognizable," died on July 29, 1894. No further events took place in Thérèse's life, other than the change to a black veil when she took her final vows. She was appointed mistress of novices; she lived in the convent for eight years, died on September 30, 1897, and was buried in the municipal cemetery. A wooden cross was placed over her grave, with her words on it: *"Je passerai mon ciel à faire du bien sur la terre"* (I will spend my heaven doing good on earth).

She was twenty-four years and nine months old at the time of her death. During her last illness, she had overheard a nun in the kitchen saying, "Sister Teresa of the Child Jesus is soon going to die, and I really wonder what our Mother will find to say about her after her death. She will find herself in rather a difficulty, for although that little Sister is amiable enough, she has never done anything worth talking about." (Ibid., p. 162) The prioress, who after letting Thérèse into Carmel had been rather stern with her, acceded to the request of two of Thérèse's sisters that Thérèse write down the story of her soul. The manuscript was to be delivered on January 20, 1896. It was delivered on time, on the Eve of St. Agnes as the nuns were going into choir. The ninth and tenth chapters were added when Thérèse was already dying. As Thérèse had seen her mother's coffin before her mother died, so she saw the pallet on which she was to be laid out; it had been brought into the infirmary. Thérèse laughed when she saw it. Shown a photo of herself, she smiled. "Yes, that's the envelope. When will anyone see the letter inside? I would like to see that letter."

Her death, from tuberculosis, was agonizing: it had been brought on by the cold in the convent—Thérèse admitted the cold was what she found hardest to bear.

The prioress decided to send out copies of Thérèse's manuscript, *The Story of a Soul,* with an account of Thérèse's last hours added. It was therefore printed, and copies went to all the Carmels in the world. It became so popular it was decided "to make the book public." So many postulants came as a result of reading it, that the Carmelites could not cope, and "many overflowed to other convents." Thérèse began to work miracles. On February 11, 1923, she was beatified, and on May 17, 1925, canonized. Over two hundred thousand applications for seats for the canonization were received; St. Peter's holds only fifty thousand. But half a million people celebrated the event in Rome, millions more all over the world. There had not been so much popular demand for a canonization, or such a popular canonization, since the days when emperors such as Charlemagne were forced onto the Church's altars only by the acclaim of the people.

St. Teresa of the Child Jesus, declared a saint by the Church and the patron of missions, owes her reputation to her book. Had she not written *The Story of a Soul*, she would never have been heard of outside her convent. She is thus a best-selling saint, in every sense of the word, and that makes her very much a saint for now. She founded no new order; during her brief life she did nothing more than "the daily round, the common task" required of her. Yet because she was able to express her interior life and sufferings in her own, simple words, she has reached out to all mankind and to our own times. And beyond.

St. Frances Cabrini (1850–1917)

No greater contrast among saints—nor even among women of any kind—could be imagined than between Thérèse Martin and Frances Cabrini. The pampered French girl, doted upon by parents and siblings, brought up in a French provincial city, had a very different background from the thirteenth child of a Lombardy farmer. Both had delicate health—perhaps their only resemblance, except that both, as early as the age of seven, were completely sure of their vocations: both wanted to be missionaries. Thérèse, in her short convent life, never left Lisieux; Frances was never still, crossing the Atlantic twenty-five times, founding an order that at her death had four thousand nuns in many different countries, visiting such then remote areas as Brazil, Argentina, Panama, and Nicaragua.

It would almost seem that the Church produced two such disparate saints in order to exemplify the two ways, that of Mary and that of Martha, and also, on the eve of the era of ERA and Women's Liberation, produced two such women in order to show that "Male and female created He them" and that, in the sight of God—and there ONLY—there is no distinction of Gentile or Jew, male or female, but all are one, as St. Paul declared, in Christ Jesus.

Mother Cabrini, like Thérèse Martin, is proof that money doesn't matter, youth doesn't matter—that you can always get what you want and become what you want, providing always you want it enough and are prepared to pay. In each case, with the total surrender of an entire life to one aim.

As F. W. Myers wrote in his *St. Paul:*

Christ has sufficed me, and Christ shall suffice
Christ the beginning, for the end is Christ.

This was as true of the reclusive Thérèse Martin, a cloistered nun, as of Frances Cabrini, rushing from Pope to cardinal to archbishop, founding schools and hospitals at giddying speed.

Frances Cabrini was a seven-month baby, born on July 15, 1850, the youngest of thirteen children, when her mother was fifty-two. Family legend has it that a flock of white doves descended on the grain Frances' father, Agostino, was threshing, and one got entangled with his flail. It was unhurt and he brought it indoors to show the children, who wanted to keep it. But he opened his window and let it fly. White doves are now painted on the old Cabrini house in Sant' Angelo, a village near Lodi, on the Lombard plain.

Frances was baptized the day she was born, for her parents were both pious. As a child she loved to pray, and regarded her confirmation day, July 1, 1857, as the day when she passed from "childhood innocence to conscious union with God." "My heart was replete with a most pure joy," she wrote much later. "I cannot say what I felt but I know it was the Holy Ghost." Her first confessor, Don Melchisedecco Abrami, permitted her to take a private vow of chastity when she was eleven, for one year. Frances' elder sister, Rosa, was more responsible for her upbringing than was their mother. Rosa was dry and sharp-spoken, and, it would seem, jealous of this lovely blue-eyed child with golden curls. When Frances was eight she nearly drowned, filling paper boats with violets (the violets were her missionaries she was sending all over the world) and sailing them in the canal near her uncle's house. She leaned over too far, fell in, and was carried toward a tunnel, in which she would have perished. She never knew who pulled her out, but had a great fear of deep water for many years after.

Frances' father's cousin and namesake, Agostino Depretis, became Prime Minister of a united Italy: Garibaldi himself came to Sant' Angelo one day in 1862, and probably the twelve-year-old Frances saw him. At thirteen she went to a Sacred Heart school for five years, taking the courses that would lead to a teacher's certificate, which she obtained at eighteen. As soon as she had passed all her exams, *cum laude*, she asked for admission into the community. The superior refused to accept her, though they all thought she was a most edifying girl, because she was not strong enough physically for the religious life. She had no choice but to go home. Which she did in the fall of 1868.

She settled down to helping her mother and Rosa with household duties until, in February 1869, her father had a stroke. He lingered for a year before dying; his wife survived him for less than a year. Now only four of the thirteen children were left at home, one of whom had polio and also soon died. In 1871 there was an epidemic of smallpox, which Frances caught while serving those who were stricken. Rosa nursed her devotedly, bathing the girl's face in milk so no pock marks would remain. Rosa ended her life in the Argentine, where her only brother had gone to teach: she kept house for him, as she had at home for all her siblings.

Hardly had Frances recovered from smallpox than the local priest asked her if she would substitute for the teacher in the public school at Vidardo, a mile and a half away. Frances agreed, and she came to the attention of the parish priest there, Antonio Serrati, who, hearing Frances was going to apply again to the Daughters of the Sacred Heart, recommended the superior reject her again on grounds of health, and he did the same thing when she offered herself to the Canossian Sisters in Cremona, who had a mission to China, where she longed to go. The reason he behaved thus strangely was that he was about to be transferred to Codogno and wanted Frances to work for him there.

At Codogno were three women living in a House of Providence, so-called. One was an heiress, Antonia Tondini, who had endowed the house with thirty thousand lire; with her lived her friend Teresa Calza, and their cook. The three women wore nuns' habits and had taken vows, but Teresa said she kept her vows—which she had made to the bishop of Lodi—in her pocket. They were supposed to take care of six or seven orphan girls, whom they badly neglected. Frances, Monsignor Serrati said, was to reform this institution. She was horrified at the idea: because the women were nuns, because she wanted to be a missionary and not spend her life in Codogno, and because she was twenty-four and the two ladies were over forty. Monsignor Serrati begged her to try it for two weeks—then she could go back to her school at Vidardo. Frances stayed in Codogno two years, bitterly resented by the two women, who were rude to her. But after two months she wore the same habit as they—a simple black gown with no veil—and took no vows. She was technically a novice, yet gathered seven pupils under her, and gradually the number of orphans cared for grew to thirty. One day in 1877, Monsignor Serrati told Frances that she was to take her vows the next day. Then he made her superior and told her to receive the profession of the other sisters. The two original House of Providence women now tried physical violence upon Mother Cabrini, and she really had a terrible time for three years.

The bishop offered to let the two refractory nuns retire from the convent, but sister Tondini instituted an action in the civil courts against the bishop for the money she had given the convent. The bishop promptly excommunicated her. Then the bishop declared the House of Providence dissolved, and in 1880, asked Frances Cabrini, "I know of no missionary order of women. Why not found one yourself?" Frances replied, "I will look for a house."

The six dark years of apprenticeship, of total obedience to Monsignor Serrati, of suffering, were over, and Frances at once showed her new independence by rejecting a house on which Monsignor Serrati had made a deposit of one thousand lire, in favor of an abandoned friary behind the Franciscan church in Codogno. Frances felt herself so unwell at this time, that she persuaded Monsignor Serrati and two other priests to become the legal owners of the property in case she died and the property would become liable for inheritance taxes. The community of seven sisters and a lay sister moved in the day the deed was signed although the building needed many repairs. They ate on a bench for lack of a table, and went to bed in the dark for lack of a lamp. On November 14, 1880, Monsignor Serrati said Mass for the community, which thereafter regarded that day as the birthday of the Missionary Sisters of the Sacred Heart. Mother Cabrini took the name of Xavier as her name in religion, but she was always referred to as just Mother Cabrini. Frances' cousin Agostino Depretis became Prime Minister for the second time in 1881, but Frances never approached him for help. Already, though she was teaching only a few orphans and training a few nuns, she told Bishop Gelmini, "The whole world is not wide enough for me." She had just turned thirty.

In November 1882, four sisters left for Grumello, where Frances made her second foundation. As early as spring 1884 Mother Cabrini found she had too many nuns to be able to house them all in the old friary, so the sisters, under the supervision of one who was a bricklayer's daughter, worked on an additional building every evening after the workmen had gone. "With very little outlay the convent doubled in size." Also in 1884 a house was opened in Milan, with eight nuns to start it. In September 1887, Frances made her first trip to Rome, to seek papal approval of her missionary sisters. Her first visit in Rome, to the cardinal vicar, was frustrating. "I will give you permission to found a house in Rome when you can show me that you have enough capital for the purpose." "How much

would be sufficient?" she asked. "Half a million lire," he replied. She
asked to see him again, then asked him to consult the Holy Father!
The third visit was different. He beamed and told Mother Cabrini to
found *two* houses in Rome, a free school for the poor and a kinder-
garten. Mother Cabrini moved in at once, sleeping with her nuns on
straw while they went daily to auctions to collect the furniture they
needed. On March 12, 1888, the rules drawn up by her at Codogno
were approved.

Bishop Scalabrini, of Piacenza, had written a book about the
plight of the Italian immigrants to the U.S.A. These were mostly
peasants, unused to living in big cities such as New York, unable to
speak English—most of them, indeed, speaking dialects other than
standard Italian. Two thirds were men, separated from their families,
many of them criminal elements. Bishop Scalabrini urged Mother
Cabrini to go to America; Archbishop Corrigan wrote from New
York offering a house. Frances decided to consult the Pope. The
Pope, Leo XIII, asked Mother Cabrini about her institute, which
now, after eight years, numbered 145 nuns. Then the Pope blessed
her and let her go. She visited her doctor, who told her that as she
had perhaps two years to live, she might as well go to America. Monsignor Serrati saw the group of nuns off on the train for Le Havre.
They spent a day in Paris, then took the *Bourgogne*, a ship for
steerage immigrants.

On arrival in New York the nuns found that Archbishop Corrigan
had sent Father Morelli and another priest to meet them but that
Morelli was to tell them there was no convent for them to go to.
The nuns went to a rooming house so crawling with bedbugs that
they could not lie down, and even while they sat in chairs, heads
resting on the table, mice ran all over them. The next day, they
called on the archbishop, who told them to go back to Italy. Mother
Cabrini refused. They had come to New York under obedience to
the Pope, and would remain. Morelli was very opposed to a
house an American named Mary Reid, married to an Italian, had
taken for the sisters, at 43 East Fifty-ninth Street, then a most fashionable district. He was afraid swarms of dirty Italian kids in such an
area would "only arouse antagonism." But he agreed to see Mary
Reid and, after doing so, allowed the sisters to take possession of the
rented house. He even visited them, giving Frances the blessed
palm he was carrying from Mass that Palm Sunday. In four months
Frances had collected four hundred destitute children. But money
was a problem. The sisters begged in Little Italy, for food as well as
dimes, and were most grateful for fruit and vegetables to feed their

children. On July 20, 1889, Mother Cabrini sailed back to Italy with two Irish-American postulants. Frances was now thirty-nine.

Back at Codogno, Frances spent a month giving spiritual pep talks to her nuns, then went to Rome and had her second audience with Leo XIII, telling him about New York, and he blessed her again. On April 18, 1890, she set off again for New York. The ship carried nine hundred immigrants, mostly Italians. Mother Cabrini had seven sisters with her. They were two weeks at sea, and on her arrival in New York, Mother Cabrini lost no time in going up the Hudson to look at an estate, Manresa, that the Jesuits were prepared to sell cheaply due to a shortage of water. Mother Cabrini changed the name to West Park, had a well dug, where enough water was found for all their needs, and used the house to take in three hundred girls from the New York slums. Frances loved West Park so much that she wanted to be buried there, and indeed was: her nuns brought her body there from Chicago. It remained in West Park until it was transferred to the chapel of the Mother Cabrini High School in New York.

Meanwhile, her fame had spread. A rich Nicaraguan wrote offering a house in Granada, begging Frances to open a school. Mother Cabrini was prepared to start a series of schools in Central and South America for the rich, for she knew their children needed spiritual education not less than the poor to whom she ministered in Italy and New York.

Back to Italy she went once more, to consult with Cardinal Rampolla about the projected Latin American foundation. Then, bringing twenty-nine nuns, she arrived in New York again in September 1891, left the nuns at West Park, and returned to New York the same evening to book passage for herself and fourteen sisters she was taking to Nicaragua. They sailed on October 10. They ran into a hurricane, but survived to land in Panama and transfer to a boat that went up the coast.

In Granada they found that many of the children who wished to enter the sisters' school were illegitimate. Frances refused to accept these, and she and her nuns were subjected once more, as at Codogno, to violence. "Night after night men fired guns around the convent and battered on the door." Frances admitted to being frightened, but would not budge, and in a few months she had so many (legitimate) students in her school that it had to be moved to a bigger building. But there were other inconveniences in Granada: earthquakes, snakes, beetles, and typhoid.

In March 1892, Frances went back to the United States, stopping in New Orleans, where many Italians had settled. But they found themselves in competition with cheap Negro labor, and found, moreover, that the white way of dealing with Negroes—lynching—was used also against them. Eleven Sicilians, acquitted of murdering the local chief of police, were dragged out of jail and hanged by a mob. President Harrison, when the Italian Government protested, said there was nothing he could do; diplomatic relations were broken off between the U.S.A. and Italy, and Henry Cabot Lodge wrote that immigration should be restricted. The local archbishop, a Dutchman, welcomed Frances and asked her to establish a mission, which she did two months later, with three sisters, one only seventeen, whom she sent ahead of her. When the nuns had collected seventeen dollars and thirty cents, they telegraphed Frances: SUCCESS! PLEASE COME. She arrived on August 6, with four more nuns, and they rented three rooms in a tenement house with a large courtyard. Soon Frances bought the whole house, and used the courtyard as an improvised chapel. Again Mother Cabrini herself went begging, this time in the summer heat. Soon the mission was a success, and became a meeting place for all the local Italians.

Meanwhile, in New York Bishop Scalabrini had started a small Italian hospital on East 109th Street. Father Morelli was put in charge, but the hospital was a failure. The bishop begged Frances to take over the hospital or it would have to close. She did not wish to, thinking the twenty-four-hour-a-day service required of nursing nuns would be bad for their spiritual life, and also disliking "anything like physical putrefaction." But she had a dream, of Our Lady with sleeves rolled up and skirt pinned back, going from bed to bed in a hospital ward. Frances sprang forward to help her. "I am doing what you refuse to do," said the mother of Christ.

Frances assigned ten of her nuns to the hospital, but Father Morelli insisted these nuns remain under his control. He had piled up debts, and the property was sold to pay them. Frances decided at that point to start her own hospital, on Twelfth Street. She had only two hundred and fifty dollars, which paid the rent for a month and bought ten beds; Frances helped make the mattresses and cut out the sheets from a bale. The sisters slept on the floor. Frances called her hospital, and all the others she was later to found, Columbus. This was an inspiration, as it pleased all the Italians, clerical and anti-clerical alike.

She had established her novitiate at Codogno, so she had to return there often. In October 1893 she went again to Rome, for Leo XIII's jubilee, and the Pope gave her a thousand dollars. She saw him again in the summer of 1894, and he told her, "Let us work, Cabrini, let us work. Then what a heaven will be ours." Frances objected. "But I *like* work so much, Your Holiness, that I sometimes wonder whether it gives me any merit. Will work get me to heaven?" "Certainly it will," Leo replied. "Heaven is for those who work like you." When she returned to New York in March 1895, the State of New York gave Columbus Hospital its "formal approbation, legal incorporation being made on 26 March."

Meanwhile, a revolution in Nicaragua closed her house there, and the sisters who had been there settled in Panama. On her way to Panama, Frances was refused entry to Costa Rica by the governor of San José. So she remained in the harbor of Limón, although the President himself sent two emissaries to apologize for the governor and tell Frances she could travel anywhere in Costa Rica she wished. She still had her pride.

The school in Panama was a tremendous success, and Frances stayed there four and a half months before setting off for Buenos Aires. Her ship went down the coast of Ecuador, but Frances would not land there, as all Church property had been confiscated and all religious had been expelled. Frances wouldn't even go on shore to hear Mass. When they got to Lima, Frances visited the Dominican Church where St. Rose's head is in a silver urn and St. Martin of Porres' remains are in another urn. The ship then went to Valparaíso, and thence Frances and her companion (she had taken only one nun with her on this trip) crossed the plains to Santiago, where she found the twenty-five-day wait because the Andes were blocked with snow "sheer waste of time." But she prayed to St. Philomena (who has since been demoted by Pope John XXIII to non-existence), and while she was praying was given a gold coin and a picture of the saint by the guardian of St. Philomena's shrine. "Keep this image in your pocketbook and you will never need money for your order," said Canon Pereira. Frances added Philomena to her list of heavenly patrons.

On November 24, 1895, the two nuns set out to cross the Andes. At first by train, then by six-mule coaches, which climbed along a riverbed to the beginning of the Cumbre pass. At 3:30 A.M. they got on mules and followed two muleteers along the edge of a precipice. Soon they had to dismount and jump across a crevice. Mother Cabrini jumped but did not clear the chasm, and would have fallen down hundreds of feet had not her muleteer caught her. She fell fainting into a snowbank but was able to ride down, through "feathery falling snow."

Arrived in Buenos Aires, she found she knew no one but a Father Broggi who had once said Mass at her Genoa convent. She found him, and he took Frances and her companion to see the new archbishop, who was most cordial and said he "would be glad to begin his episcopate with the foundation of a house of the Missionary Sisters." Father Broggi parked the two nuns with the Sisters of Mercy until they got a convent of their own. Frances chose a house after seeing sixty: it was expensive and in the center of town. The Argentinians were impressed that a woman showed such energy and enterprise, and sent their children to her school in droves.

As soon as Frances was sure the school was a success, she sailed for Italy. There she went to say good-by to Leo XIII, who was now eighty-eight. Then she went to Paris, where she lodged with a Mde. de Mier, whose sister was in Frances' school in Panama. The cardinal of Paris was away, and his vicar-general would not allow Frances to make a foundation until he returned and gave his permission. So Frances went to England for ten days, went to Mass in London at Farm Street, the Jesuit church, then on to visit Cardinal (then Bishop) Bourne in Southwark.

She spent 1899 founding schools for poor Italian children in New York and also in Newark. Then, in September 1900 she took ship again for Le Havre, where she learned she had permission now to go to Spain, where, Queen María Cristina wrote, Mother Cabrini would be most welcome. The queen, however, was not amused when Mother Cabrini resolutely refused to let one of her nuns live in the palace in order to teach Italian to the princesses. But still, Mother Cabrini opened a college and a school in Madrid, and an orphanage —and two orphanages in Bilbao. These became, as Mother Cabrini had hoped, reservoirs for providing nuns for Latin America.

She traveled again by ship to Buenos Aires, and used all the nuns, now expelled from Panama because of a civil war, to work in her Argentine schools. She opened new houses on the Pampas and on the Paraná River. Then, though she was feeling far from well, she went on to Rio de Janeiro, and found to her delight she could understand Portuguese; then to São Paulo, and back to Italy, where she nearly died, recovering only after eating an orange sent her by the now 93-year-old Leo XIII from the Vatican gardens. She visited England for two weeks, and in that time opened a house at Brockley. Then she went West to Denver, Colorado, where there were many Italians working in the mines. The sisters visited the miners—which meant going down in bucketlike contraptions hundreds of feet in the depths of the earth and then walking along dark galleries. The superintendent was pleased with the sisters' interest in the poor Italian miners, and Frances realized how much they needed a hospital and a school for their children, so often left destitute when their fathers were fatally injured.

She bought a property on the edge of town against the bishop's advice, telling him that her children would then have an orchard and a farm. But the town moved quickly out toward her place, and it became immensely valuable.

She was asked to found a hospital in Chicago, and she bought the North Shore Hotel, six stories of gray stone, for ten thousand dollars down. The asking price was a hundred and sixty thousand. The owners tried to cheat her of twenty-five feet of frontage; the contractors also tried to cheat her. She quickly and quietly routed them all, took over the conversion of the hotel into a hospital, and finished the work in eight months instead of twelve. In Seattle she founded another hospital, a small orphanage, and a parochial school; she also built a wooden church for the Italian immigrants.

She visited Italian prisoners, in Sing Sing and elsewhere, sending her sisters in to give what comfort they could to the men three times a week, and arranging for an Italian priest to confess them. She and her nuns assisted those condemned to death—not only Italians but also others. One young Negro handed his crucifix to one of the guards as he climbed into the electric chair; "Give it to the Sisters," he said.

For the twenty-fifth anniversary of the founding of Frances Cabrini's institute, there were celebrations in the eight countries to which it had spread, and in the fifty houses where almost a thousand sisters worked.

She could now have retired—to Codogno or to Rome. Instead, she went to Brazil, where a new foundation was decimated by smallpox. Mother Cabrini herself nursed the sick sisters, applying castor oil and whipped cream with a feather, to prevent the sisters being pock-marked—as her own sister Rosa had done to her with milk, half a century before. She herself declared, "While I work, I am well," but nevertheless contracted malaria. As soon as she recovered, she returned to the U.S.A., for two years. She really wished to retire, to spend what was left of her life in prayer. But the nuns from every one of her institutes wrote to the cardinal prefect of the Congregation of Religious, and he prepared a decree to be issued on her sixtieth birthday, July 15, 1910. He then summoned her, and told her, "You have governed your Institute so badly, you are to remain Superior General." The nuns present applauded the cardinal's joke. Before

Frances returned to the United States, she asked to see Antonia Tondini, the deposed superior of the House of Providence, now no longer a nun, under whom Frances had spent those long-ago six sad years. Frances knelt to the old woman, well over eighty, and asked her pardon "for anything I did that grieved you." Antonia melted, called her "child," and embraced her most affectionately.

Frances was now collecting money for a new Columbus hospital in New York, and managed to get an annual subsidy of five thousand dollars from the Italian Government. She was very frail, and even thought herself dying; but a stay in the Colorado mountains restored her. In 1913 she went to Seattle to buy a new orphanage. She sent her nuns to look and they found a place, a large house standing in its own grounds. Next day, she and one sister went to look at it, thumbing a ride instead of taking the streetcar. "The place belongs to my husband," said the lady who had stopped her car for them. She was so intrigued with the little nun that she persuaded her husband to sell the place for a hundred thousand dollars—and an anonymous benefactor came forward with the sum.

The war found Frances already an American citizen, but concerned with Italy still. She never missed daily Mass and Communion, nor to be present at the nuns' recreation, but on Friday, December 21, 1917, she spent a busy day wrapping candy for the five hundred children at her school on Erie Street in Chicago. She died of a hemorrhage alone in her room on December 22, and was canonized in 1946. Her feast day is December 22. If, as in the Middle Ages, when every trade had its blessed patron, a patron were to be chosen by real estate brokers, it should be she.

All her miracles—and she did many, during her lifetime and after —were most practical. Money would be found in a sister's purse; wine and food where there was none before; a sister with agonizing varicose veins put on a pair of Frances' white cotton stockings and was instantly cured; a young nun blinded a new-born baby in one of Mother Cabrini's hospitals by using a 50 per cent solution of nitrate of silver instead of 1 per cent, to wash out the infant's eyes. The doctor said, since the cornea was gone, nobody could do anything. The delinquent sister put a relic of Mother Cabrini to the infant's eyes, and next morning they were intact and perfectly normal. The doctor testified at Mother Cabrini's beatification, in 1928. There were, and are, many more miracles Frances Cabrini has worked and works.

Why is this first U.S. citizen to be canonized relevant for us today? Firstly, because she is so contemporary: all that traveling, that busyness, is so 1970s, though she died in 1917. Secondly, in this age of seeking elsewhere—in India, in China, and Japan—for salvation, she proved that the old ways—of Martha and of Mary—are still valid. As St. Augustine put it: God did not say, go to the Orient to find Him, nor voyage to the West: to Him who is everywhere present, one comes by love and not by sail.

Conclusion

"Wherefore seeing we also are compassed about with so great a cloud of witnesses"
>   Hebrews 12:1

> A noble army, men and boys
> The matron and the maid
> Around their Saviour's throne rejoice
> In robes of white arrayed.
> They climbed the steep ascent of heaven
> Through peril, toil and pain,
> O God, to us may grace be given
> To follow in their train.

>   from   "The Son of God goes forth to war"

Every saint is always relevant, because T. S. Eliot was right when he wrote, in "The Cocktail Party," that:

> "The best of a bad job is what most of us make of it
> Except, of course, the saints."

>   Anne Fremantle